D0855839

Paul Tortelier
A Self-Portrait

By Paul Tortelier
How I Play, How I Teach

By David Blum
Casals and the Art of Interpretation

Paul Tortelier

A Self-Portrait
In Conversation with David Blum

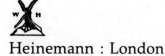

Heinemann : London

William Heinemann Ltd
10 Upper Grosvenor Street, London W1X 9PA
LONDON MELBOURNE TORONTO
JOHANNESBURG AUCKLAND

First published 1984
SBN 434 78860 0

Musical illustrations by Dr Malcolm Lipkin

Printed in England by
Butler & Tanner Ltd, Frome

To my friends, the young, who carry
our hope for tomorrow.

Contents

viii Contents

List of Plates

Acknowledgements

In the course of preparing this book I interviewed many people who kindly shared their reminiscences of Paul Tortelier with me. I have found it worthwhile to include in the book a number of these stories, many of which Paul had forgotten. They are highly characteristic of him and, I believe, add a complementary dimension to the conversations. (These anecdotes are indicated by means of special indentation.) I wish to express my gratitude first of all to the members of his family: his wife Maud; his children Anne, Yan Pascal, Pau, and Pomone; his sister Geneviève; and his cousin Madeleine Robinson. Secondly to his friends and colleagues including Claudio Abbado, Rudolf Caspar Baumberger, Pio Chesini, Chüän Ju Shih, Gordon Clark, Karl Engel, Willem Hielkema, Pierre René Honnens, the late Ivy Muriel Kirkwood, Véronica Krüger-Lewis, Arto Noras, Geoffrey Pratley, Raphael Sommer, Mary Symons, and Christoph Widmer.

Among others to whom I am indebted for kindly providing information and assistance are Mildred Clary; Kenneth Corden, Producer, Music and Arts for BBC Television; John Drummond, Director of the Edinburgh International Festival; Denham V. Ford, Honorary Chairman of the Sir Thomas Beecham Society; John Pattrick, General Manager, Classical Division, EMI Records; the staffs of Ibbs & Tillett and of the BBC Written Archives Centre.

I also wish to thank the following people for their many helpful suggestions: Peter Gras, Geoffrey Byrne-Sutton, Eve

Wakelin Harris, Antony Hopkins, Hilary Rubinstein, and Louise Bloomfield of William Heinemann Ltd. I am grateful to Bryan Crimp for compiling the Discography which appears as Appendix II. My thanks are also due to Susan Holgate and Caroline James for their secretarial assistance.

Above all, I am grateful to Paul Tortelier for his unfailing patience, helpfulness, candour and good humour.

D.B.

Preface

A room in the Paris Conservatoire one day in the early 1960s;
shades of Cherubini, Auber and Fauré look on. It is 9 a.m. as
Paul Tortelier begins to give a lesson. The gifted young Arto
Noras has brought the Third Bach Suite. 'Let us look at the
opening phrase,' says Tortelier.

'These twelve notes are very simple,' he continues; 'they could
be played by a beginner. But to find their melodic form, to
express their rhythmic élan is not as easy as it might appear.'

Professor and student work at that one phrase for more than
the allotted hour, searching for its true character, moulding its
proportions. In fact they are still at it at lunch time. Tortelier
invites Noras to return with him to his flat. After having a bite
to eat, they return to the passage playing it again and again
throughout the afternoon. The miniature world of these twelve
notes has become a model for the examination of many aspects
of bow technique and interpretation. Evening comes on . . .
Finally, at eight o'clock, the professor exclaims, '*Voilà*, I am
satisfied! At last you play this passage as I ideally hear it. And
now that you have mastered it, you are ready to play it any way
you like, should you feel it differently than I do.' This is
quintessential Paul Tortelier.

Complete identification with the task at hand – that is a key to his character. Those who know him describe this trait in different ways depending on their viewpoint. Colleagues speak of an 'absolute integrity'. His family refers to his 'being total in every way'. Students call this trait 'intransigence', 'perfectionism', or 'illumination'. He himself calls it 'hereditary fanaticism'. A close friend describes it as a state of *thereness* in whatever he is doing: writing the text of a peace anthem; studying a score; learning to play croquet, or engrossed in an interesting conversation. Once, when conversing with a friend while jogging, he fell badly but picked himself up and carried on for half an hour; not until arriving home did he notice a deep gash in his knee. His visits to our home – given the intensity of his personality and his un-forgettable midnight concerts – leave us exhilarated but utterly exhausted. One feels as if a meteor has passed through the house. Above all, he is *there* on the concert platform, when he enters into an all-absorbing oneness with the masterpiece he is playing. I remember his coming offstage after having performed the Schumann Concerto, and telling me, with a sense of wonderment, that he had felt when playing as if he had been Schumann himself.

It is often the case that his *thereness* fails to correspond with what is expected of him at a given moment. As his wife Maud knows – and as his mother knew – he is *there* when practising or composing. Surely no musician has ever let so many meals become cold.

The serenity of a Bach Sarabande, the intoxicating gaiety of the Paganini Variations on One String, the trials and tribulations of that complex hero *Don Quixote* – Tortelier enters into every mood, *becomes* the music he is playing. Not unsurprisingly his own character is many-faceted, some aspects seeming contra-dictory – but all come together to make a fascinating whole. He is never happier than when, surrounded by friends, he can tell amusing stories and act out all the roles to perfection. Yet he is equally happy to be lost for days on end in composition. At such times it requires some tact to pull him back to the external world. His very element is the concert platform. Nevertheless, he has done what few artists would dare to do: withdraw from his immensely successful career for nearly a year at a time – on one occasion to fulfil his idealistic dream, to live on a kibbutz; on another, at the age of 57, to enhance his skill as a composer by studying counterpoint. His outspokenness is legendary. He has sung his own text for the 'Marseillaise' on French television, ironically heralding the triumph of industry over nature, of commercialism over art. A Swiss critic has spoken of his 'magnificent insolence'. All the same, Tortelier refers to himself as being shy – and indeed he is. One summer day we sat in the lobby of a small Parisian hotel involved in a conversation which lasted several hours. Despite the sweltering heat he would not remove his jacket; he was, after all, wearing braces. His origins are of the common people; he feels this deeply, has always lived simply, even uncomfortably, and invariably travels second class.

Yet there is something unmistakably aristocratic in his manner, as in his dress which is tasteful and meticulous. (He refers to the dances in the Bach suites as 'rustic – yet elegant' and complements this statement by quoting Rodin: 'In true grace there is strength.') He has no use for formal religion; none the less he greatly enjoys playing in churches. He despises television; yet he has been called – with justification – 'God's gift to television'. His impracticality is such that he requires a nursemaid whenever someone is available to fulfil that role; however, he has a canny way of managing to get things done by himself when he has to. Sometimes he seems withdrawn from the stream of life, but this can be misleading to those who don't know him well. As Maud says, 'Although he rarely reads the newspaper, hears the radio or watches TV, he somehow picks up the news and makes a synthesis of events. Some people take him for the typical absent-minded artist. But he's really at the centre of things. He's led there by his intuition about people. He arrives by intuition where others arrive by logic, and his is the shorter route.' He is an agnostic, but it would be difficult to find a more reverent man, reverent of those values in life, nature and art which risk being cast aside in the world of today.

Both as man and musician Paul Tortelier has a special gift of communication. He has an ability to feel into and for the other person. Once, on an aeroplane, he sat next to a man who seemed deeply distressed. He turned out to be a Breton fisherman who had learned that day that his son had been drowned at sea. Paul took him to his own house in Paris where he could spend the night before having to face the terrible journey home. Paul upbraids himself for being 'stingy' – a remnant, he says, of his impoverished childhood; yet I know many examples of his concern and generosity. Most people who have worked with him closely, including myself, have always found him to be a warm and considerate friend.

Yet those who disagree with one of the musical or social ideals to which he is dedicated arouse his warrior instinct. He can then become maddeningly obstinate and may easily tax one's patience. And heaven protect the student who comes to him without sufficient commitment. (Given Tortelier's standards, the degree of commitment has to be considerable.) 'Indifference – ' he cries out, 'that is the greatest artistic crime!' A girl once played the Khachaturyan Concerto for him in a cold, *indifferent* way. When she finished, there was a long silence – normally a bad sign. Paul finally sighed: 'Forget a little about your cello for a while. Have a love affair; it will do your playing a world of good.'

Hard as he can be as a teacher – 'I am severe, very severe' – he is hardest on himself. This is a man who does not, who cannot spare himself. He is moved by a superior force; he is the servant of a gift that directs his energy and fulfils its goal through him. His extraordinary technique is largely self-created, and forged from an unremitting expressive urge.

Within the powerful framework of his conception of a work, there is always room for an element of improvisation. He may decide on a change of bowing or fingering five minutes before a concert. He is always probing, always searching; interpretation never stands still. Demanding – indeed imperious – as he can sometimes be, he is self-effacing before the works of the great composers. He often asks those present at his rehearsals to give him any musical suggestions they may have. When I had known him but a short while, I myself was put to the test. He was rehearsing Beethoven's A major Sonata with his daughter, Pau. When they finished, he asked for my critical comments. I hesitated. The performance had been superb, yet there were some details – small matters of nuance and balance – which I thought worth mentioning. But could I trust his sincerity in having asked me this question? I took the risk. He enthusiastically thanked me for bringing these points to his attention and re-hearsed the passages in question not only once but several times. Having gone over a particular phrase repeatedly with great care, he asked me, 'Is it better now?'

'It was beautiful to begin with,' I replied, 'but it's even better now.'

'Is it only better,' he persisted, 'or is it as good as it could be?'

'It's as good as it could be.'

'Then,' he said, turning to Pau, 'we may proceed.'

David Blum
Vandœuvres
Switzerland 1983

I

A Montmartre Childhood

Looking back, I have the feeling that certain important events in my life were in some way brought about by more than casual chance. For instance, for someone destined to become a musician, it may be considered a good sign to have been born on 21 March, the day on which Bach was born. That is also the first day of spring; however, the year of my birth, 1914, marked the beginning of war. It's a striking contradiction: a time of renewal of life, a time of destruction. But this at least helps me to remember the date of my birth, because I have a bad memory for dates, and perceive time as something uniform.

I was born in Paris at the foot of Montmartre, at 7 rue de Trétaigne. It's curious that our neighbour at No. 9 should have been Charles Kiesgen, Pablo Casals's impresario who was one day to introduce me to my idol. Well, who's to say what hidden forces govern our lives? Was it mere coincidence that I lived for a while at 8 rue de Panama, and my future wife at No. 9, though I never knew Maud at the time? These are but a few of the strands which have been drawn into the pattern of my life, guided in some mysterious way by the cello.

You told me at the time we visited the flat in which you were born, and in which you spent the first ten years of your life, that essentially nothing had changed there in over sixty years. As you put it to me, 'It was then, and it is now, no more than a humble worker's dwelling.' Another family now lives in those three small rooms, with their children playing in the dark corridors. Were you aware of being a poor child?

1

No; the flat in which I lived with my parents and my sister Geneviève was typical of our social milieu. We belonged to the majority – to the working people who, for the most part, made up my world, and with whom I've always felt at one.

My father, Joseph Tortelier, like his father before him, was what we call in French a *menuisier-ébéniste* – a carpenter-cabinet-maker. He kept a workshop at 120 rue Marcadet near to the rue des Saules, a street well known for its cabaret *Le Lapin Agile*.

Was Montmartre still a picturesque quarter at that time?

People tend to romanticize Montmartre because of the famous artists who once worked there. The top of the hill still retains something of an artistic character. But there was nothing at all picturesque about our quarter. In any case, if there were any artists still working in Montmartre when I was a boy, I was completely unaware of their existence.

Montmartre was a strange mixture. The poor and the bourge-oisie lived side by side. For instance, the Kiesgen house – where I used to play with their son Camille – seemed to me quite luxurious; it was made of hewn stone, had ornamented bal-conies, and was even equipped with a splendid old-fashioned lift. Our house next door was built of rough concrete, with an ugly flat façade. Needless to say, it had no lift. In fact we didn't even have a shower; we had to wash ourselves in the kitchen. However, everything is relative. We were well off compared with my aunt who lived in Pré St-Gervais, a slum on the out-skirts of the city. In her house five people were crammed into two small, unheated rooms with no electricity or running water; you had to go down from the third floor to the lavatory in the yard.

Where did your parents come from?

My mother, whose maiden name was Marguerite Boura, had family roots in both Burgundy and Lorraine. My father's family came from Rennes in Brittany.

Are there specific character traits associated with those regions?

Don't forget that Lorraine is the country of Joan of Arc. The people from there are known to be stubborn. One calls them *têtes de Lorrains* or *têtes dures* – 'hard-headed'.

But the Bretons are even worse: *tête de Breton* – even harder! Now you can understand my temperament.

There is also much fantasy in the Breton spirit.

Oh yes, a lot of fantasy. They are a hard-working people, but not too well disciplined or well organized: the Celtic character.

Many Bretons think of their province as being independent of France. Do you consider yourself to be more Breton than French?

I certainly don't have the sort of nationalism that characterizes many Frenchmen. I never did. It's strange, but even when I was a child and attended a cycling competition, in contrast to my friends who cheered for our own country, I supported the Dutch team. I don't know why. The sonority of the Dutch name pleased my ear, and that was enough for me. Incidentally, my name is very similar to the Dutch word *Torteldier* which means turtledove.

Has it no Breton origin?

It may derive from *Tourtelier* which applies to a sort of baker – a pie-maker. In any case, my Christian name was given to me because of my father's admiration for Paul Reclus, the son of Elysée Reclus, the well-known geographer and anarchist. Paul Reclus was a remarkable man, extremely kind and intelligent. Since he worked as an engineer for the French railways, he had the right to travel first class without payment. Nevertheless he travelled third class because he preferred to be with simple people. It's true that well-off people can sometimes be a little distant; there is more communication among the rich.

There is a charming story about Albert Schweitzer. When a friend asked, 'Doctor, why do you always travel Second Class?' he replied, 'Because they have discontinued the Third Class.'

That is just how I feel. When there was a third class, I always travelled third class. And now I travel second class. I keep to the tradition of my namesake.

When did your father's family leave Brittany?

My grandfather moved to Paris, where my father was born.

Do you still have relatives in Brittany?

Some cousins still live there. I love Brittany. I recognize at once the Breton type, the same sort of man as my grandfather: an energetic man – not necessarily physically strong – but with an invincible will and determination.

My grandfather, like my father, was named Joseph. No self-respecting carpenter in Catholic Brittany could be named otherwise. From him derives the strain of high idealism that runs in our family. Let us call it the Don Quixote tendency. My grandfather was imbued with an exceptional sense of mission to help the common man. Philosophically he was an anarchist, believing in a harmonious society in which people voluntarily help each other without governmental control. Together with Jaurès, the great socialist and founder of the newspaper *l'Humanité*, he was one of France's leading spokesmen on behalf of the working class, noted for his power of oratory. He made a special trip to America to help organize a trade union, and was a leader of the first general strike in France, which was a milestone in the emancipation of the worker. This, mind you, happened at the end of the century, when workers were not organized and their plight was miserable.

Did your family have a musical background?

None of my family had formal musical training, but they had a genuine love for music. For instance, my grandfather was a passionate admirer of Debussy's music. He discovered the beauty of *Pelléas et Mélisande* at a time when it was not generally appreciated. Even today it's not appreciated everywhere. This was all the more extraordinary because he had no musical sophistication in the ordinary sense of the word. He only played on a wooden flute, and never ventured beyond simple songs like *Plaisir d'amour* – but he played with love. Even in his old age when he had barely any strength left, he put his soul into his little flute.

My parents had a longing for culture, though they were virtually uneducated. They attended a series of orchestral concerts given for people of the working class called *Les Fêtes du Peuple*, conducted by Albert Doyen, and there they discovered

Beethoven. One of my father's great favourites was the *Pastoral* Symphony because it so fully expresses the radiance of nature, and my father, like Beethoven, loved nature almost religiously. I am sure that the *Pastoral* Symphony has done more than any other work to popularize great music. My father's other favourite was the Ninth Symphony; he believed in the power of joy. That was his credo – his Bible. Despite their poverty, my parents also managed to attend some of the Concerts Lamoureux conducted by Camille Chevillard who introduced pieces by Wagner in orchestral excerpts. While my mother was at first particularly attracted to opera, she eventually grew to appreciate not only symphonic music, but also chamber music, and the Bach Cello Suites. She once attended a concert given by a well-known Lieder singer, Marya Freund, and was forever after in love with Schubert.

Both my parents played the mandolin in an amateur music ensemble made up of workers. My father also taught himself to play the violin. While I don't recall hearing him play, my sister, who accompanied him in Mozart's E minor violin Sonata, often speaks of his musical sensitivity.

Your parents seem to have had an innate sense of good taste.

Good taste is important. A degradation of taste has occurred in our time. I have a feeling that this may be because we are gradually losing our roots. Although my parents lived in Paris, they still had a strong connection with nature. My father was only one generation removed from his ancestors who were Breton peasants, and a single generation separated my mother from her ancestors in Lorraine. They still had the common sense of the peasantry which seems to go with good taste, which we call *sapience* – an instinctive knowledge of the fundamental laws from which we have developed. What is true for nature and for the earth is also true for man and art.

It was such a moment of truth that brought the cello into my life. My fate was sealed long before my birth; it was sealed on the day (in 1905) when my mother heard the cellist Francis Touche play in a café. He was leading a group of four musicians in an arrangement of a Beethoven symphony. That was a lovely time when such masterworks were also performed by chamber music groups in the home. Amateur music-making is of the greatest value, but nowadays we have adopted a more intellectual approach. We live in a *civilisation bavarde* – a civilization that talks too much. We want to *know*, but at that time people wanted to *enjoy* – to enjoy music when they played it, to enjoy it when they heard it. My mother immediately fell under the spell of the cello. She was touched to the core of her being by its warm voice. There and then she decided that when she gave birth to a son, he would become a cellist. Her first child was, however, a girl – my sister Geneviève, born in 1906. That was something of a disappointment as far as the cello was concerned, because in those days girls rarely took up the instrument. (Geneviève learned to play the piano, however, and did have a go at the cello when she was 14, but remained a modest player.) Finally, eight years later, my mother's dream was fulfilled: the future cellist was born.

Wasn't it unusual for a child from your background to play the cello?

Very much so. Even today many French people don't know what a cello is, let alone play it. When I take a taxi, when I take a plane, the taxi-driver or the customs officer will invariably ask, 'What have you got there – a guitar or a double-bass?'

When your mother made her plans for you before you were born, did it occur to her that difficulties might arise if you were not musically inclined?

She never doubted, not for a moment. However, she had to wait until I was 6 years old before I was big and strong enough to begin to play the instrument. Meanwhile I was the *enfant chéri* of the family. If it was my vocation to become a cellist, that of my mother was to fulfil all the requirements of *l'amour maternel* – to be in every way the best mother possible. They say that she nursed me until I was 18 months old. Granted that she was dedicated to my nourishment, but I do think this must be something of an exaggeration. For my sister, too, I was a dream come true. She treated me as her favourite doll; she remembers singing to me until I would coo with delight. I was spoiled, to say the least, by both women in my family.

What are your earliest memories?

I recall, when very young, being taken down into the cellar. We huddled there in the dark, worried that the Germans might shell Paris.

I also remember being given the honour of meeting Sarah Bernhardt when I was 3 years old. I was with my family in a village called Osny, near Pontoise. The war was still on, and the famous actress had made a patriotic film bearing the noble title *Mère française*, which included some sequences shot in that village. When the filming came to an end, the local mayor decided to honour Madame Bernhardt in a special ceremony, and, for some reason, I was chosen to present the official bouquet. As we approached the great lady, my father holding me in his arms, Sarah could not resist kissing me. But when I saw her face, completely covered with make-up, an old woman pretending to be young, I opened my big eyes in terror and cried out, '*Je ne peux pas, Sarah!*' – 'I cannot, Sarah!'

And what did Sarah do?

Luckily she only laughed. Children are especially perceptive of truth or artificiality. They see clearly, with open eyes.

After having looked through the photos taken of you when you were the enfant chéri, *I don't wonder you were chosen to greet the great Sarah. Where did the charming costume come from which you wore as a school boy?*

As my father's great love was Russia – he was more Russian than the Russians – I was dressed accordingly. My mother made shirts for me *à la russe*: a blue blouse with a high collar and with buttons running down the side. I never wore any other style. The overshirt which I wore for school was cut in this way, and when I went out to some nice place at night I wore a similar blouse made of black velvet.

As my mother wouldn't cut my long curls, and as my blouse resembled a short dress, I was often taken for a girl. People used to call me *Mademoiselle*, but I wasn't offended. I thought this was probably because I was handsome, and I felt rather proud of it.

Do you know that in the west of Ireland mothers used to keep the boys dressed in long skirts like girls until the age of twelve so that the fairies wouldn't come down and snatch them away?

My mother did in fact try to protect me – not against the fairies – but against the much greater threat of girls, by having me wear short trousers well into my teens so as to keep me looking younger than I was. This custom only came to an end when I began to play the cello in cinemas and such places where I was obliged to wear long trousers.

When I was about five, I was given piano lessons, for which I seemed to have little aptitude. I continued with the piano in a lack-lustre way, but, after all, I had been destined for the cello.

The day finally came when my mother decided I was ready to begin cello lessons. She approached Béatrice Bluhm who was first cellist in the orchestra of *Les Fêtes du Peuple* and asked if she might consider teaching me. A half-size cello was acquired and the lessons began.

In selecting Béatrice Bluhm my mother had made the best possible choice. I shall speak of her in some detail later. Every decision my mother made regarding my musical education revealed a remarkably acute intuition. She put me into the hands of only the finest teachers, and also persuaded me at a much later stage to enter the harmony class at the Conservatoire – that fearsome, awesome class.

Did your mother seek advice from some musician about these decisions?

I never knew. In any case, she made all the right choices.

Was your talent for the cello immediately apparent?

I was gifted with a good ear, and, in a cellistic sense, gifted with my hands. They were of the necessary size and had the natural reflex and coordination to play the instrument well. These are important factors. But, of course, what can you do without working?

My mother made sure that I practised at least two hours every day. She always saw to it that I made the best possible use of my time. She would have agreed wholeheartedly with the words attributed to Bach: 'Time is God's most precious gift. It is the only thing not given to us twice.'

Was she sufficiently perceptive musically to help you with the cello?

Her ear was excellent and she could tell whether I played out of tune. She could also tell from what she heard whether or not I was concentrating. She learned *solfège* when I did, to help me. But subsequently she didn't study harmony, counterpoint and fugue. When it came to music, her reactions were based more upon instinct than knowledge, but were none the less very true.

Did you take to the cello immediately when you began to play?

I don't remember ever questioning the role of the cello in my life. In any case, a child of 6 cannot know for sure what he wants. The only thing which is certain is that I had a passion for games, especially games of skill such as draughts. I could have played games all day long. And I had an intense love for sports. This fulfilled two needs: first of all, to expend my energy; and, secondly, to win. As cello practice took me away from my beloved games, I first thought of it as just a damned thing created solely to poison a boy's life. It took half a dozen years before the instrument became a bearable companion, another half-dozen before this demanding companion became a friend, and yet a few more years before I began to feel something of what Rodin so admirably expressed when he said, '*Les vrais artistes sont en somme les plus religieux des mortels.*' ('The true artists are in fact the most religious of mortals.')

In his book *Les Hommes de bonne volonté* Jules Romains depicts a little boy growing up in Paris, just as I did – a child, who is always running through the streets. We call such little creatures *poulbots* (after the French painter Poulbot who specialized in drawing the street urchins of Montmartre). I tended to be lazy, and, since the street held such fascination for me, it was difficult for my mother to keep me at work. When she went out to buy food, or for some other reason, I would jump up from my practising the instant she left and run to the window which overlooked the street from the third-floor landing. I didn't dare risk going out onto the street for fear she might catch me. I just

looked out longingly. If I saw her coming, I would dash back to
my cello. When I was about ten – I'm always unsure of dates – we
moved to a ground-floor flat behind my father's workshop in the
rue Marcadet. At last having easy access to the street, I would
seize every opportunity to dart out and play football or whizz
along on my scooter between the pedestrians when I was supposed to be practising.

*What sort of punishment would you get if your mother caught
you?*

She would shout so much that I was terrified. However, she
rarely slapped me.

*Children are often discouraged by parents who are too severe, yet
you managed to carry on with your music. You must have respected
and loved your mother in spite of everything.*

Yes, I loved her dearly. And apart from her insistence upon
my practising, she was always very kind. She spoiled me with
cakes and other goodies. I was taken to the movies.

Luckily, with time, my laziness tended to diminish, but as a
child I would never have played the cello had my mother not
constantly reminded me, *'Paul – ton violoncelle'* – 'Paul – your
cello'. That became the *Leitmotiv* of my life. I heard it fifty times a
day. Neighbours who lived above our room still remember the
phrase. I too can still hear my mother's voice reiterating it.
Nowadays, although I'm no longer lazy, I sometimes tend to get
diverted into other activities, and then my wife will say, just as
my mother used to, *'Paul – ton violoncelle'*.

On one occasion, which I remember very well, my mother
decided to make an experiment. I wonder how she had the
courage to do it. She decided not to say anything about the cello
to me for a whole day, in order to see whether I had developed
any sense of responsibility. On that particular morning I got up
from breakfast, waiting for the command – but it never came. I
could hardly believe it. She was playing a game with me, and
purposely left the room because, had she stayed there, I would
have found it strange that she said nothing. So after a quarter of
an hour I began to play on the floor. I amused myself the whole
day with my trains or with card games and didn't touch my cello

once. My mother was strong enough to resist the temptation to say '*Paul, ton violoncelle*'. At the end of the day she was very kind and pretended not to have noticed anything unusual. She always laughed when, years later, she would recall this incident. She liked to tell the story to show how much I needed a vigilant mother.

What advice can you offer parents of musically gifted children? To what extent should they insist upon the child practising?

It's difficult to answer precisely. The goal is of course to develop the child's self-motivation. Yet, given all the distractions which can easily tempt a youngster, some parental supervision is often necessary. Of course, much depends on the character of the child.

Your mother was lucky. Her child was exceptionally gifted.

And I managed to submit.

How did you find time to do both your school work and musical studies?

By leaving school shortly after I started. When I was 9 my parents removed me from the state school and enrolled me in a private school. I left school entirely when I was 11, and that was the end of my institutionalized academic education.

In removing her son from school, and having him study the cello, piano, and *solfège* at home all day long, my mother was taking a great risk. In other words, while her father had gambled on horses in a most unfortunate way, she decided to gamble on the cello. It is only fair to say that, if this plan worked successfully, it was partly due to the strong spirit of competition which existed among the students at the Paris Conservatoire at that time. I enjoyed the challenge and approached it like all other games: with the intention of winning. As my harmony teacher, Jean Gallon, used to say, 'When one comes to the Paris Conservatoire one already begins to make progress just on opening the front door.'

Wasn't school compulsory in France up to a minimum age?

I don't know. For my father, who rebelled against capitalism in industry and every kind of conformity, nothing was really compulsory. He saw no more the need for school than for military service or vaccination. He was utterly convinced as to the wisdom of my leaving school. As for my mother, she understood that in arranging for me to have private lessons in French, arithmetic, and English, with a little geography thrown in, I would have enough to make my way in life. Most important of all, she realized that I would save much time by having private teachers.

How did you get along with your tutors?

There were two ladies, one for French, the other for English. It's to their credit that they managed to get along moderately well with *me*, for I had very little interest in what they taught, and I never knew my lessons. My teacher of English, Madame Mondain, had been born in Tahiti and used to tell me amusing stories about the Tahitian queen Pomaré. In exchange, after the lessons, I would amuse her and her two children, both musicians, by telling 'Marius' stories (tales of a fictional hero from Provence who has an irrepressible imagination and gets into all sorts of unexpected scrapes). These stories maintained my popularity wherever I was invited over a period of several decades.

This private schooling for two years, and later the private tutoring – all this, plus the music lessons, must have put a heavy financial burden on your family.

My father came from one of those Breton families whose existence was a continual battle against poverty. Pierre Jakez Hélias has magnificently described such a family in his book *Le cheval d'orgueil – The Horse of Pride*. Thus my father was very strict with the family budget, and my mother felt that she could not ask him for the money. She had somehow to find the money herself, so she decided to take in boarders – six young musicians who lived nearby and came to us for their meals. (One of these, the oboist Etienne Baudo, eventually married my sister; their son is the conductor Serge Baudo.) In our tiny kitchen my mother managed to feed ten people: my father; my sister, herself, and me, plus the six boarders. As the boarders themselves were very poor, she charged a low price for the meals, just enough for her to make a little profit. She had to make a long journey each morning to *Les Halles*, the central marketplace of Paris, because the food there was cheaper than anywhere else. As every *centime* counted, she would take the very first Métro in the morning, because the first was cheaper than the second. As this train left at 5.30 a.m. she had to be up at 5.0. She would walk from our house to the nearest Métro station – at Marcadet – which took her at least twelve minutes. Then she had half an hour in the Métro before reaching *Les Halles*. The actual shopping took another three-quarters of an hour, and then she would return. So, altogether, two hours just to get enough food to last out the day. When she arrived home it was 7.30 or 8.0. You or I would be dead-tired and ready to go back to bed. But this was just the beginning of my mother's day. The winters in Paris during my youth were much colder than they are now. It was nearly always freezing, and my mother would come home with what we call *l'onglée*, which means that her fingers were completely numb and hurt when they thawed out. Her nose and ears were frozen too – yet she managed to carry I don't know how many kilos of food.

In the afternoon she helped me with my lessons, looking after my arithmetic and other studies. Twice a week, when I went to the *solfège* class in the centre of Paris, she would accompany me, which took three hours. One of our boarders was an oboist named Jean Devergie. This young man, who was eventually to play an important role in my life, had a nose for business; he had made himself well known in Parisian musical circles by always being available to replace his colleagues when they fell ill. He would sometimes accept two or three engagements for the same night, keep the best-paying job for himself, and try to find substitutes for the others. When in such a predicament, he would ask my mother to find other oboists. If there were two or three days to spare, she would write a quick letter asking, 'Could you play at the *Opéra* Tuesday night?' But sometimes the day arrived and a replacement could not be found. Since we had no telephone, she would have to go personally to the homes of various oboists – many of whom lived far from us – to see if one was free. That was not all. My father kept furniture on display in his shop. Each time the doorbell rang, my mother would have to answer it, welcome the customer, and try to sell him something.

My father was very demanding. He insisted that she polish all the furniture till it was spotless, and, of course, she had to clean the house every day, as well as wash all the family's clothes by hand.

Did you help out?

I never touched a thing; I never washed a plate; I never made my bed; I never did anything. She did it all. I don't know what she couldn't do. For me it was a real Latin upbringing in which the man was spared all menial chores. It was great for my cello playing, but left me with a permanent inability to cope with household affairs.

Your friends say that whenever you stay with them you make your bed perfectly. Apparently you learned that one domestic art.

Do they say that? Well, perhaps it's true. But that's all I ever learned to do. For instance, my cooking is as primitive as can be.

What do you cook?

Oh, well, I . . . boil potatoes, and eggs . . . and I have once or twice put oil in a pan and cooked beans. My mother was an excellent cook. She even managed to make tasty affairs of the simple meals we shared with the boarders, often over-stuffing them with five courses, after which they found it difficult to play their instruments. Her speciality was pastry. She could make anything you saw in the window of the finest *pâtisserie*. She also made chocolate truffles and wonderful caramels. It's little wonder that I was a rather plump child – not really fat, just nicely rounded. To this day – though I can't find anything in the kitchen for the life of me – I have an infallible nose for pastry. Wherever it's hidden, I go straight towards it. A few years ago I even made one foray myself into the realm of the pastry chef, and people tell me it was a great success.

One day Paul announced to his family that, following in his mother's footsteps, he would become a pastry chef for the day. For this august occasion he chose an old French speciality: *le pet-de-nonne*. He shut himself away in the kitchen; first the eggs, flour, butter, salt, oil, and sugar had to be found. The flour – boiled in water and mixed with eggs – had to be made into dough, which then had to undergo a further alchemical transformation, that of being fried in oil and sprinkled with sugar. An hour later Paul emerged, proudly bearing the finished *pets-de-nonne* which everyone agreed tasted delicious. Triumphant, Paul returned to his cello and the family cautiously entered the kitchen which now looked like a battlefield. The whole place was covered in flour, and all the saucepans were burnt. It took two hours to get it clean again.

Given your mother's overwhelming work-load, did she manage to maintain some degree of cheerfulness?

My mother worked so hard that she used to say, 'Let's hurry up so that we can get to bed early.' She would never stop working the entire day, and that would be her only reward: simply to go to bed. She had no fear of death. She would tell us, 'Death is a marvellous thing. Ah, to have a good sleep at last!' That was all. But she was always happy when she worked, always cheerful. She loved keeping this boarding house; she loved feeding the students and being surrounded by youth. And for me there was an ambience of festivity all the time. People tell me that when I give a concert it is a kind of jubilation. Well, in my childhood every mealtime was a jubilation because of the presence of these flute and oboe players who were 18 or 20 years old and who were always in high spirits. Most of them were from the southern part of France: two were from Marseilles, one from Bordeaux. But another was from Valenciennes in the north – so it became a battle between north and south. And I laughed and laughed because I loved to watch this fight. Jean Devergie, whom we called 'Jeannot', would sometimes challenge me to run out to the tobacconist's, buy cigarettes for him, and be back again within three minutes. As long as I could break a record I was the happiest boy you could imagine.

Best of all were the days of special celebration, such as Christmas when all our friends and neighbours would crowd into my father's workshop to sing and make merry. The greatest event was the *Revue des Insectes* which my sister and I organized along with all the other children of the street. Our kitchen was temporarily transformed into a tailor's shop filled with magically coloured cellophane costumes complete with wings. I was to be a cricket dressed in black, and Geneviève a cicada. We even built a hive for our stage-set and put on a play we had written about insects. Geneviève accompanied us at the piano while we sang and danced.

Have you maintained a tradition of such celebrations within your family?

It's difficult for us to reserve definite occasions for certain things as some families do. We are not disciplined enough for that; fantasy is always interfering. However, we have sometimes staged little skits for our private amusement. Once, in Israel, we put on a mini-production of *Le Cid* by Corneille. We've sometimes had masquerade parties. On one such occasion in Paris, the sculptor Léon Séverac and I appeared as Roman gladiators, wearing only our shorts, my thin frame contrasting with my opponent's gigantic hairy chest. Just as we began to duel with kitchen utensils the new Swiss housekeeper arrived. She didn't stop blushing for the two years she stayed with us.

It was during my tenth year that Jean Devergie had come to our house as a boarder. He himself was then 20. I came to love Jean Devergie with an intensity that has never been surpassed in my life except by the love I have for my wife today. I loved him almost more than my own parents. After all, my parents held no mystery for me, while 'Jeannot', with his dark complexion, looked like a Sicilian bandit who had stepped out of a fable. Devergie was, in fact, from the south; like his good friend Etienne Baudo, he was from Marseille. Both came from simple backgrounds; their mothers were fishmongers in the street market. These two young men first took up the oboe so as to have an easier time in the military service where they would be allowed to play in the band. They both developed into excellent players.

Devergie not only struck up a friendship with me, but he helped me with my music. For example he would ask me to maintain a single note with an unwaveringly beautiful sonority – *un son filé* – for about a minute, the sort of thing he did on his oboe. He was strict with me – far more so than my father who wasn't hard on me at all. Between my mother and Devergie I really had to practise.

Did he help you with interpretation?

Not at all; he was only interested in the instrument, but it was useful that he heard me practise because he could correct me and watch over my work.

He seems to have appreciated your talent.

Oh yes. He was proud of me and liked to show me off. Whenever friends came to the house he would ask me to play. I had to be ready to be put on exhibition at any moment. But that was really good training. I cannot play *The Swan* by Saint-Saëns without recalling Devergie.

It is unusual for a young man to have that kind of friendship for a child.

Yes, it's true. Of course, I wasn't his only interest. As I later learned, he was running after women; in fact he was a sort of Don Juan. But at that time I believed he was living only for me; I thought that I was everything in his eyes.

The greatest moment of all came every Wednesday night. That was when 'Jeannot' would take me to the Select Cinema where he played the oboe. At that time, of course, the films were silent. He would place me in an extra chair in the orchestra pit so that I didn't have to pay and could see the screen which was directly above my nose. After three hours of straining my head to look at the film, I had a pain in my neck, but I was happy all the same. Coming home I would skip along all the way from Place Clichy to Montmartre. I had an unbelievable passion for the cinema. How I would laugh at the antics of Charlie Chaplin, Harold Lloyd and Max Linder! Douglas Fairbanks, John Barrymore and Tom Mix became my heroes; Mary Pickford, Florence Vidor and Lillian Gish, my heroines. I remember Lillian Gish in *Orphans of the Storm* and in *Broken Blossoms* – a touching film in which Richard Barthelmess played a Chinaman. I loved the serials and would wait in suspense during the entire week to find out what happened. Many years later, when I was playing in the Boston Symphony, I saw one of my idols in person. Heifetz came to play as soloist and was accompanied by his wife, Florence Vidor. I was astonished that a mere musician like Heifetz could dare marry such a star.

Did you play for Heifetz?

Oh yes; he suggested certain technical exercises – scales in octaves and such things – and he recommended that I work to intensify my vibrato. But he seemed rather insignificant compared to his wife.

Do you still enjoy the cinema?

I now go very rarely to films – perhaps once a year. If there were still film-makers like Charlie Chaplin, I'd find the time to go more often. But nowadays films tend to be so banal, so pseudo-sophisticated, so standardized that you know ahead of time what you're going to see. There will be a strip-tease in it, whatever the subject, even if it is about the Bach family, and there's bound to be a gun somewhere, perhaps hidden in the harpsichord.

Jean Devergie was a *bon vivant*; he was a gourmet and he loved to smoke. Needless to say, smoking became a temptation for me. Sometimes I would steal a little money from my mother's purse to buy cigarettes. I once hid the money behind the lavatory but, alas, my mother discovered it.

Was she very angry with you?

Luckily, she only laughed. She knew about the stealing but not yet about the smoking. It was a more serious matter when one night I fell asleep while smoking secretly in bed. It might have been the end of me, but I only succeeded in burning a hole in the sheet. That was enough to reveal my secret and I got a good kick the next morning.

But that wasn't the end of my mischief. On another occasion I was given one of the two slaps I ever received from Jean Devergie. Oboists are, as you know, forever anxious about their reeds; they treat them with religious awe, devoting infinite care to their construction. Once, when Devergie was out, I stole into his room and opened the charming little box in which he kept his precious reeds. They looked like jewels, placed as they were in their setting of blue velvet. I thought that I too might have the pleasure of playing with them and scraping them with a knife just like he did. Did I get it after that!

When did you earn your second slap?

That was a long time later. Devergie stayed with us for three years until he was engaged to play second oboe in the Boston Symphony. When he left Paris I cried for days. I could not bear the separation; it was a *chagrin d'amour*. I wrote letter after letter to him. My life seemed broken. About three years later, when I was 15, we spent the summer at Dinard on the Breton coast. Devergie, who was taking his holiday in France, was playing in the casino orchestra, and I ardently looked forward to seeing him again. When the time came, however, I was a little disappointed. He seemed so much more interested in girls than he was in me that I thought of him as virtually unfaithful. Of course, he still liked me. Once when I was swimming out in the sea I began, in fun, to gesticulate wildly just as if I were drowning. Seeing me in what appeared to be a desperate plight, he immediately dived into the water and swam out to rescue me. When he finally reached me, I told him that I had only been playing. His face was ashen – he had been terribly frightened – and he was absolutely furious. My second slap was well deserved.

Jean Devergie had great faith in me as a cellist. Some years later he recommended me to Serge Koussevitzky, and was thus responsible for my going to America to play in the Boston Symphony. During the first year my mother and I spent in Boston, we lived in Devergie's house. He had married an Irish-American girl, and they named their first boy 'Paul'. It was a great friendship.

II

A Cabinet-maker's Dreams

My father believed in two things only, but these with his heart and soul: Swedish gymnastics and the eventual arrival of the golden age of collectivism. I have already mentioned the trait of idealism carried over from my grandfather. To this should be added the fact that many of our Breton ancestors were priests. Although my father had lost all sense of traditional religion, his vocation was, none the less, to convert others – to convert them to Marxism. This was for him a way of perpetuating the human and social message of Christianity. He had something of a visionary about him. You could call him a Christian without the religious side.

While my father rarely spoke of music or art, he would spend hours on end discussing the social order, philosophy or ethics. When we lived in the rue de Trétaigne, we had a close friend on the first floor, a socialist, with whom he would enter into endless polemics. He also had many Jewish friends, just as I have, and they introduced him to the teachings of Karl Marx. One of these was the shoemaker, Mr. Kaït, who lived just across the way from my father's workshop. Our simple rooms seemed luxurious compared with the poverty of this man and his family of four children. His wife always looked as white as death; he himself had a worn, haggard look, and would go unshaven for a month. Yet he shared my father's idealism. Forgetting the hardship they each had to endure, they would sit up long into the night, planning the redemption of society through a system of social equity based upon the principle of human love.

To the same extent that my mother was determined to make a cellist of me, my father was determined to make a man of me. He had a Spartan view of education and wanted to develop the masculine side. My mother stressed the artistic side which, if there is no other influence, can weaken the personality since it develops sensitivity at the expense of vitality. My father's chief concern was that I should get out on to the street every day, where I could have sun and air. You can imagine that it didn't require much effort on my part to fulfil his wish. When my mother went on an errand, my father would often come to me and say, 'Paul, leave your cello for a while; go out and play.' I had marvellous health, unbelievable health. My father told me to wash in cold water and not to wear warm clothing. I never wore a vest or jacket, and needed no more than a shirt on my chest the whole winter despite the extreme cold. When I went out I always ran; I never walked. Even today I hardly ever walk; if I take a 'stroll' with a friend, he ends up running alongside me.

During the late 1970s Paul's friend and colleague Raphael Sommer was staying at a hotel in Nice near the Tortelier house. At 6 a.m. he heard a knock on his window. He opened the shutter with some trepidation; there to his amazement he discovered Paul standing on the terrace. Having found the front entrance closed at that hour, Paul had scaled the rear fence and – not knowing which room was Raphael's – had climbed over several balconies and knocked on two or three windows until he found the right one. It was time to go jogging!

My father acted as my mentor in his beloved Swedish gymnastics, and we rode bicycles together. To this day, when I cycle uphill, I remember my father having taught me to ride in a zigzag pattern to make the climb easier. Once, when I was 10 or 11, I had an accident. My bicycle wheel got caught in a tram rail, and as I fell I smashed my knee against the pedal. That was the first time I ever had to go to hospital. I had my leg in plaster for a month and I still have the scar.

One of the disadvantages of having moved into the ground-floor flat in the rue Marcadet was that our quarters were very cramped. We had only two small rooms – a bedroom and kitchen – tucked away behind my father's workshop. All these artisans lived in rooms behind their shops as they do in an Arab Souk. We had no sunshine there and, given the Parisian climate, our rooms were damp a good part of the time. As a result, when I was 13 I came down with rheumatic fever and was nearly paralysed for a month. Curiously enough, my mother had had the same illness herself at the age of 13. There seemed to be a veritable chain of 13s. My illness prevented me from participating in the cello competition which was to be held on Friday the 13th, and for which I had drawn the number 13. Furthermore, I took my cello lessons from my beloved teacher Feuillard in Room No. 13. So, you see, it was the thirteenth day, I was 13, I was number 13, and in Room 13.

My rheumatic fever left me with a heart murmur which had at least one good result in that it excluded me from military service, which lasted three years and could be ruinous to a musical career. In any case, my father, like Casals's mother, was unalterably opposed to militarism and would have gone to any lengths to keep me out.

That was the only serious illness of my life, and I have only missed one concert because of flu. If I've generally enjoyed good health, I owe it to my father.

My mother was a large, sturdy woman, with a bosom in the style of Mae West. My father, however, was small as many Bretons are, small and thin – so skinny that his bones showed through, as mine do. His back was a little bent. Despite his slight appearance, he had amazing physical strength. Jean Devergie and Etienne Baudo – also men of considerable strength – liked to challenge my father to a match of hand wrestling. This game was normally played by two men who would sit facing one another, then grab hands to see who could first force the other's arm down to the table. Instead of beginning in the usual position with the forearm held vertically, my father took a handicap by beginning with his arm already down on the table in the loser's position. At this point he would ask the two men, Devergie and Baudo to grasp his hand and, pitching his might against their combined strength, would force their two arms all the way back across the table and pin them down on the other side. Such was the pressure on the table that on one occasion we heard an impressive crack. You could not fight a man of such strength. He had strong legs as well. He was proud of an enormous leap he had once made. In the middle of the night, after having danced for many hours, he leapt over six chairs. Although the floor was polished, he carried out this feat so skilfully that he didn't slip at all.

In addition to doing repair work, my father made such things as dining-room tables and wall cabinets. All his work was done by hand, and only in his later years did he make a concession to the machine age by buying a little electric saw. He never wore a coat and tie – except on Sundays when, although he didn't go to church, he put on his best suit in keeping with the French tradition.

My father would deliver his work to his clients himself on foot, pulling a wheelbarrow to which the furniture was attached by two straps. Sometimes he had to climb the rue Ramey – a steep hill – like a horse. He was a ceaseless worker. At midnight you could still see his light burning; yet he was up every morning at five.

You also wake up at five in the morning. Is that an inheritance from your parents?

Both my parents required very little sleep, and I am the same. Five hours usually suffice.

Given all your concerts and travelling, is that really enough?

If I do need a little more, I find it everywhere except in bed. As soon as I sit down in a car or in a plane I fall asleep. I don't waste time; the moment you drive me to a concert I'm snoring away. But in bed I cannot sleep for long. I'm usually up at the crack of dawn composing or writing letters.

If you hadn't become a cellist, do you think you might have been a cabinet-maker like your father and grandfather?

My father would not have been unhappy if I'd followed in the family profession. Sometimes he would show me how to handle the wood, and how to take care of my fingers when approaching the blade.

Do you feel that your father was something of an artist in his own way?

He had good taste as well as enormous patience. He worked with great precision, looking for perfection in whatever he did. Sometimes he would even caress his furniture.

Is there perhaps some connection between your father's fine craftsmanship and your artistry on the cello?

Perhaps in a general sense, but my father was an excellent designer, and I cannot design.

You design with your bow; you design the musical phrase.

Yes, but I can't design with a pencil; I couldn't draw a map if you asked me to. Away from the cello I am very unskilful with my hands.

My father's gestures were soft and sensitive, whether he dealt with a cabinet or with me. He never laid a hand on me. He was like an angel with children. They could come into his shop and be all over him when he was trying to work, and he would say nothing. I sometimes really tortured him. If his head happened to be turned away from me and I wanted him to answer a question, I would reach around, grab his beard and jerk his head towards me. He would never complain; I could do anything. He wanted to make me happy and was never more pleased than when he could make me laugh. I always enjoyed myself with him.

Some of the happiest memories of my childhood are those of holidays we took each summer by the sea, for instance at Cabourg in Normandy or Les Sables d'Olonne on the Atlantic coast. My father loved practical jokes. I recall one such occasion when, on the beach at Cabourg, he suggested to me and a group of my friends that we come up to him as if we were strangers and insult him. Imagine our joy when we shouted derisively, 'You bearded old fool, you old crock, what are you doing here?' And our joy became all the more intense when the people around us, justifiably scandalized, tried to stop us. Papa meanwhile stimulated their reaction by saying, 'Isn't it shameful? Such kids! What sort of parents do they have?' Then, when we could find no more words to express our wickedness, when the situation had become sufficiently tense, Papa suddenly said with great simplicity, 'Well now, children, let's go home.' You can picture the amazed faces around us, and our pleasure as we gathered round my father. This epitomizes his spirit.

Though my father was, as I have said, amazingly patient with children, this patience quickly gave way with my mother. For some reason they just couldn't get on together; they were always arguing. They eventually separated. One of the contributing factors – a last straw – was Sebiro, my father's assistant carpenter. Sebiro resembled an old drunken version of D'Artagnan in *The Three Musketeers* – the same flowing moustache, the same tilt of the head. He would have been an unbearable companion for anyone but my father who, possessing the soul of a missionary, had decided to save Sebiro from spectacular alcoholism. It was hopeless to try to reform Sebiro who spent more time begging at the entrance of the Métro Lamarck than helping in my father's workshop. The climax came one day when he actually set the workshop on fire. At that point my father resolved to get rid of him, but it was too late. He had been patient with Sebiro for too long and could not bring himself to let him go.

My mother had a helper of sorts in Sebiro's sweetheart – also an alcoholic – a pathetic little creature who looked like a mouse, and who sometimes begged alongside Sebiro at the Métro. She was the only household help my mother ever had. The arrangement lasted no more than a few months, and it's doubtful whether it was really very useful. All Sebiro's sweetheart could do was to wash dishes. You can imagine the couple. Sebiro was successful with women of this type. I recall his bringing home another girlfriend, a dirty, fat woman who must have been in her late 60s, whom he called with great respect *La Comtesse de la Faucherie* – which means something like 'The Bankrupt Countess'. *La Comtesse de la Faucherie* had a royal manner which compensated for her ruined clothes. He would say to her between hiccups, 'Countess, your desires are orders before which I bow.' It was a great moment in the small kitchen of 120 rue Marcadet, where my mother was feeding a dozen people, when pearls of that sort dropped from Sebiro's mouth.

When I was 14 my parents finally separated.

How did you feel about that?

It didn't come as a shock because since I was about 9 they had mostly been living apart. Although my father had kept his workshop in our flat, after finishing work he would go to our former apartment; eventually he moved to another house where he kept a room. I can't say whose fault it was that their marriage failed. At the time, I was on my mother's side because it's normal, I think, for the boy to be rather close to the mother and the girl close to the father. I also stayed with my mother because she did so much for my musical education while my father was quite detached from me in that respect. So when they separated, my mother and I found new lodgings in a kind of hotel farther up along the same rue Marcadet. We continued to keep some boarders, but now only three or four. My sister had now married and lived independently from us, so my mother's load was a little lightened.

Did you maintain a close relationship with your father after your parents were separated?

You know how children are. They forget; they are busy. I was 14 at the time and already earning my own living. But my mother was fair; she reminded me to visit my father. Sunday was supposed to be my day off, but all the same I had to play my cello in the cinema. It was between the film showings that I would go to chat with my father as we walked around a billiard table.

He eventually met another woman who was devoted to him, and who lived with him until his death. She fancied herself to be something of a chef. One day when I was invited to lunch she fed me *Tripes à la mode de Caen* – a French speciality with a very rich sauce. That evening I returned home only to find that my mother had prepared the same dish for dinner. Fate or chance? That's the trouble with having two mothers. As a result I couldn't face another plate of tripe for half a century.

My father spent his last days in dire poverty, living in a little watchman's hut which overlooked a timber yard.

After all his years of labour hadn't he managed to save any money?

Poor Father! He kept all his money in his shop, simply because he was opposed to capitalism and its banking system. As a result, all he had saved by the sweat of his brow during several decades was stolen in one day.

By a capitalist or a communist?

That I don't know. Perhaps by Sebiro . . . though I doubt it. After that he put his money in the Workers' and Peasants' Bank run by the Communist Party, and his money was lost once more. So he died as poor as Job, I'm ashamed to say, because I failed to give him any help. Luckily he was not alone. He did have the woman with him who had cooked the tripe. She once said to me, 'You know, your father is a Christ.' That was so in many ways. He was a marvellous man, something which I didn't then fully value. At that time I appreciated immediate results, such as my success in the cello and harmony examinations. I didn't realize that what my father taught me would enrich my later life.

Would you expand upon that?

He was a humanist and transmitted his ideals to me. I would say that without ideals I couldn't play one note as I do. However well I might play the cello, it wouldn't sound the same. This idealism was the food my father brought to me, but, at the time, we mocked him for it. He was mocked the way Christ was mocked in the streets. I don't say he was actually a Christ; I simply quote the words of his second wife.

Despite the fact that he ended his life in dire poverty, he was not, then, an unhappy man.

No, not at all, except that during his last years he endured terrible physical suffering, which he bore with great fortitude.

He died in 1945. It is to my everlasting regret that I was not with him during his final moments. He had been suffering from a liver complaint for which he'd undergone an operation that simply left him in a more pathetic condition. I am ashamed not only that I failed to help him financially, but that I didn't cancel a concert I was scheduled to give in Lyon at the time of his death. Of course, it is easy for me to say that now when I have more offers of concerts than I can cope with. But up to that time I had the greatest difficulty finding engagements. By then it had been fifteen years since I had left the Conservatoire, yet I had hardly performed anywhere as a soloist. I knew my father was failing, but I thought I would have enough time to play the concert. When I returned it was too late. Profoundly moved by his death, I wrote a suite for unaccompanied cello, based on the model of

Bach, but in my own way. I tried in this work to express my grief.

There was one ray of consolation. My father lived just long enough to see the Liberation. That was a supremely happy moment for him.

III

Accepting my Destiny

*Do you remember your first cello teacher, Béatrice Bluhm, with
whom you began to study at the age of six?*

Oh yes. She was like a mother. She was admirable. I remember
her with great tenderness.

Were you a difficult child to teach, temperamentally?

She knew perfectly well how to deal with me, But, as far as I
can recall, I was generally polite and respectful.

What did she emphasize in the lessons?

What I remember most clearly is that she took great care with
my bow stroke right from the beginning. She followed the
sound principles of the Franco-Belgian school which is based
upon flexibility of the wrist and suppleness of the arm. Of course,
what makes a school is the teacher, not the country. There are,
none the less, some typical French characteristics, particularly
in the use of the bow. This may have something to do with the
technique of fencing which the French have developed to a high
degree. Don't forget that France is the country of the Three
Musketeers and D'Artagnan. Even today – though we get few
gold medals at the Olympic games – if we win at all, it is in
fencing. Manipulating the bow is very much like fencing; you
need a strong, yet supple wrist, with quick reflexes.

I also remember Béatrice Bluhm's studio. It was not luxurious,
but in its harmonious arrangement of tapestries and paintings it

had an alluring artistic atmosphere which appealed to me. And I
still remember the sort of clothing she wore. Nothing was stiff;
there was a feeling of suppleness, of freedom. And this feeling
of suppleness related to her cello teaching as well. The cello is a
difficult instrument to play at any age, but particularly for a
child. There are thick strings to press down and long distances
to reach between the notes. The great danger is to strain the left
hand. If a teacher puts too much stress on stretching the fingers,
stiffness can easily develop. It is not good to be too strict about
these extensions. So, for example, where a long reach was required from one note to another, Béatrice Bluhm would make a
kind of articulated *glissando*, a quick and supple movement of
the whole hand. Some people might object, musically speaking,
but she avoided stretching the tendons, and for a child's hand
this was crucially important. She also allowed me to play with
vibrato quite early, and that was all to the good. Vibrato helps
assure the suppleness of the hand.

I think that women have a particular flair for playing and
teaching the cello. They teach you how to feel; they create
images for you. I notice this in my wife's teaching, and I recall
that Béatrice Bluhm taught in much the same way. One sometimes sees a woman holding the cello so tenderly that you have
the feeling she is cradling a child. It is something physically
natural for them.

At that time, as I have said, very few women played the cello.
It was supposed to be a man's instrument – like the trombone –
requiring great strength. Women also tended to react with a
certain prudery about playing an instrument which required
sitting with their legs apart, an unnatural thing at that time
when ladies did not wear trousers. In fact Béatrice Bluhm
normally played the cello with her legs together, as a woman
would do when riding side-saddle. The fashion of the time with
its narrow skirts certainly didn't help matters. I think that the
changing role of women in society, the gradual establishment
of professional and physical equality with men, has been a
factor in the modern woman's acceptance of the cello. Nearly
as many women as men now play the instrument. And, speaking qualitatively, the female sex may even have the edge. A
year or two before he died, Casals commented to me, 'Have

you noticed that, in general, women are more gifted for the cello than men?'

Béatrice Bluhm had two sisters: Sasha and Nora. Considering the time in which they lived these three sisters were rather emancipated. For instance, one of them had a child without being married, and raised the child herself. That was Nora, a vivacious person without inhibitions. As for Sasha, she had the beauty of a Nordic goddess; all three were strong women, and as blonde as could be.

Together with Nora's daughter Lola, the Bluhm sisters formed a string quartet. They had a house in Sèvres on the outskirts of Paris, near the woods, not far from Meudon where Rodin had worked. It was like an Impressionist painting to see them in their beautiful garden in spring, wearing lovely, light dresses. They had carnation-pink complexions and blue eyes. They could truly have stepped out of a painting by Renoir. I recently met one of these ladies again after many years; it was Sasha who had been the first violinist of this quartet. She was now over eighty. 'You know, Paul,' she said, 'when you were a child, you came one Sunday to a little party we gave, and played a transcription of the *Prize Song* from *Die Meistersinger*. Although you were only 8 or 9 and had never heard any Wagner and knew nothing of his style, you felt completely the spirit of the piece, the singing line, the sense of majesty.' This shows that style is not something which comes exclusively from study. Style is also something you have to feel intuitively.

How long did you study with Béatrice Bluhm?

Until I was about 9. At that point she suggested that I should go to Louis Feuillard. She felt she hadn't enough to give me for my future, and believed it to be the right moment for me to move on. Although she continued to follow my progress with interest, she wasn't at all possessive.

Just the opposite of many teachers.

Indeed! She was a remarkable woman. And fortunately for me Feuillard proved to be no less remarkable a man. I studied with him privately from the age of 9 until I entered his class at the Conservatoire when I was 12. I continued with him there until, at 14, I went on to study with Gérard Hekking who taught the older students at the Conservatoire.

As Feuillard was a renowned teacher and extremely busy, wasn't it exceptional that he should have accepted you as a student when you were only 9.

He had very few pupils of that age.

Did he recognize your talent at once?

Yes, I think so.

What sort of a man was he?

Feuillard's appearance somewhat belied his exceptional qualities. He was small, modest, sober, not at all prepossessing. He was a bachelor in the sense of being a widower entirely dedicated to his students, and he followed the highest principles, like a man of the church; you never saw a woman other than the housekeeper in his house. And he was old-fashioned in his dress, with a little bow tie and a typical stiff collar, most severe in appearance.

A bit like Anton Bruckner.

Very much so. But behind this somewhat forbidding exterior he possessed a heart – the best heart you could imagine, and a warmth, betraying his Burgundian origins (he was born in Dijon). He had kind eyes; there was light in his eyes. He had no children of his own, and he soon became like a second father to me.

Feuillard had an extraordinary pedagogical sense. His teaching material is now famous; it reflects the power of his love. He had the intuition and intelligence to know how to deal with youngsters. He knew that they must not be presented with a thick book of études, that playing page after page of the same sort of exercise can become tedious. They should be given just what is needed – no more, no less – and it has to be pleasant.

My son began his cello studies with Feuillard's Young Violoncellist's Method. *At the top of each page there are two or three exercises going to the heart of a new idea, and at the bottom of the page this idea is incorporated into a short piece. The student can thus quickly assimilate the whole page.*

It is extremely important to isolate technical problems – not to leave the student in a state of confusion. If, when playing the piano, a hand goes wrong, one knows at once which one it is. With a string instrument this is less obvious. So Feuillard would first ask the student to play the passage *pizzicato* to be sure that the pressure of the fingers of the left hand was adequate.

If it sounded well and, of course, in tune, it meant that the left hand was correct. In this way the youngster could discover where his difficulty lay: in the bow or in the left hand. A very simple method, but most effective.

Tell me something of Feuillard's course of study.

He was strict concerning his 'Daily Exercises', and in playing them through every morning I developed the dexterity of my left hand. I still know the whole volume by heart. Otherwise, there was no rigidity in his approach. He knew that I was not yet ready to interpret the Bach Suites when I was 12 or 13, but none the less he let me play them. He may have had deeper reasons for this, but his immediately expressed goal was to develop my bow technique. People study Bach now because they know it is good music and 'one must play only good music'. All this is a little snobbish. When we were young we did not question whether it was good to play Bach because he wrote good music, or bad to play Romberg or Davidoff because their music was less good. We played what was good for the wrist, for sonority, for intonation, for the smooth change of bow at the heel. Feuillard understood the art of variety in teaching. He knew, for instance, that the studies of Popper have different qualities from those of Grutzmacher; they have charm. So he had me play scales, Ševčík, Romberg, studies by Popper and a host of other composers, as well as Bach. If Feuillard understood that a child's interest must be maintained, and that he must have pleasure in studying, that was perhaps his Burgundian side. For now we come to it: to enjoy life when one works! He had such a fragile nature, such a fragile physique, but he was full of fire and enthusiasm.

The Burgundians are a highly sensual people. They are known for their enjoyment of good food and wine. One reads of this in *Colas Breugnon* by Romain Rolland. Maurice Maréchal, the leading French cellist of his epoch, also came from Burgundy. Feuillard used to cite Maréchal as an example exhorting me to 'Play with warmth – more warmth!' He would say, 'When Maréchal plays this passage in the Schumann Concerto he makes a lovely *glissando*,' and my dear Feuillard's face would light up in ecstasy. All this was very sensual, despite the fact that Feuillard's appearance was that of a humble solicitor.

Many years after I studied with him, he asked me to make a contribution to his last work *La Technique du Violoncelle* which comprises eight volumes of outstanding classical *études*. He crowned this skilfully graded collection with his own transcription for cello of the Chaconne from Bach's D minor Violin Partita. Wishing to give my *étude* a place of honour at the end of the final volume, just before the Chaconne, he asked me to write the most difficult piece I could invent. I did so, indeed, composing a two-page waltz in the key of C sharp minor, consisting of the most unusual combinations of double stops taking one through every register of the cello. Its difficulties are so extreme that for many years I was virtually the only person who could play it.

Whose was the first beautiful cello playing that inspired you? Was it Feuillard's?

Feuillard was a great teacher but he was not a great performer. He was too frail, and you need to be very strong to play the cello.

Surely when you were young you must have heard somewhere a cello sonority which moved you, and which you wanted to copy.

No, I don't remember when I first heard such a sonority. Perhaps it was my own.

Did you not hear Maréchal?

Not when I was young. Feuillard just spoke about him, but I never heard him then. I didn't go to concerts. It was another life completely.

Was it because you couldn't afford to go?

I didn't have money, I didn't have curiosity, and, in any case, I had little time. I was hardly aware of the cultural attractions Paris had to offer. I knew nothing of art, of history, or of the world at large. I only knew that I had to play: *'Paul, ton violoncelle'*. My ignorance was, of course, pitiful. But on the other hand I think there's a risk when, as nowadays, people tend to know too many things. They know so much that they lose track of essentials. One learns and learns, but one doesn't have time to think. 'To everything there is a season,' it says in the Bible – 'a time to every purpose under the heaven.' Now, if you try to teach an adolescent science, maths, history, geography, literature, philosophy and I don't know what else, as well as providing a musical education, then he disperses his energy. It's better to be simple to start with. Acquire what is essential, and there will come a time when you will understand all the things you need to know. In fact it's better when one's philosophy develops through the experiences of life rather than through studying books. In any case, in those days the cello was my only concern. Nothing else really mattered; any other learning was kept to the bare minimum.

During the period you studied with Feuillard at the Conservatoire, how long did you practise each day?

I usually did four or five hours, but, of course, I didn't have school.

Did you remain in close contact with Feuillard even after you were no longer his student?

Until the end of his life Feuillard retained his friendship for me, and I my love for him. He took pride in watching me develop. He had great trust in me, and during his last illness he asked me to take over his class and replace him as teacher. My relationship with Feuillard extended beyond the cello. For instance, perhaps noticing how little educated I was, he felt that I should enrich my culture. He once showed me his library of books, and told me of his liking for Maupassant. 'Even though I have so little time for reading,' he said, 'when I am tired I can pick up a Maupassant story and assimilate a full experience in a short period of time.'

And now I own those very books, for when he retired and went to live in his country house in Louveciennes, a suburb of Paris, he left me his fully furnished apartment, including his library which he kept in bookcases made for him by my father. Feuillard was not a rich man; but he none the less asked me to pay only a nominal price for his apartment, *une bouchée de pain*, as we say in France.

Did Feuillard live to see your success?

It is a great sadness for me that Feuillard died before my career began to develop. He was always looking out for concerts for me. He fought hard to get me a modest tour of Burgundy. But though Burgundy was his homeland, though he had contacts there, those engagements never materialized, which shows how badly situated I was as a soloist. He couldn't possibly have imagined my eventual success. I have often thought, after a concert in London or Tel Aviv, Rome or Paris, 'If only Feuillard were here, how happy he would be!'

It was different for my mother. She outlived Feuillard, shared my success with me, and even came to England when I played there. She felt sure that I would have an international career.

When did Feuillard die?

It was during the war, I believe in 1941. I wish he could have watched his own funeral, because it was just like one of the Maupassant tales which he so loved. As I have said, Feuillard was a widower with no children. His nearest relatives were two cousins, far removed, who had naturally assumed that they would be his heirs. But Feuillard was advised by a close friend, 'There is only one right thing to do. Your housekeeper, Alphonsine, has dedicated forty years of her life to taking care of you; she should be your heir.' Feuillard agreed, and to the cousins' dismay, changed his will in Alphonsine's favour, leaving her his house in Louveciennes.

On the day of the funeral, the hearse arrived at Louveciennes to take the coffin the twenty-five kilometres to Paris for the service. Ironically enough, although the cousins were not the heirs, they were, as closest family members, obliged to pay funeral expenses. Owing to war-time restrictions no trains were running, nor was any spare petrol to be had; this vehicle there-fore provided the only means of getting to Paris. I had been asked to play a Bach *air* during the service, but first I went to Louveciennes to accompany Feuillard on his final journey. The coffin was brought out of the house. The cousins and their families followed, and grouped themselves around the coffin in the hearse. Alphonsine came last, attired in mourning – entirely in black, with a black veil, such as the women wear in Italy. She closed the garden gate behind her. But as she prepared to climb into the hearse, one of the cousins rose to bar her way. 'Stay out,' he commanded in bitter tones, 'There is no place for you.' I offered her my seat, but she refused it, saying, 'You have to play at the service.' So she tried to force her way into the hearse. As she was a vigorous woman, it soon turned into a real battle. They fought for several minutes, all shouting at once. Sadly we had to leave without her. I sat in front next to the driver who told me, 'I have seen many things in my life in this job – but never anything like this.' It could indeed have been a scene from Maupassant. Had Feuillard read it, how he would have laughed – not of course at the plight of Alphonsine – but at the way it revealed the truth about human nature.

Well, to return to my story: at the age of 14 I completed my studies with Feuillard, having obtained a first medal with 'first mention' in his class, and I continued my studies at the Conservatoire with Gérard Hekking.

What do you feel you gained most from Hekking?

Above all, rhythmic élan and variety of colour. Hekking had a wonderful feeling for colour. In addition to playing the cello he was, in fact, a painter. He could play Debussy's Sonata in an incomparable way, as this is a work which requires an imagin-ative tone palette. And when it came to rhythm, there were then only two players who could really make Bach dance: Casals and Hekking. Hekking, being Dutch, had the kind of vigorous rhythmic feeling one finds in paintings by Brueghel. This rhythm is something you have to have in your blood. There was always a pulse. Freedom in between the beats – but never disturbing the regular lilt of the dance.

What Casals called 'a rubato which is not a rubato'.

Exactly.

What was Hekking's character like?

The opposite of Feuillard. If Feuillard was the retiring solicitor, Hekking was the Grand Seigneur. He was very handsome, seductive and, in fact, a sort of Don Juan. The girls were all in love with him, and his many adventures made it rather hard going on his wife – but he had great charm and a wonderful smile. He sparkled with wit, and his smile would often light up with malice. Feuillard – although highly intelligent – was not really witty; his jokes never had bite to them. Hekking knew how to use his wit. But he also learned that irony can, on occasion, be one's worst enemy. As he liked me very much, he counselled, 'Paul, no matter what you think of a colleague, you must always speak well of him' – advice which he himself did not always take to heart.

Have you always followed that advice?

I have tried. Whenever I've recalled Hekking's words, they've acted like a brake and have helped me avoid some difficult situations – some, but not all.

The brilliant young cellist, Leslie Parnas, winner of the first prize in the 1957 *Concours International Pablo Casals*, was playing the Dvořák Concerto under the direction of a well-known conductor. The concert was being broadcast. Not only Paul, but Casals himself was in the audience. As the performance progressed Paul became increasingly agitated. The orchestra repeatedly covered the soloist and sometimes drowned him entirely. Paul knew full well how difficult it is for a cellist to play under such circumstances. He identified himself with Parnas to such a degree that he could bear it no longer. In the hush between the second and third movements he addressed the conductor from the middle of the hall: 'Pay attention, my friend, the orchestra is a bit too loud.' An acutely embarrassing silence – and the Finale began. Not surprisingly, the conductor felt that he had been given an elementary music lesson in public. After the concert he stalked the corridors brandishing his baton menacingly in case he should meet his critic. Meanwhile, Paul had gone to Casals. 'Maître,' he asked, kneeling before him, 'can you forgive me for this action?' The great man replied, 'What you did was justified – it was a cry from the heart.'

Are you discreet with your criticisms when you teach?

When I teach? Oh, no. I am severe, very severe.

Did you have any particular technical problems at the time you were studying at the Conservatoire?

I had a problem with the strength of the bow. To gain more power I did something unorthodox and put my little finger underneath the screw at the very heel of the bow.

I noted with interest, in a recent concert, that in a certain forte *passage you did just that.*

Long ago I did it because I was young. Now I do it because I am old. It helps me concentrate the strength of the bow. But it's a technique to be used only on rare occasions. I must be rather careful, especially when I get excited, not to apply an excess of pressure to the string. This is particularly important when recording. In a concert hall you have to send the sound out boldly; you have to articulate to reach the last row. But when you make a recording, the microphone will pick up the slightest unpleasant friction of the bow. Recording is really such a problem. It discourages you before you succeed; it's absolutely merciless.

When did you leave Hekking's class?

At 16 when I took my first prize (again with 'first mention') at the Conservatoire.

Wasn't that very young to be awarded such a high distinction?

Normally one would be 18 or 20. I had tried for the prize the previous year, when I was 15, but had fallen short of gaining it, despite the fact that Fernand Pollain – an eminent cellist – thought I should have received it. This failure served to arouse my competitive instinct. Thus, when I took part in the examination the following year, I absolutely made up my mind to win, in fact completely to outdistance all the others.

This led to a rather amusing situation. For this examination we were obliged to play the first two movements of the Elgar Cello Concerto. I felt even then that the haunting lyrical 9/8 theme of the first movement should be played with the greatest purity; I wanted to avoid the customary *glissandi*. This isn't to say that I never make *glissandi*. They're natural to the singing voice, and, when used in their proper place, provide the string player with a beautiful means of expression. But each passage has its own character, and I feel that *glissandi* are not appropriate to this particular theme. As I am blessed with a large hand, I was able to devise a special fingering which enabled me, by the use of extensions, to avoid all slides. In those days I used even more extensions than I do now. My fingering was, of course, not the traditional one, and I decided to keep it to myself, taking care not to show it to my colleagues who were preparing the same piece. The only problem was that we had to perform the work in Hekking's class. So I learned two sets of fingerings, dutifully adopting that used by the class when playing there, the other being my own which I worked on privately.

Had you devised this fingering yourself?

Partly, but I also had the help of a Mr Foussard, the first cellist in the Théâtre Marigny, one of the places in which I was earning my living at the time. Some forty years later, when I was playing the Elgar Concerto in the Royal Festival Hall, my old friend Foussard was in the audience. When the concerto ended, I beckoned to him to come up to the stage, embraced him, and told the audience, 'I wish to introduce to you a colleague of mine. You may find it strange that I should greet a colleague like this, but Mr Foussard is a French cellist who helped me with my fingering in the Elgar Concerto so that I was able to obtain my first prize at the Paris Conservatoire in 1930.'

For the Scherzo the fingering was entirely my own. In this movement the *sautillé* bowing is particularly difficult. My way of making use of all my fingers in whatever register I was playing enabled me to minimize the movements of the left hand, and I could thus concentrate more fully on the bow.

What was Hekking's reaction when he saw your fingering?

I had wanted to try out my fingering at least once in public prior to the examination. So I waited until the last moment, and used it at the general rehearsal. Hekking was in the hall and I remember his surprise as he watched me play. He had a light smile on his lips and a brightness in his eyes. It says much for his generosity that, rather than resenting my impertinence, he respected me for trying out new ideas and developing my own technical approach.

Did you have any further cello lessons after leaving Hekking's class at the age of 16?

No, strangely enough. Occasionally I went to play to Hekking, but only occasionally. I had no real teacher. The essential thing is that I was well taught from the beginning. I am indebted to Béatrice Bluhm and to Feuillard. By the time I was 13 or 14, I had a good bow technique, sure intonation and clear articulation. And I am grateful to Gérard Hekking for all he conveyed to me in the way of rhythmic vitality and variety of coloration.

Didn't you want to know about schools of cello playing outside France?

No, not really. I travelled only for the necessity of earning my living. Perhaps the French school of cello playing was enough for me. I never had the curiosity so prevalent today to learn from other schools. I was already, perhaps unconsciously, preparing my own 'school'. Even when I was 12 I wanted to interpret in my own way. I didn't do this for the sake of being contradictory. I did it because I wondered, 'How can this be made to sound more beautiful?' And Feuillard let me be free; he was very liberal in this respect. He let me change the printed bowings and, on occasion, the nuances. Later, of course, I realized that in most cases it's better to play as written. But at the time it was a sort of creative exploration around the original, and I think it was good for me. I was already searching for my own way of playing and interpreting, not to be different from the others – just to be better.

IV

Earning a Living: Paris circa 1930

From the age of 12 or 13, I had to help out by partly earning my own living. For two years I had a job on Fridays, Saturdays and Sundays, playing accompaniments to silent films in a cinema in la Plaine St-Denis, the poorest quarter you could imagine – and what a really dirty and terrible place that cinema was! Two full-length films were shown, starting at 8.30 p.m. and ending at nearly midnight. My mother would stay up for me with a nice cup of *café au lait*, and I wouldn't be asleep until 1.0 a.m. On Sundays films were shown continuously from 2.0 p.m. until midnight. Normally my duties began only in the evening, but on one occasion I replaced a man who had fallen ill and I had to stay the full time. By the end of that day I was so tired that, in order to carry on playing, I had to rest my bow-arm on my knee and move the knee instead of the arm in order to push the bow across the strings.

It sounds like a scene from a Dickens novel . . .

Luckily I didn't have to do that daily; otherwise I would already be in the cemetery. But, in fact, some people worked like that every day.

Wasn't it absolutely exhausting to have such a job?

Not the best thing for a boy studying at the Conservatoire, but it had two compensations. First of all it taught me to sight-read. A pile of music would be placed before me on an especially large music stand. I had to be ready to change instantly from a quick piece to a slow piece depending on what was happening on the screen. In the poor cinema of la Plaine St-Denis we were only three musicians – a piano trio – but in more respectable cinemas the orchestra consisted of ten or twelve musicians: an oboe, a clarinet, a cello, two violins, a piano and so on – a heterogeneous ensemble to say the least. We played some Beethoven, some Wagner, and reams of tenth-rate, if academically correct music written for the silent movies by specialists – French composers who made money doing this kind of thing, and whose names are forgotten today. The conductor had a button on his desk which controlled a red light. He watched the screen constantly. We might be playing some sentimental music for a love scene, but if a horse began to gallop, he would press the button and within half a second the orchestra had to attack a *prestissimo*. When a new film was shown there would be a new pile of music before us and you never knew what was coming. It seems amusing in retrospect, but in fact it was a rather painful experience.

The other compensation was that it gave me further access to the magic world of the motion picture. In one of these cinemas I could just see the screen from my position, and, as I was 14, you can imagine my temptation to look up. I gradually became clever enough to play in the key of the piece that was being performed, without playing what was written – just an improvisation – so as not to lose sight of the film. But one night I suddenly felt a hand on my shoulder. It was the director of the theatre who said sternly, 'You are here to play, not to look.' Even after that, it was hard for me not to resist peeking at the screen.

Once when I was 13 I was asked to replace a cellist playing in an orchestra for an elegant party at the Hôtel Continental.

This was a big occasion for me and I made sure to arrive at the appointed time – a difficult thing for me to do. But when the door-keeper saw me he refused to let me enter the hotel. It took some minutes to convince him that in spite of my youth I was really supposed to be there. When I was finally allowed in, I saw the orchestra already assembled at the far end of a vast ballroom. I was dazzled by the bright lights, by the lustrous silverware, by the magnificent gowns of the ladies. I had never seen anything like it. As I crossed the full length of the floor, everyone turned to look at me. I was still a small boy, wearing my long trousers for the first time, and the cello I carried was about as tall as I was. I was terribly embarrassed and blushed even more when I saw that the members of the orchestra were also staring at me, wondering who this child could be who dared to arrive late. I began to sight-read the pieces and all went well, so well in fact that I was bold enough to ask whether I could play a solo. More scepticism. But finally they let me play *'The Swan'* by Saint-Saëns, and I had my greatest triumph.

When did you have a chance to play in a good orchestra?

Not for some time. I first had a series of jobs in brasseries in various parts of Paris, one such place being the Dreher in the Place du Châtelet, an establishment well known for its music. Famous musicians, such as Jacques Thibaud, had played there in their youth. Our programmes consisted of excerpts from such pieces as *Manon* or *Rose Marie*. I also played in La Lorraine, where people leaving the Salle Playel would go to have supper. On another occasion I played in a brasserie where the composer of 'La Madelon' was engaged as pianist. Do you know 'La Madelon'? It's a song that was popular during the 1914–18 war, like 'If You Knew Susie . . .'

There was a little organization which provided musicians with a list of jobs available from night to night. I played in a number of brasseries, substituting for cellists who couldn't fulfil engagements. Each place had a style of its own. I once went to a brasserie in the rue de la Jonquière where I was to play with two Hungarians specializing in gypsy music. When I arrived I asked for the cello part for the pieces we would play. But they only laughed and said, 'We never play with music.' I told them that I hadn't ever played spontaneously like that. 'Well then, you must try!' And they launched into a Csárdás. I had to improvise a cello part the whole evening to gypsy melodies that I had never heard before. Somehow I managed and they seemed pleased.

Do you think that your playing in the brasseries may have contributed to your ability to communicate to the public with your cello?

I have never thought about it like that, but I believe there could be something in what you say. After all, performing in public night after night was quite different from practising in a small room. The arrangements I played were pretty awful, but some of the melodies were first rate. A musician must always find the soul of a melody and let it speak directly to the public. My experience was undoubtedly helpful in this respect.

For instance I once played in a brasserie near the Gare de l'Est, together with a Monsieur Halleux, a pianist, and Madame Halleux, an enormous lady who played the violin with a nice fat vibrato. They were specialists in operatic *pot-pourris*, not only *Manon* and *La Bohème*, but *Lakmé, Carmen* and all sorts of operas which I had never heard. Don't forget that at the time, when I was 14, I had never seen an opera in my life. They told me that I played the cello well enough but that I knew nothing of the lyric tradition, that I didn't take enough liberty. They showed me where I must sustain the high notes, make a *rallentando* here, an *accelerando* there . . . and I felt completely at sea. But little by little I began to catch on. Learning to play in an operatic style was valuable to my sense of projection of tone and line. It was helpful to have to play the cello as if I were a singer.

All music is related to song; some instrumentalists tend to forget that. As a conductor, I find it invaluable to sing through any piece I'm preparing. Singing goes right to the heart of expression.

I know that a student is talented if he can sing expressively – with or without a decent voice. The ancient Chinese put it very beautifully: 'The harmony of the heart produces the harmony of the breath which produces the harmony of music.' If one understands that, one needs little more. Breathing is at the root of music. Pianists and string players are handicapped by the fact that their performance is not based upon breathing; wind players and singers are closer to natural phrasing.

It is also important for string players to find an equivalent to the singer's *parlando*. When I play Beethoven's Variations on *Bei Männern, welche Liebe fühlen* from *The Magic Flute*, I follow the text in my imagination, and shift my finger in accordance with the accentuation of the words. When I recorded a cello transcription of *Après un Rêve* by Fauré, I studied the words carefully to be able to come as close as I could to the spirit of the song.

I actually did sing during one of my engagements – and with considerable success if I may say so. When I was 17, I spent the summer in Luchon, playing in a café orchestra. There was a garden behind this café, and, on the rare occasions when it wasn't raining, the proprietor would engage two or three singers and put on a little operetta. For one such *revue* he needed someone able to impersonate Maurice Chevalier. As I adored Chevalier and knew all his songs by heart, I volunteered. Donning appropriate straw hat and dinner jacket, and surrounded by young girls dressed in peasant costume and men strumming tennis rackets as if they were banjos, I entertained the audience with Chevalier favourites such as 'Valentine' and 'Les Ananas'. It's amusing that many years later, on occasions when I would talk to an English public about a musical work, I was often compared to Maurice Chevalier. Was it my accent perhaps?

When I was about 18 I finally got my first job with a real orchestra, as sub-principal cellist with the Orchestra de Radio-Paris. The radio was not then a governmental institution, but a private broadcasting station. Eventually I also joined the Orchestra de la Société des Concerts du Conservatoire, one of the finest ensembles in Paris. Its principal conductor was Philippe Gaubert, a first-rate musician, a composer, and the outstanding flautist of his time. I have already spoken of the natural agility of the French hand for the bow, but France is also famous for its many fine wind players. This may be partly due to the way the tongue is used in the French language. In any case, playing in this orchestra was an important step forward in my artistic experience, since it acquainted me with a whole repertoire which I never knew existed. One of my earliest discoveries was the *Siegfried Idyll*. How moved I was! I also played in the Orchestra de la Société Philharmonique conducted by Charles Munch, and in the Concerts Straram. Both were *orchestres de luxe* which met for short seasons. Under Walter Straram's direction I made the thrilling discovery of Richard Strauss's music. His tone poems were quite new to the Parisians, fed as they were on a steady diet of Beethoven, the *Unfinished* Symphony of Schubert and the *Pathétique* Symphony of Tchaikovsky. A certain amount of contemporary music was played in private circles and in the

Paul's father, Joseph Tortelier,
towards the end of his life.

Paul's mother,
Marguerite Tortelier (*née*
Bovra) at 75.

Paul, aged 4, with his sister
Geneviève.

Paul (*right*) with his first cello teacher Béatrice Bluhm (*centre*) and
another student, c. 1925.

Paul wearing his best velvet *blouse russe*, c. 1924.

Paul aged 18.

salon of the Princesse de Polignac – Poulenc, Honegger, Milhaud. (The time of Bartók had not yet come – in France at least.) However, it was mainly when playing under the direction of Roger Desormières and Nadia Boulanger that I discovered the *musique moderne* of the epoch, in particular Stravinsky because he was Nadia Boulanger's idol. By the time I had heard *The Firebird, Petroushka, Le Sacre du printemps* and the *Symphony of Psalms*, as well as *Don Juan* and *Till Eulenspiegel*, I began to consider Stravinsky and Strauss as worthy of taking their place among my musical gods. I would have been amazed had I been able to foresee that only a few years later Strauss himself would hear me play *Don Quixote* under his own direction.

During the same period I became acquainted with some chamber music by another composer who attracted me greatly: Paul Hindemith. This favourable impression was reinforced when I heard his *Concert Music for Strings and Brass* and *Mathis der Maler*. By then the harmonies of Strauss and Stravinsky were familiar to my ears – these composers had almost become classics – and Hindemith offered a new musical experience. Fifty years later I am still fascinated with his music which I consider among the most important of the twentieth century.

Did you ever play at the Opéra?

No, I only played *Carmen* and some operettas during a season at a French spa. I did, however, perform some orchestral excerpts from *Tristan und Isolde*. That was enough to sweep me off my feet. But I had no idea what the whole of *Tristan* was like. I only saw the complete work when I was 60. I have no time to go to the opera. If you have a career like mine which requires travelling, if you have a family, if you have students, if you compose – you are lucky to find time to sleep five or six hours a night. It's my dream to have a three months' holiday to spend as a tourist in Vienna, going to the opera every night.

V

Jean Gallon

In a competition of exceptionally high standard, an adolescent of 16, possessing every gift, played this expressive English music with passion. Monsieur Tortelier has energy in his bow, a beautiful sonority, a sense of rhythm, and a taste for contrasts. He is destined for a most brilliant future.

Henri Malherbe, *le Temps*, 25 June 1930

After I had won my first prize I was ready to launch out upon a solo career. Yet, despite the favourable reviews I received, and a performance of the Lalo Concerto that I gave at the Concerts Lamoureux, I found no way to move forward into the professional musical world. I was no more than a boy from a working-class home, and had none of the proper contacts. I have already mentioned Feuillard's futile efforts to find me engagements. So I had no choice but to continue on my round of brasseries and orchestras. After two years of this, my mother, whose intuition never failed when it came to my musical education, decided that it would be beneficial for me to enter the harmony class at the Conservatoire. Although untutored in such matters, she somehow understood that the study of harmony would be of vital importance to me.

However, when I began the course, I felt that I was entering into a period of martyrdom, and in fact I was to some extent right. The average time required to complete the course was three years. Some students devoted five years to it; if you were gifted you could get through it in two years, but very few did.

48

Even before applying for the course, we had to have a thorough preparatory background in the basic elements of four-part harmony: consonance, dissonance, sequences, imitations, modulations. We had to be able to realize a non-figured bass and make a reasonable harmonization of a given melody. Only then were we admitted to the course, and it did indeed prove to be hard work, particularly during the first year. I was, as we say in French, a *primaire*; I wasn't intellectually prepared in the manner of those students who had gone to university. I was also at a disadvantage in not being a good pianist; if you play the piano you have the harmony in your fingers as well as in your head. For instance, Liszt is said to have tapped his fingers on the table when composing. I should add that the presence of a cellist in the Conservatoire harmony class was a rarity. Until then, only one cellist had succeeded in obtaining the first prize in harmony: Paul Bazelaire, who became a well-known performer and teacher with Pierre Fournier among his students. It was Bazelaire whom I succeeded when many years later I myself became a professor at the Conservatoire. Well, owing to these various factors, I almost gave up in the first year. I couldn't even finish the examination. The second year went better; I was awarded a *premier accessit* which is a sort of honourable mention. That was already something, but in the third year I made a great effort and won the first prize.

Of course what was important was not the first prize in itself – although I was proud of it because I had been a dark horse coming from behind; it was the fact that the prize was obtained in the class of a truly extraordinary teacher: Jean Gallon. During the course of his long career, Gallon counted among his students not only two of the outstanding French composers of the twentieth century, Olivier Messiaen and Henri Dutilleux, but a host of others who eventually became well-known professors of music, such as the present director of the Paris Conservatoire, Raymond Gallois Montbrun. It is sometimes difficult to judge whether it's the teacher who makes the student or the student who makes the teacher; there is no clear-cut boundary. As Dominique Hoppenot puts it in her book *Le Violon Intérieur*, 'The teacher is not above the student; he is merely ahead of him.' Gallon responded with typical modesty when, at his eightieth birthday party, he said of one of his many successful students, 'Oh, that one; he would have succeeded just as well if he had studied with my *concierge.'* At such moments Gallon's face would break into a wide grin and his huge chest – for he was a large and powerful man – would shake with laughter. Not only in his exacting and patient teaching but in his general appearance he reminded me of J. S. Bach.

Gallon helped me to understand music in another dimension: from the point of view of the composer. Of course, he was teaching harmony, not composition nor even counterpoint. But there is no compartmentalization in music, just as there is none in anything in the world. The way he taught the limited field of harmony was so intelligent that it opened doors to other fields. When you left his course, you had also acquired a feeling for counterpoint and for musical architecture.

What was his philosophy as a teacher?

He believed that liberty is not licence. Today the credo is freedom in everything. 'Why should we study in the classical way?' they ask. 'Why follow the rules of the old masters when we can write as we please?' I would answer, 'Would you give a baby whisky to drink?' A beginner in harmony has to drink milk first. During the Renaissance, the great painters began as apprentices, preparing the colour for their masters. All the great composers began with milk – with their mother's milk, I should say – Bach, Mozart, Beethoven – they all began with strict rules. It's the same with the cello. Think of what would happen if I were to say to a beginner, 'Playing the cello is something entirely natural, so hold the bow in any way you please.'

Gallon would remind us that *'les entraves sont salutaires au génie'* – 'fetters foster genius'. We wrote only for the human voice – a limitation, yes, but also a good discipline. The voice cannot leap at random and must remain more or less within the compass of a twelfth. This creates problems, but it is by overcoming such problems that you develop your strength. You think, 'Ah, if only I had a violin here, I could give it a wonderful high note, but all I have at my disposal is a soprano voice which I cannot place higher than G.' You have to find a solution and then sometimes you succeed in making it beautiful. Gallon would insist that one expressive note is worth a dozen banal notes.

As Sibelius put it: 'Every note must be experienced.'

C'est ça. Gallon warned us not to strive for effects through artificial means. While valuing the animating power of counterpoint, he asked us not to introduce it at the expense of harmony just for the sake of being brilliant. Similarly, every modulation had to be meaningful. When he said, 'If you modulate too much, you don't modulate at all,' it was a principle that was valid for your life – in many ways. He would cite the wonderful passage in the development of the first movement of Beethoven's *Pastoral* Symphony where the motif below is repeated over twelve bars in an unchanging Bb major, only to shift suddenly, as if illuminated by light, into D major. The whole process is repeated with an even more unexpected shift from G major to E major. These modulations are rendered particularly effective by their economy.

Gallon was concerned with more than strict rules. If he discovered parallel fifths – forbidden in the textbooks – he didn't mind so much. To him there were major sins and minor sins. To have written a parallel fifth was a minor sin; to have missed a modulation was a major sin. And it was a major sin to make errors in taste. If you were asked to write a piece in the style of the religious music of the sixteenth century, and you inserted a sensual harmony in the style of Schumann, he would say, 'I am reminded of a priest who, while celebrating mass, suddenly reaches for face powder and puts on make-up.' Above all, Gallon stressed that harmony was more than a cerebral process. For instance, he would play a melody by Beethoven or Fauré and ask us, 'What notes do you *feel* should be in the bass?' The study of harmony under Gallon was fascinating, especially in the third year. By then you felt you were something of a composer and could bring your own personality into play.

How did your cello studies progress at the time?

During the last year I had to work so hard on harmony –
sometimes spending eight hours a day on the exercises – that
I completely gave up practising. I did, however, continue
playing the cello to earn my living. As before, I played in
a brasserie every night, but now I was in three orchestras as
well. It was, however, only on Monday, Wednesday and Friday
that everything accumulated. On those days I would usually
rehearse from 9.0 a.m. until noon with the Société des Concerts
du Conservatoire. I would then rush to the radio to perform a
lunchtime concert of light music. A brief interval for the 1.0
news gave me a moment to work on my harmony exercises.
Then from 2.0 to 4.0 p.m. I would attend the harmony class.
Gallon, who would not tolerate latecomers, normally locked
the classroom door at 2.0 p.m. sharp. For example, a student
from an upper class family which always lunched at 1.0 p.m.,
invariably arrived at the class a few minutes late, and thus
found himself locked out for most of the school year. However,
as my radio concert didn't finish until 2.0 p.m., Gallon made an
exception and allowed me to come at 2.15. At 4.0 I would have
a *café crème* with a *croissant*, and play cards with my friends. At
6.0, I was in a brasserie playing popular songs, waltzes and
marches until midnight – except for an hour's break for dinner,
I had to do my harmony work late at night. Sometimes I wrote
all night long, and on mornings when I had no orchestral
rehearsal I would say, '*Maman*, please wake me at noon because
I have to finish my exercise for the 2 o'clock class.' And while I
copied out my work, my mother would feed me my lunch with a
spoon.

*I don't know which is more remarkable: your indefatigable energy,
then as now, or your good fortune in always having a devoted
woman at your side.*

I have worked hard; I have never stopped working – but that's
just a way of life with me. However, it's true, I have been
blessed with good fortune: first with my mother and then with
Maud.

Was it then that you made the acquaintance of Henri Dutilleux?

Dutilleux was a fellow-student in the harmony class, but he had started one year after me. While I was doing the course over three years, he completed it in two, so we finished together. He would coach me in harmony, and we soon became great friends. When Dutilleux entered Gallon's class his exceptional gift as a composer was already apparent – his fine sense of construction, his special feeling for harmonic colour. In recent years I've had the privilege of playing his work for cello and orchestra *Tout un monde lointain* (based on poems by Baudelaire).

During the final year of the course Dutilleux and I took our Easter holiday at the home of his parents in Douai in the north of France. We enjoyed ourselves so much at the nearby seaside resort of Audresselles that we decided to extend our stay two days after the beginning of the new term. Arriving at Gallon's class on the Wednesday instead of the Monday, and a little late at that, we found the door locked. We were both terribly embarrassed, and didn't know what to do. Our friends gave us the harmony exercises when they came out of the class, and we therefore arrived well prepared for Friday's lesson. But to our consternation, Gallon would not let us in. 'I think you two require a full week's rest,' he commented drily. 'You need not bother to come to class today.' He had never done such a thing before, and we were quaking in our boots. The following week we returned and were admitted without comment.

The final examination lasted eighteen hours – from 6.0 a.m. until midnight. We had to arrive with our pockets empty and without books. And the piano was locked – no help there! We were given two musical texts, one being a bass of about forty bars which had to be harmonized, the other being a melody to be completed in four voices. It was so difficult that I only completed the fair copy of my work a few minutes before midnight. I had not stopped since 6.0 a.m. and had only eaten a few cherries and drunk a cup of coffee. Dutilleux took the exam on the same day, and when we finished we staggered out of the room like drunkards. Some days later, after it had been announced that Dutilleux and I had both won the first prize, Gallon addressed the whole harmony class. Recalling our prolonged holiday over

Easter, he said: '*Ils ont pèché ensemble, ils ont expié ensemble et ils ont triomphé ensemble*' – 'They sinned together, they atoned together and they triumphed together.' He grinned and his great chest shook with laughter as he led our comrades, less happy than ourselves, in applause.

Gallon always treated his prize-winners to a dinner at a fine Parisian restaurant. He was a true gourmet; one felt this not only in his approach to food, but in his teaching of harmony. A student was once recommended to him who seemed to have all the necessary qualifications. Gallon interviewed him and found him to be intelligent, serious, musical, and gifted with a fine ear. Yet he turned him down. When asked why he had done so, he answered, 'Because he is a vegetarian.'

I was privileged in having Jean Gallon's friendship until the time of his death in 1959. The three years spent in his class opened the door for me to become a composer, and gave me invaluable insight as an interpreter. I shall speak of these matters at greater length, but for the moment I can only stress that this study proved indispensable to my artistic development.

Do you find that young musicians nowadays tend to omit such essential studies in their impatience to build a career?

It is not good to move too quickly and too early. Rather than flitting from one teacher to another, or from one competition to another, I wish young musicians would delve into the study of composition. Sometimes when I am asked by a student at a master class, 'Where shall I go next? With whom should I study?' I answer, 'You are better off studying harmony and counterpoint in a conservatory, providing there are good teachers. Take your time. Be content with less.' But few have the patience to do it.

A somewhat different attitude from what one normally finds today.

Perhaps I, too, would have lacked that sort of patience had I been immediately successful as a soloist. As I have said, I was ready, but had no such possibilities. Well, thanks to that bad luck I had the good luck to finish my three years' harmony course. During that time I stayed quietly at home. I once told Jean Gallon that I hoped to take a holiday away from Paris during the summer. And do you know what he said? 'If I were you I would stay in Paris because in the summer it's very calm and peaceful here. You can put your knowledge in order, and classify what you have learned. In the morning you can study, and in the afternoon you can take walks in the cemetery of Montmartre.'

VI

Sallying Forth (Don Quixote I)

My confinement to Paris soon came to an end, however. During the autumn of the year in which I had won the harmony prize, I was engaged to play in the orchestra of Monte Carlo as solo cellist. Could that have been in 1934?

It was 1935.

Ah, dates are a torture for me! In any case, my playing was known to René Benedetti, one of the finest violinists in France, who many years later became my son Pascal's teacher. Benedetti recommended me to Mr. Putmann, the administrative director of the Monte Carlo orchestra. I took an audition and got the job. This orchestra had a fine reputation. The permanent conductor was Emil Cooper, a Russian, a good musician who took a kind interest in me. He noticed, for instance, that I rarely used the very lowest part of the bow and suggested that I shouldn't hesitate to begin my bow stroke right at the heel when necessary. I paid attention to that; it's by collecting such pointers that you develop. I discovered a new approach to music through such conductors as Toscanini and Bruno Walter.

What were your impressions of those two great musicians?

I had already performed under Toscanini in Paris when he was invited to conduct the Orchestre Straram. Even today, after nearly fifty years, I can exactly picture Toscanini as he walked to the podium. Those ten seconds were unforgettable; there was something in his manner that riveted the attention of the orchestra even before he began to rehearse. As he stepped quickly across the stage – a slight, and fine figure – the forward bend of his body betrayed a solemn intent of purpose. His baton, held in his right hand was tucked under his right arm. His head, noble and severe, graced with white hair and moustache, emerged from a white scarf just showing above the closed collar of a black jacket. I remember his curious eyes – the eyes of a man, then nearly 70, who was half-blind – that seemed to look straight through you, and which took on a fierce intensity when he conducted.

Once on the podium, he would quickly glance left and right (to the first and second violins respectively), and then in the twinkling of an eye he would alert the orchestra to attack the overture by tapping the back of a music stand with the tip of his baton as elegantly as one would light a match.

His memory was, of course, legendary. Only rarely would he call out for one of his large, beautifully bound scores to consult a detail. He would then hold it right up to his nose, studying it with one eye, having placed the baton under his left arm just like a French peasant carrying an umbrella. For one of his Paris concerts Toscanini had programmed Debussy's *Nocturnes*. Now, in the opening section called *Nuages* there is a cor anglais solo which recurs throughout the movement:

The player, in his attempt to make a nice crescendo, failed to articulate the first note clearly. The Maestro soon fell into a rage, breaking his baton, stamping on the floor and yelling *'Per Dio, Per Dio!* It's always the same; I never hear the first note. Make the crescendo afterwards, but play the first note distinctly.' At this moment of crisis, Toscanini demanded his score, and seeing that Debussy had neglected to put an accent over the first G sharp, cried out in his Italianate intonation. 'Ah, Dayboossee – Dayboossee – when I get up to heaven I will have something to say to you!' I have no doubt that he's telling Debussy about it at this moment. And how right Toscanini was! The first note of a phrase is like the first letter of a word. If it isn't pronounced clearly enough it can lead to a misunderstanding.

Apropos of this, there's a little story I'd like to tell you. Once, when I was 17, while taking the train from Perpignan to Prades, I struck up a conversation with two young men riding in the same compartment. They told me they were studying geology in Rome. I thought it peculiar that my question as to whether they had met any attractive girls there was met with stony silence, as was my comment upon the perfect neatness with which they had packed their suitcases. It all became suddenly and embarrassingly clear to me when they removed from those suitcases two long black frocks. They weren't studying geology – but theology.

This proves two points I like to make. First of all, we must always give attention to the beginning of the sound; secondly it's better not to belong to any 'ology' at all.

While I was in complete accord with Toscanini's concern over the first note, I was less happy with his way of making his point. When the Maestro was invited to conduct in Monte Carlo his programme again included *Nocturnes*. So I alerted my friend Abrial, our fine cor anglais player, as to Toscanini's wishes, and he prepared the passage to perfection. I was pleased that for once Toscanini would obtain what he wanted. Poor Abrial! No sooner did he play his triplet than Toscanini threw the same fit that he had in Paris: the broken baton to the accompaniment of 'Per Dio, per Dio!' Had he listened carefully enough to Abrial's playing? I'm not so sure. In any case he was carried away by his obsession. His theory was right, but it was a pity to humiliate someone who had played correctly.

Of course, I learned a great deal from Toscanini. He was not only concerned with precision; he had a wonderful sense of line and an incredible vitality. However, I was frankly not always enchanted with his interpretations. I was a little disappointed in the cello section solo in *La Mer*. Toscanini didn't quite have the feeling for that lovely passage. It was a little abrupt, a little stiff; it didn't fully convey the sense of flowing waves.

In contrast to Toscanini's authoritarian, volcanic personality,

Bruno Walter was of a kind and gentle disposition. He wore the same sort of black jacket as did Toscanini, but more simply, without the elegant white scarf, so that, given his dark sad eyes, his dark hair and dark complexion, his whole appearance had a sombre cast. However, this would be alleviated by the delicate smile that would play on his lips when he conducted a passage of special loveliness. If one judges a conductor by the precision of his beat, then Toscanini was the better of the two. But, artistically speaking, I preferred Walter's conducting – the way he modelled the musical substance with fluid gestures, the way he phrased with his stick as a string player would with his bow. He had the required firmness, delicacy, and spirit to render the splendour of Haydn's and Mozart's music, and he had an extra-ordinary ear for balance. In his hands Wagner's music became wonderfully transparent. In the *Meistersinger* Prelude, for in-stance, where there is so much counterpoint, one discovered many things one had never noticed before. However, the musicians in an orchestra don't always fully appreciate the conductors with whom they work. Several members of the Orchestre de Monte Carlo could not understand Walter's art because his baton 'technique' did not always correspond to the expectations of the materialistic eye. To tell the truth, without my intervention some of them would have gone so far as to ridicule him during the rehearsals.

I had one meeting with Bruno Walter, and a memorable one it was. I was 16 at the time, and he was 75. I had the audacity to ask him for an appointment to discuss the interpretation of the Siegfried *Idyll which I was to conduct with a youth orchestra I had formed in Los Angeles. He received me most graciously in his home, and spoke at length of his admiration for Wagner's work. When I described the opening tempo as 'slow', he pointed out that Wagner's indication* Ruhig bewegt *means 'quietly flowing' which has an entirely dif-ferent implication. He went to the piano, and with unforgettable simplicity and reverence played half the work through to me. Inci-dentally, I have never heard more beautiful piano playing. Greatly moved, and abashed at the realization of how much I had yet to learn, I apologized for having taken up so much of his time. Busy as he must have been, he assured me that I should not worry about that. 'There*

*is always enough time,' he said. His words revealed not only his own
kindness; they were the expression of a past epoch in which patience
and generosity were a natural way of life. This moved me most of all.*

I can well understand your feelings. Like Pablo Casals, Bruno
Walter was a man who combined the finest human and artistic
qualities.

Was it not in Monte Carlo that you met Richard Strauss?

Yes; it was announced one day that Strauss was coming as a
guest conductor. That provided me with one of the decisive
experiences of my life, for I was asked to play the cello solo in his
Don Quixote for the concert. My first problem was to get hold of a
score. At that time the work was virtually unknown in France.
There was no recording of it, and I only managed to obtain a
pocket score two weeks before the concert.

Did you find it terribly difficult?

It was difficult to hear with the inner ear simply from reading
the score, especially in the opening which is so complex and in
which Strauss so admirably depicts Don Quixote's confusion.
So much is going on at once. In those two weeks I learned the
piece by heart – not only the solo part, but the orchestral cello
part as well. Strauss was amused when he learned of this, and
told me that I naturally need not play the *tutti* passages.

Were you nervous?

I was nervous before the first rehearsal, wondering whether I
would get lost with all the sounds of the orchestra around me.
But I didn't. Strauss was surprised that I played the work from
memory. I had wanted to make an impression upon him; that
was my pride.

A justifiable pride. What did Strauss think of your performance?

He seemed very happy with it, and made only one suggestion.
This was in reference to the first variation, which depicts Don
Quixote when he first sallies forth in search of adventure. At that
point neither he nor Sancho have reason to believe that things
will turn out badly for them – the attack on the windmills, etc.
They are confident and happy. Now, Strauss told me, 'Play this

variation like an amateur. Don't produce such a nice tone; don't be too careful.' I understood at once what he meant. The cello should depict Don Quixote in his carefree state, relaxed in mind, and not too neat in appearance.

It is remarkable that you could already fully grasp the dramatic characterization of that difficult piece. That's not easy for a young man to do.

It's not at all easy at the age of 23 to portray the death of an old man, particularly such an idealist as Don Quixote. But I believe I managed to convey this even at the first performance. After the concert I noticed a diminutive lady applauding vigorously. She came backstage afterwards and paid me a great compliment. It was, she said, the first time she hadn't found the work too long and fragmented. It had sustained her interest because I had, she felt, realized the work's dramatic character and understood how Don Quixote's psychological development is expressed throughout by the cello. I told her that the work was, in my view, a masterpiece whoever might perform it, and I begged her to forgive me because I wanted to get the composer's autograph on my score before he left the hall. 'Well,' she said, 'that's easy enough. I will take you to him myself; he's my husband.'

Frau Strauss's sharp tongue was legendary. Apparently the composer of Elektra *enjoyed being hen-pecked.*

Let's hope he enjoyed it. Strauss wrote the following dedication on my score: *à Paul Tortelier – l'excellent Don Quixote – un grand bravo. 12.3.1937.* He also sent me an inscribed photograph which hangs in my study.

Don Quixote seemed destined from the beginning to play an important role in my life. When I was a boy, it was my favourite book. My father had given it to me; an idealist himself, he loved the story. I remember that book well; it was illustrated by Gustave Doré. When I play Strauss's work, I still have those drawings in my mind's eye.

How many times have you played Don Quixote?

I have never counted. However I'm sure that I have made the greatest number of recordings – three times. The first was with

Sir Thomas Beecham before the advent of long-playing records, the second with Rudolf Kempe with the Berlin Philharmonic, and the third was again with Kempe, but with the Dresdener Staatskappelle orchestra which Strauss himself had often conducted.

Have you a favourite among these recordings?

The last is possibly the best. I don't remember the first one, as I haven't got a copy, but I suppose somebody must have it.

What were your impressions of Strauss as a conductor?

Like Hindemith, he conducted very sparingly, with small, precise gestures. He trusted that his own music would produce the effect he wanted if the musicians responded intelligently to what is marked in the score.

Ah, but as Strauss himself remarked, 'There are few who can read the score.'

It's true. Reading a score with understanding sometimes requires strong deductive powers. Composers often leave us clues as to what they want, and, like good detectives, we have to be on the lookout for them. Strauss, for instance, leaves us such a clue in *Don Quixote* just as we pass from the ninth variation marked *Schnell und stürmisch* – fast and stormy – to the tenth variation marked *Viel breiter* – 'much broader'. The question is: how much broader? At this moment Strauss gives the lower strings and woodwind eleven notes to play within one beat:

Any conductor who is himself an instrumentalist will understand that he has to put the brakes on to give adequate time for those eleven notes; in so doing, he establishes just the right tempo.

We also find such a clue in the first movement of the *Eroica*.

Just where the *fugato* begins – a serious and complex passage in which the orchestra must take care not to rush – Beethoven gives the cellos the following notes:

Up until then the quickest note value in the movement has been the semiquaver. In writing a semiquaver triplet – for the one and only time in the movement – the composer is literally helping you to hold your arm back. Any true musician will sense its meaning. I could cite many other examples. Once, after a master class I gave for BBC television, a critic wrote that Paul Tortelier reminded him somewhat of Sherlock Holmes. I was very proud of that.

A Holmes who plays the cello rather than the violin.

Voilà, my dear Watson. The search for the right tempo never ends. It's said that a student once asked a great conductor, 'What are the most important aspects of interpretation?' – to which the Master replied, 'Three things: the tempo, the tempo, and the tempo.'

While in Monte Carlo I played in a series of quartet concerts given mainly for elderly ladies in fur coats. At that time the Côte d'Azur was a place inhabited chiefly by retired English people. As I was supposed to play a solo piece at one of the concerts, I was obliged to go to the administrator's office to give him the title. This Mr. Putmann was a bureaucrat of sorts, and not very well liked. I was frankly terrified to speak to him; he had cold eyes which froze my blood. I consulted the first violinist of our ensemble, Marcel Reynal, as to what I might play. Now Marcel, being a practical joker, said, 'Tell him that you'll perform *Le vol de la balle* – 'The Flight of the Ball'. This title was inspired by a game of table football we played at a local café; we would play so energetically that the ball was always flying up in the air. 'But who should we say was the composer?' I asked. 'Why, Aperlo, of course.' That was the café proprietor's name. Mr. Putmann had passed by the Café Aperlo every day for the past twenty years. 'And what if he agrees to my playing it?' I queried with waning enthusiasm. 'Well, in that case you'll just have to compose the piece,' Marcel answered reassuringly. I could not give up then; I couldn't lose face, so I braced myself, entered Mr. Putmann's office and confronted those cold eyes. 'And what will you be playing, my dear Tortelier?' I looked directly at him and said without flinching, '*Le vol de la balle* by Aperlo.' He was caught off guard, unsure of how to respond. He hesitated . . . 'Well . . . perhaps it is not the best piece for the occasion. Couldn't you think of something else?' It was a narrow escape. I was very happy that I could return to my friends and say, 'I did it' – and that I didn't have to play a piece which doesn't exist.

It's rather a pity you didn't have to compose Le vol de la balle. *I'm sure it would have been quite a virtuoso piece.*
How long did you stay in Monte Carlo?

Only two seasons. It was towards the end of my second year there that I received word from Jean Devergie that there would be an opening in the cello section of the Boston Symphony for the following season. I auditioned for Koussevitzky when he visited Paris that summer. He engaged me and I went that autumn to America, taking my mother with me.

While in Boston I learned to play Tchaikovsky with Koussevitzky – not only Tchaikovsky, but Brahms, Sibelius and other great composers whose music was largely neglected in France. Koussevitzky was also a champion of contemporary music; for instance, he played a great deal of Hindemith, which allowed me to increase and deepen my knowledge of his works.

Did you find it difficult to adapt to American life?

There was little risk of my being homesick because Koussevitzky was so partial to French musicians – both string and wind players – that a third of the Boston Symphony's personnel must have been French. I made friends quickly and my colleagues and I had some happy times.

During our first year in Boston, my mother and I went to night school in an effort to improve our English. I had already embarrassed myself in a restaurant by ordering 'soap' rather than 'soup'. For once I should have retained the French pronunciation! (Indeed, English pronunciation has always been a problem for me. An audience in Leicester once laughed when I announced the title of my composition called *Weightlessness*. I was rather taken aback until it was explained to me that I had said 'Wetlessness'.) Our teacher was proud of Mother's rapid progress, and at the end of the course awarded her the highest mark while I failed miserably. But the funny thing is that when the director of the school made a nice speech in her honour, I had to translate it into French for her, as she could not understand a word of it.

Professionally speaking, it was a quiet period for me. We had no more than one rehearsal a day, and on concert days there would be no rehearsal. On Friday afternoons we played for the ladies, the men being at the office. It seems to be a speciality of American women to help the arts. In any case, the circle around Koussevitzky consisted mainly of women.

Nearly every American orchestra has its women's committee. It is an indispensable institution. I have even heard the president of such a committee, bedecked with flower hat, say to a major American orchestra, 'I hope you won't mind if I tell you that you are all my players!'

Did Koussevitzky live up to his reputation as being one of the most autocratic of conductors?

Louis XIV walking through the Hall of Mirrors at Versailles could not have been more majestic than Serge Koussevitzky as he slowly made his way to the podium. Like the Sun King, his posture was such that even though he was actually rather short, he looked tall. He was always elegantly dressed and impeccably groomed. He wore reading glasses at rehearsals and contact lenses for concerts, and never conducted without the score. Often at concerts he grew so excited that his aristocratic face became as red as a tomato, and the veins in his temples seemed near to bursting; yet his bearing always remained regal. When he turned to the violas on his right or the first violins on his left – which he often did, pivoting on his heels like a dancer – he revealed to the public his distinguished profile.

Despite such mannerisms, he was undeniably a great conductor. He had such power of emotional communication that you couldn't help but play with all your soul. He could have made a chair play! Despite his surplus of temperament, he maintained good taste. 'Don't play too sentimental!' was an admonition we heard hundreds of times. If, when on tour, we had no more than half an hour to rehearse before a concert, he preferred to play through the slow movement of a symphony for the sake of singing expression rather than the more intricate Scherzo or Finale. Thus he maintained the Boston Symphony's reputation for warmth and beauty of tone, above all in the great romantic symphonic repertoire.

His recordings bear witness to this in their unbroken expressive line. Take for instance Sibelius's Seventh Symphony with the BBC Symphony Orchestra – a performance of blazing intensity.

I couldn't agree more. He was unsurpassed in such music and knew how to make an orchestra play gloriously.

He arrived at rehearsals fit and eager and sat perched upon his high stool looking like a gourmet ready to taste a delicious dish with which the meal was to begin – often a Haydn symphony. He was very hard on us. Like Toscanini he was a perfectionist and could go over a single passage relentlessly. He spoke his own mixture of English, French, and German with a Russian accent. '*Kinder*,' he would say angrily ('Children' – that's what he normally called us), '*Kinder*, I shall repeat it tousand times . . . until I *won't* have it!' Nobody would dare laugh at such linguistic idiosyncrasies for he inspired fear rather than love. Little wonder that his musicians spoke of him as *le Dompteur* – the Tamer.

I, however, did manage to tease Koussevitzky once without paying the price, when I appeared in a 'floor show' given by the orchestra members for the the Pension Fund – a show for which I myself had thought up the title 'Gone with the Woodwinds'. All of Boston society was there, with Koussevitzky seated in the first row. I put on a sketch with a colleague named Langendoem who portrayed a ridiculously incompetent student playing Gounod's *Ave Maria* for a famous cello teacher. I was the *Maestro* in the grand Italian style, attired in a magnificent dressing gown and adorned with a superb black moustache.

When Langendoem's playing drastically surpassed the limits of good taste, I cried out in desperation, 'Don't play too sentimental!' Everybody was amused and even *le Dompteur* himself smiled.

Did Koussevitzky take an interest in your playing?

Yes, he even once asked me to play as soloist, which caused something of a scandal, as I was not the solo cellist of the orchestra. I played a work dedicated to me by Thomas de Hartmann, a Russian composer of the old school. Eventually Artur Rodzinski heard me and offered me the position of solo cellist with the Cleveland Orchestra, but Koussevitzky would not release me. I was a little angry with him for that, and finally left the Boston Symphony at the end of my third season. It was 1940; the war had just entered a new phase. My mother wanted me to take her home so that she would not be separated from her family.

One of the most memorable events during my stay in Boston was the lunch I had with Stravinsky at the home of Mrs Whitmore, a patroness of the orchestra, who thought it would be nice for me to make the composer's acquaintance. What an occasion that was! Stravinsky knew that I was an aspiring composer and spoke to me most encouragingly without the least pretentiousness. He made a most interesting suggestion, that, above all, I should study counterpoint. Knowing that I was a Frenchman, he probably realized that my musical culture might be more developed on the harmonic than on the contrapuntal side. The French are not contrapuntalists by nature as the Germans are. My friend Marcel Bitsch has published a treatise on Bach's *Art of the Fugue*, and has done much for the teaching of counterpoint in France. All the same, it is probably not in the French character to manipulate contrapuntal voices in the manner of Bach, Wagner, Strauss or Hindemith. In any case, Stravinsky declared, 'Counterpoint is the welfare of music.' He added that he was not satisfied with Petroushka because it lacked contrapuntal interest. Then he said, 'Wagner did one hour of counterpoint every morning.' I smiled to myself thinking, 'He is supposed to hate Wagner's music, but none the less he secretly admires the giant.'

One is often attracted to one's opposite.

That's certainly true. Stravinsky's advice amused me very much because, in recommending counterpoint, he was emphasizing just the thing that wasn't his strong point. It's true that later he became rather preoccupied with counterpoint, but rhythm and harmony were his real strengths. This reminds me of a story about Surcouf, a famous pirate from my native Brittany. During the Napoleonic wars Surcouf captured an English ship, but the English captain, being a proud man, would not bow to Surcouf or to anyone else. He maintained a most disdainful air and, with a gesture of defiance, said, 'You fight for money but we fight for honour.' To this Surcouf replied, 'Yes, everybody fights for what he lacks.'

VII
Amours et Amourettes

Rodin said, 'An artist is a man who has the luck always to be in love.' As far back as I can remember I was in love. I recall standing by the window of my father's shop each morning waiting for a certain girl to pass by on her way to school at the end of the street. I must have been about 10 at the time; I was enchanted with her.

You didn't run out into the street when she came by . . .

Oh, no – I was much too shy!

What did she look like?

She was a brunette and she wore a dark brown leather coat. That's all I can remember of her. I have been in love ten times at least. I agree with Rodin.

When did you first begin to overcome your timidity?

A girl my aunt employed as a servant helped me along in that direction. Being alone with me one afternoon, she suddenly felt a vocation to initiate me into the mysteries of Eros. This turned out to be a rather innocent adventure such as is described in the story of *Daphnis and Chloe*. One normally thinks of a man 'corrupting' a girl – but in my case it was the other way round. This happened several times with girls when I was quite young. Until I was 15 I was desperately awaiting the great occasion, stimulated once in a while by a girl unwilling to go that far. However, during that difficult period, and for a long time afterwards, my mother did what she could to keep me away from young girls. After all, at that time a *jeune fille* was someone you would have respect for. My mother was a very moral person, and I was so infused with morality that I was afraid to touch a girl. So, if I had adventures, it was more often with women in their forties, and my mother would not object. I had to make do with several such short-lived adventures. On their side, the girls did not seem to be particularly attracted to a rather shy young man still under the protection of *Maman* Tortelier. Altogether, therefore, I spent little time engaged in the Frenchman's favourite pursuit.

At what point did your mother begin to relax her vigilance?

By the time I was 21 she realised that I had to be free. She knew that she could not suppress my romantic inclinations, but she wanted me to fall in love for good, and not waste my time and energy flitting from one girl to another. It was, of course, in her nature to be overprotective. However, to be fair to her, she had already encouraged me when, at 18, I had my first experience of a deep sentimental love. The object of my affection was a charming, dark-haired girl from Nice, a gifted cellist who was studying with Hekking as I myself had done. She had been seriously ill – which greatly touched me – and when she recovered I found that I had fallen in love with her. During the following year we were very close, almost engaged in fact, and my mother was happy about it. Mother and I were invited to spend a holiday in the home of my girlfriend's parents in Nice, so matters were obviously getting serious. It was no fault of my mother's if this romance didn't continue. On the contrary; it was I who broke off the relationship. Years later, when I received an honorary doctorate from Leicester University, the wife of the chancellor – a well-known scientist – told me, 'A woman who marries a man of science marries someone who already has a mistress.' Composition was my mistress and a demanding one she was, drawing me to her with a mysteriously compelling power. One day my girlfriend's brother came to visit me. 'My sister is surprised that you no longer call,' he said. 'She's had no sign of you for days; you don't seem to be impatient to see her.' 'No one has replaced her in my affections,' I replied, 'but something has happened that I can't really explain. I'm so absorbed in my study of harmony that I find myself thinking of her less and less.' 'In that case,' her brother said, 'I think it's best that you break off the relationship.' She was a little older than I was and she couldn't wait for me. I was distressed to have to reject her in this way.

Have you seen her since?

Yes, on one occasion I met her by chance at a concert. She had married happily, and was most charming when she spoke with me.

Soon I too was to know what it is to be rejected. One day my aunt – my mother's sister – came to our house in great agitation. 'Help me,' she implored; 'Madeleine has joined a theatrical troupe and they are going to take her away to South America. Anything could happen to her!' This Madeleine, my cousin, was Madeleine Robinson, then 16, who was trying to become an actress. She was a beautiful, vivacious and intelligent girl, whose short life until then had been a struggle against hard times. Her parents were separated and her mother was now ill with cancer and had to spend long periods in hospital. Their home in Pré St-Gervais could not have been more wretched.

Madeleine's mother had tried to reason with her to no avail. In the hope that she might listen to someone closer to her own age, it was decided that I should go to speak with her. So I went to the theatre where she had been engaged. Not having seen her for some time, I could hardly recognize her with her face covered with make-up, so sophisticated had she become. Though barely 19 myself, I told her firmly that if she – then utterly unknown as an actress – were to go with this group to South America, she had no idea of the dangers she might encounter. My mother would offer to take her into our house, and if she really wanted to become an actress, she should find a first-rate teacher, study the classics, and dedicate herself completely to dramatic art. I obviously pleaded my case convincingly, because she agreed to come to our home. Her worry about breaking her contract was dispelled when I pointed out to the theatre director that Madeleine's signature was not valid as she was still a minor.

Madeleine stayed with us for several months, and began studying with Charles Dullin, one of the most gifted men in the history of the French theatre. Dullin directed the *Théâtre de l'Atelier* where he produced plays by such masters as Pirandello, Chekhov and Ibsen, which were novelties in Paris in the early 1930s. His portrayals of *Volpone* and Harpagon in *l'Avare* made a deep impression upon me. Madeleine made remarkable progress and, as you know, became an extraordinary actress of great power and personality. She has a strong character and has never hesitated to speak out frankly in defence of what she believes in.

My mother had made an effort to keep me away from young girls and, as I have said, I was exceedingly shy. Suddenly I had my beautiful cousin Madeleine in close proximity every day. While I had begun with nothing but the purest platonic admiration for her, I gradually found myself falling in love, a sentiment which, much as she liked me, she did not reciprocate. I should have been controlled enough to behave towards her in a gallant, dispassionate manner. However, I could not help but express my feelings. This became something of a problem – not only for her but for my mother too, who was growing increasingly alarmed – and Madeleine eventually found it best to leave our house to avoid such complications. Luckily her career was already set on the right path.

I was more successful in my romantic endeavours when during my stay in Boston I met a lovely girl, a fine pianist, the daughter of a patron of the Boston Symphony. My relationship with her might have developed further had the war not caused me to return to France with my mother.

In Paris the following year I fell in love with the girl who was to become my first wife. Again, I was in love with a brunette, also from the south of France, and also a talented string player, though this time the instrument was the violin rather than the cello. Prior to the wedding, I had to fulfil my future father-in-law's request that I be baptized. It was a peculiar ceremony. I wonder what sort of faith the priest himself possessed when, just before the solemn moment, he told me, 'Simply bend your head forward as if you were having a shampoo.'

My first wife and I were not sufficiently mature to succeed as a couple. She came from a well-to-do family and was only seventeen at the time of our marriage. Suddenly she found herself living with a young musician who came from a world utterly different from her own. Our marriage was a romantic dream. The reality proved more difficult than either of us had foreseen: To make matters worse, it was wartime, with all its strains and tensions. We had a child, a girl whom we named Anne, but owing to wartime conditions we reluctantly decided that it would be safer to send her to stay with my parents-in-law who lived in the provinces. They had food, a farm, and the possibility of bringing her up under more favourable circumstances.

I cannot say that my parents helped the marriage along. My father unwittingly alarmed my bride with his talk about the workers rising up against the bourgeoisie. Anyone who can speak, as he did, with such conviction about the need for a profound change in society risks being looked upon as a dangerous or violent man. My father was anything but that; he was an anti-militarist who could never have hurt anyone. I wonder how he would have behaved in a real revolution.

My mother was not very happy about the marriage. She felt the class difference keenly and, rightly or wrongly, had the impression that my wife acted snobbishly towards her. The real problems were not these, however. They centred on our basic incompatibility. We were divorced in 1944. It was never fated that things should work out between us.

Among your public there are, I am sure, a vast number of women greatly intrigued by what they may imagine to be the amatory side of your character.

I don't want to disappoint them, but apart from a relationship I had in my twenties with a *prima donna* (who temporarily provided me with some glamour), and a couple of passing adventures during my Monte Carlo and Boston years, I cannot claim any special prowess à la Don Juan.

During the course of your career have you ever been the involuntary object of unwanted female attention?

Oh yes, a number of times. Already in my early twenties, certain mothers decided that I was a good marriage prospect, and tried to push their daughters on me; I managed to resist their advances. And in later years, on two or three occasions, women have taken me by surprise by expressing an interest in me – even without their mothers' encouragement. Indeed, my first mistress predicted rightly that I would be successful with women after I reached the age of 40. But by then it was too late; I was already rapturously and irrevocably in love with Maud.

VIII
Maud

The period 1940–44 was a bleak one in my life as it was for the whole of Europe. There were of course others who suffered far, far more than we did but in Paris under the occupation conditions were bad enough. Heat was nonexistent and food was scarce. My mother had to wait in line for up to seven hours to obtain the barest necessities. Having a wife and child, and not wanting to live at the expense of my wife's family, I had somehow to eke out a living. The only job available to me was a position with the radio orchestra. Aside from this I taught from time to time as a replacement at the Conservatoire. With no solo concerts, my career had no opportunity to develop. My marriage, having proved unhappy, soon ended in divorce.

With the liberation of France the whole of life changed, and my professional and personal existence began to take on a new meaning. I was asked once again to play in the Orchestre de la Société des Concerts du Conservatoire, as I had done a decade before, but this time in the position of principal cellist. The orchestra was now conducted by Charles Munch.

What was your estimation of Munch?

An exceptional personality, at his best in Berlioz, very fine for Brahms. I don't share the general view that he was the ideal interpreter for Debussy's *La Mer*; I found the last part a little lacking in poetry, but this is a detail. He was a man of rich temperament. In contrast to Koussevitzky, whom he succeeded as director of the Boston Symphony, Munch had a way of putting his musicians at ease. I'll give you an example. The orchestra had assembled for a short rehearsal before a concert. Munch arrived and, leafing through the score of a symphony, said, 'My friends, we need not rehearse the first two movements . . . nor even the Finale, for we played this work a few days ago and I trust you. Let's only play a bit of the Scherzo if you don't mind – for my sake.' One of the musicians replied, '*Maître*, we needn't do that either, because we trust *you*.' Such a joke would have been unthinkable with Koussevitzky. Munch was very kind to me and asked me to play the Haydn D major Concerto several times.

But the most important happening for me in the spring of 1945 was of a personal nature: my meeting with Mademoiselle Maud Martin.

How did it come about?

Through another event in my life that seemed dictated more by fate than by chance. Paris is a big city; I don't know how many thousands of streets it has. Thus it is really amazing that we had lived on the same streets without knowing one another. As a child Maud went to the Ecole Lucien Lafflessele in the rue Labat, the same school that I had attended some years before. She eventually moved to 9 rue de Panama; when I was 15 my mother and I had lived at number 8. When Maud entered the Paris Conservatoire she was placed in Class number 13, the same class I had been in. We never met because though we had always been in the same place, it had never been at the same time. She was following my footsteps at a distance of thirteen years.

Maud first knew about Paul before he was even aware of her existence. As a 15-year-old cello student at the Conservatoire she attended a concert which Paul gave in the Salle Gaveau. She was particularly struck by his performance of a transcription of Sarasate's *Zapateado*. In fact, this brilliant virtuoso piece moved her to tears precisely because, as she recalls, 'He played it with such charm and lyricism as to make me forget that it is a virtuoso piece.'

Maud then performed the first of what were to be innumerable acts in support of Paul's career. Her father was leader of the second violins in the Orchestre des Concerts Colonne, and was a member of the orchestra committee. Maud often went to practise her cello in the foyer of the

Théâtre du Châtelet while the orchestra was rehearsing. Once, after a meeting of the committee, finding herself among its members in a bistro, she dared to intervene in the discussion, objecting to the orchestra's practice of always inviting the same soloists. Praising Tortelier's talent, she made a plea to have him engaged.

Had I not composed *Le Pitre* – 'The Clown' – one of my *Trois P'tits Tours* I might never have met Maud. Can you think of a better reason for being a composer? This very piece had been assigned to the cello students participating in the 1946 competition – no, it must have been 1945, as it was just after the end of the war. Maurice Maréchal asked me to visit his class to give some advice about the style of my composition, and on this occasion he asked one of his students to play it for me. And whom did he choose? – his favourite student, Maud Martin. The moment I set eyes upon her I was absolutely stunned. I fell in love with her at once. As we say in French, *J'ai eu le coup de foudre*. I was struck by lightning. Nobody who has ever lived has had a stronger *coup de foudre*. I cannot depict her physically; I would need to be a Balzac – or a poet, Baudelaire – to do that. And I cannot paint her as Renoir would have done. But many people who knew her when she was 18 did indeed think she had stepped out of a painting by Renoir or by Greuze. She was a vision; she was a delight. I was walking on air.

Was she immediately attracted to you?

That she never told me.

Maud's first personal impression of Paul had, in fact, been rather negative. One day, as she and her mother were leaving the Conservatoire, they saw Paul down the road talking to a friend. 'If I were twenty years younger,' confided Maud's mother, 'that man would interest me.' 'Would he?' queried the daughter; 'I think he looks a bit cold.' He seemed to her 'a little severe in his intense manner of discussion. His eyebrows were then black, and from a distance his eyes also looked black. Only if you got close up could you see their ethereal blue.'

When I first met Maud in the classroom, I had found the position of her first finger faulty, and had suggested that she change it. One day when I returned to the class she said, '*Maître, j'ai pensé à vous.*' She had been thinking of me. What did this mean? Perhaps no more than that she had given consideration to my suggestion about her finger placement . . . I thought that I must somehow arrange to be alone with her. I had first to overcome my shyness. I have always been shy and still am. However, I finally found the courage to invite her to take a drink with me together with some other students at the Café de l'Europe. Afterwards I accompanied her to the Métro station. At last alone with her! Those five minutes were enough for me to be completely enchanted by her personality. I desperately wanted to declare my love to her, but could think of nothing better to say than to advise her that, after taking a shower, ten minutes of a good friction-rub on the back and shoulders with a towel was worth an hour of scale practice.

Not a word of love had been spoken, not a kiss had been given, and I had only met Maud on brief occasions in public when the summer holidays began. Three months' separation – and I had not succeeded in going beyond the vague preliminaries of courtship. Many things can happen in a young girl's life during the summer months (I learned that from my daughters) and I don't recommend falling in love just before this period if it cannot be spent with the beloved one. How embarrassed, puzzled, not to say worried I was when October finally came and I wondered how to contact Maud Martin again in our big, busy city. Indeed, without the unwitting help of my colleague André Navarra who had the marvellous idea of giving a cello recital in Paris that autumn, Maud and I might have had a different destiny, unless one considers fate to be a programmed enterprise. Joy burst in the deepest corner of my heart when, a few seconds after I was seated in one of the *loges* around the *fauteuils d'orchestre* of the Salle Gaveau, I glanced up at the balcony and there discovered a pair of blue-grey eyes and met a most gracious smile. Immediately everything became possible. Life was like an enchanted sky in which to fly. There she was and there I was, and there we were for each other. The confirmation of this came after the recital when I met her in the foyer and she allowed me to see her home.

> Maud had attended the concert with her sister. She suddenly saw Paul looking at her. At that moment she felt the first stirrings of love. But, as she was very young, and was in great awe of his artistry, she could hardly imagine that he might be interested in her.

The Luchon revue, 1931. Paul is holding a straw hat in imitation of
Maurice Chevalier.

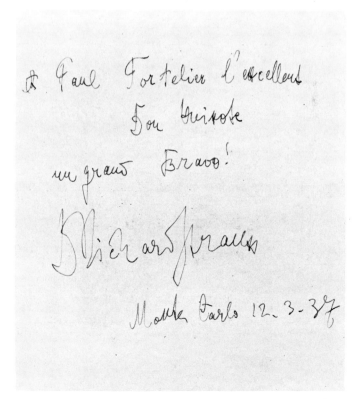

Richard Strauss wrote this inscription on Paul's score of *Don Quixote*
after Paul played it under his direction in March 1937: 'To Paul
Tortelier, the excellent Don Quixote, a great bravo!'

Mother and son in Boston in 1938, after Koussevitsky had invited Paul
to join the cello section of the Boston Symphony Orchestra.

Maud Tortelier (*née* Martin) at Prades for the Casals Festival, 1950.

Announcement put up by the musicians at Prades to celebrate the birth of Paul and Maud's daughter Maria de la Pau, 1950.

Paul and Maud with Pablo Casals in Zurich, 1951.

The Tortelier histrionic talents displayed again – this time with June Rotenberg in a revue given for Casals, Perpignan, 1952.

The weeks that followed were like a dream. One night stands out with particular intensity. We had spent the evening in the company of my mother at our flat in the rue Léon-Cogniet, the flat which Feuillard had given me six years before, and where Maud was to reside for another twenty-three years. It was late when she left us to return to her home in the rue de Panama, a considerable distance across Paris, but she was in time to catch the last Métro. (By the way, I am surprised that I would let her go home alone after midnight!) I suddenly realized that our clock was slow and that she would, in fact, miss the last train. Worried that she would be forced to walk all the way home, I rushed out in order to find her. I ran along the deserted streets, but there was no sign of her. I began to wonder how she could have gone so far, for I had been running faster and faster down one boulevard after another, and yet she was nowhere to be seen. I raced along the Boulevard de Clichy and by the time I reached the Place d'Anvers I could only believe that my loved one had evaporated into thin air. I collapsed in utter exhaustion, thinking that I had better make an appointment with Dr. Soulié to have my heart examined, and turned back filled with anxiety. I sometimes think of that moment when I play the passage in *Don Quixote* (after the tenth variation) in which the Don, having been defeated in battle by Samson Carrasco, stumbles along in a pathetic retreat. But what a miraculous apparition met my eyes when, arriving again at the place de Clichy, I saw Maud cycling towards me from the opposite direction! Seeing her before she saw me, I whistled the first six notes of my cello concerto – a motif she knew well – to which she replied by whistling the completion of the phrase.

The bicycle explained the mysterious adventure. Having missed the Métro, she had returned to my flat, borrowed my mother's bicycle, and set out in search of me. But as she had taken another street, we had missed each other. Now all I had to do was to go along Maud's route once again – all the way to her home this time. As I held Maud's hand in my right hand and my mother's bicycle in my left, I wondered if I really needed to pay a visit to Dr. Soulié after all.

> Paul never told Maud in so many words, 'I love you'. His way of saying 'I love you' was, '*Je serai pour vous ce que vous voulez que je sois*' 'I will be for you whatever you want me to be.'

After a three months' courtship we were married – on the 9th January 1946.

I'm surprised and delighted that you are at last sure of a date.

Oui, oui – I hope it's right. If it was not the 9th, it was the 6th, but it was during the first part of January – of that I'm certain.

How did your mother feel about Maud and her new role in your life?

She was fond of Maud right from the start, and tried as much as possible not to intrude upon my relationship with her. For instance, two months before our marriage I was returning to Paris from a short trip. I had sent Maud a note asking her to meet me at the Gare St-Lazare. My mother, not realizing this, also came to the station, but, upon seeing Maud, quickly withdrew without letting her presence be known.

Before the wedding my mother did everything she could to make us happy. The reception was held in our house and she presided over it with great joy. After we were married, however, the temptation to mother me as before was stronger than her will, and this of course created difficulties for her new daughter-in-law. She interfered with Maud's happiness by constantly disputing the management of the household. Maud hated doing household work, but she liked it even less when her mother-in-law did it. My mother had always been in charge of the family finances, and it was painful for Maud to have to ask her for money, or to request permission to use things in the kitchen. Though they admired each other enormously, the two women in my life were constantly arguing. It is especially difficult for women to get along together, living at such close quarters, when they share so many personality traits and, above all, when much of their activity centres around one man.

While Paul's mother was always most affectionate with her son, she was less pleased when other signs of affection were displayed in the household. One day she had prepared soup for lunch and was carrying the large tureen from the stove to the kitchen table where Paul and Maud sat together. Just then Paul took Maud's hand in his own. Paul's mother happened to see this and, at that moment, the bowl dropped right out of her hands onto the floor. On another occasion – it was a Sunday morning –

Paul and Maud wanted to remain together in their room a bit longer. Suddenly they heard a harsh banging, followed by the stentorian command: *'Paul – ton violoncelle!'* *Maman* Tortelier had knocked so hard with her set of big household keys that a permanent indentation was left on the door.

So the three of us lived together *appassionato* for a few years until I understood – at long last – that matters could not continue as they were. We found my mother a flat on the sixth floor in the same building. This made things easier, although she still let her presence be known. As she was always up at 6.0 a.m., she would come down to tidy up our kitchen. Sadly enough, she was gradually becoming deaf, and failed to realize that she made so much noise with the pots and pans that it became impossible for us to sleep.

How did you cope with these difficulties?

I could escape from all this when travelling with my cello. But when I was home, on more than one occasion I became extremely upset. Furthermore, my habit of answering *'Voilà'* to the tenth call for breakfast, lunch or dinner, which had so irritated Mother before my marriage, became worse and hardly bearable for Maud. These *voilàs* were uttered mainly when I was composing, and during the first years of our married life I was feverishly writing a Double Concerto for two cellos and orchestra. One night the atmosphere in the household became particularly tense. In the morning I took the manuscript of the concerto, almost completed, and hurled it into the collective dustbin outside the house. This gesture was a sort of semi-suicide for, in this concerto dedicated to Maud, I had given the best of myself. I had worked on it for over two years at every free moment with care and patience so that it should truly be a piece worth playing. An hour later I could not help telling Maud what I had done. She rushed downstairs to try to save the manuscript. Fortunately, the dustbin hadn't yet been emptied, and she was able to rescue our concerto from oblivion.

To be an understanding wife, a devoted mother, an outstanding cellist and an illuminating teacher may seem beyond the capacity of any one person. However, that is what Maud has achieved. She has never faltered or hesitated in fulfilling this quadruple role. To begin with, she showed great courage when she advised me to risk embarking on a soloist's career. That meant resigning my position as principal cellist of the Société des Concerts du Conservatoire from which I derived three-quarters of my income. Our son, Yan Pascal, had just been born, and the future could only be called uncertain.

Those who know Maud cannot help but be struck on the one hand by her unusual warmth and vivacity, on the other by the unfailing ease with which she steers the family through the storms of daily life.

A typical Tortelier family scene:
Paul is in his study, composing; Maud is in the kitchen, preparing lunch for the family. A call is heard: 'Maud, please come. Tell me if you think trumpets are right for this passage.' She protests; the steaks will be burnt. He persists; the trumpets cannot wait. Finally she fulfils both chores. She helps orchestrate the new piece and yet manages to serve lunch on time. Everyone enjoys an excellent meal – everyone, that is, except Paul who arrives at the table ready to begin the meal just as dessert is being served.

Maud is my constant helpmate. She has many qualities which I lack.

For example?

She is blessed with emotional equilibrium while I veer from mood to mood. She remains gracious and accessible while I can become tense and difficult. She has quick eyes; I have slow eyes; she picks up anything that I cannot find. That's a great help because I'm always losing something and she lays her hand on it at once. She has an inborn common sense that I lack entirely. She has a memory for things which I forget – and I, believe it or not, sometimes remember things which she forgets. She drives a car beautifully, and I am a public menace behind a wheel. In order to reach our home in Nice one has to negotiate several hairpin curves. Luckily I have Maud as my chauffeur or I would never get there.

You're not the only cellist who has had difficulty driving. Piatigorsky once told me that he was afraid to make left turns; he always tried to arrive at his destination by making right turns only. When returning home, he would sometimes miss his driveway and end up driving across his lawn.

My first experience behind the wheel was not an auspicious one. I was 14 at the time, and taking a driving lesson. I overshot a curve, confused the accelerator with the brake, and smashed into a brick wall. I was relieved to see that the wall was undamaged, when suddenly a man dressed in a butcher's smock appeared from round the corner waving his arms frantically. He pulled me into his shop, and there I saw to my horror that the whole inside wall had caved in. Bricks, eggs and meat were strewn all over the floor.

I was granted a licence in Boston in 1939, but I didn't drive again until 1959, and then ventured on to the road with the greatest trepidation in a tiny *Deux Chevaux* which hardly moved no matter who was behind the wheel. It finally broke down on a country road about sixty kilometres north of Paris, near Novillers-les-Caillous which was, at that time, the simplest little village in the world. The breakdown proved fortuitous. Just down the way we saw a house for sale which was to become our country home.

Yes, there are so many ways in which Maud complements me! As you know, when I go into the kitchen I can find nothing at all – except the cake, and when I see the cake my mouth begins to water. Now, my wife reacts similarly to meat, even raw meat. It's the Parisian custom that children munch on long loaves of bread as they bring them back from the bakery. Well, when we lived in Paris and Maud went to the butcher, she would nibble on the meat as she walked home. Like my parents, I am an early bird, up at 5.0 a.m. every morning. Maud has always preferred to stay in bed until 10 a.m. except of course when the children had school; sleep is precious to her.

Paul and Maud came unexpectedly to London one day. Their hosts apologized that they had nothing larger than a single bed to offer for the night. 'That's all right,' said Paul happily. The next morning he was up early, bleary-eyed. To his hostess's query as to how he had slept, he answered, 'Just come and see for yourself.' They entered the room where Maud lay fast asleep. 'Look at her!' exclaimed Paul, the sight challenging his descriptive powers in English. 'She *mingled* with the sheets – and, *alors*, she knocked me onto the floor.'

Maud is not only my personal companion in every conceivable way, she is also my musical companion.

How has her playing developed since you first met her?

At the beginning her playing was quite different from mine, but little by little we have adjusted. Not only has she learned from me, but I have learned from her as well. Again and again I have benefited from her critical sense. She was present, for instance, when I recorded the Bach Suites, and that was a great help because one does not realize exactly what one is doing when recording. One is so subjectively involved that it's easy to lose an objective viewpoint. Before I made that recording, Maud suggested that I study for one week without vibrato so that I should find all the expression with the bow rather than getting agitated with my left hand. That was an excellent piece of advice.

I feel guilty that the requirements of being Madame Tortelier and bringing up our children might have limited Maud's career. In order to practise, she has to steal half an hour as often as she can between her never-ending household chores. But the moment she picks up her cello and begins to play it, joy radiates from her being. One of our greatest pleasures is in performing together – works for two cellos by Vivaldi or Handel, or my Double Concerto. That work, rescued from the dustbin, has been played in many parts of the world, including Russia.

Whenever you perform together, people are struck by the communion of thought and feeling that exists between you.

How could it be otherwise? Fate intended that we should be together. And when fate speaks one must listen.

IX

A Door Opens (Don Quixote II)

In 1945 as an expression of the *entente cordiale* between France and England there were exchange visits between the Orchestre de la Société des Concerts du Conservatoire, of which I was principal cellist, and the London Philharmonic Orchestra. Charles Munch and Sir Thomas Beecham also exchanged their batons: Munch conducted the English orchestra in Paris, whilst Beecham conducted the French orchestra in London. After our first rehearsal with Beecham, a colleague of mine in the orchestra, who knew of my ambition to become a soloist, urged me to ask Sir Thomas to hear me play. I was rather sceptical, but one must always try. So I summoned up the courage to ask Sir Thomas and, to my surprise, was granted an appointment to visit him the very next morning. When I arrived at his luxurious flat, he greeted me in his dressing gown, lit a cigar, and asked me to play. I obliged with a few works of my own which he seemed to enjoy. He then said, 'My boy, write your name in this book.' I duly entered my name in his address book and was cordially ushered out.

Some weeks later, a friend in Amsterdam asked me to participate in a concert of contemporary music given in the chamber music hall at the Concertgebouw. I played a nocturne by the French composer Jolivet. The audience was small – but what mattered most was the presence of Frank Onnen, a well-known journalist and musicologist. He arranged for me to have an audition the next day with Eduard van Beinum, music director of the Concertgebouw Orchestra. I played a Bach Prelude for him, and also a new concerto which had been written for me by Jean Hubeau, one of the most gifted musicians in France. Van Beinum seemed to be very enthusiastic, and he asked me to give him my address, just as Beecham had done a short time before. When I returned to Paris, I had nothing to hold on to but hope, and I had been hoping for a long time already. I was 32; I had been playing in orchestras for sixteen years and had no solo career at all. Without the story I am going to tell you now, my life might never have changed in that respect.

After my audition for van Beinum I returned to Paris and continued playing in my orchestra. For many weeks nothing happened. Then, one day, a letter arrived bearing a Dutch stamp. That was something for me. I almost never received letters from abroad and a Dutch stamp had special significance. I opened the letter feverishly. It was signed 'Eduard van Beinum': 'Will you agree to play Hubeau's Concerto with the Concertgebouw Orchestra?' Would I? I couldn't believe my eyes. At last I had an engagement. Unknown as I was, van Beinum was willing to engage me on my merit – an example of typical Dutch honesty. However, when I came to play this work in Amsterdam, van Beinum fell ill. And who was engaged to conduct the concert in his place? Sir Thomas Beecham. Although Beecham had heard me play, he really couldn't imagine what my abilities might be as a soloist, since I had only performed some short pieces in a small room. But there, in Amsterdam, he heard me with orchestra, and observed that I had a success. 'My boy,' he said, 'come to see me tomorrow morning.' Now this time it was he who was asking me, not I asking him. The next day I went to his hotel; it was a morning I shall never forget. Once again, he was in his dressing gown – yes, with a cigar in his mouth. 'I like your playing,' he said. 'You played very well indeed last night. Do you know Strauss's Don Quixote?' My heart skipped a beat, but I managed to reply nonchalantly as if it were something banal for me to be asked such a question, 'Yes, I played it with Strauss.' Beecham's eyes lit up. 'You have played it with my friend, Strauss. When was that?' 'Oh, years ago,' I replied unexcitedly. 'My dear, that is most interesting. I am organizing a Strauss festival to be given in London next autumn. Could you be free to play *Don Quixote* with me?' I responded as matter of factly as I could, 'I will look at my diary.' My diary was of course empty. I consented, and he concluded the interview by saying, 'All right, we shall try to arrange that.' Now a great hope came to my heart, though it was still nothing but hope. Yet months went by without a word from Sir Thomas.

Now, the third link in this chain of good fortune came when the French conductor Jean Martinon, who was making his début with Radio Eireann, invited me to come to Dublin to play the Haydn D major Concerto. You may recall that the father of my childhood friend, from the days when we lived in the rue de Trétaigne, was Charles Kiesgen who became one of the great impresarios of the day, handling such artists as Casals, Thibaud, Cortot, Kreisler and Segovia. He did not represent me, as he took only the big names. But, as I knew him well. I told him of my engagement in Dublin and asked if he could help me find an impresario when I passed through London. He gave me a letter of recommendation to Ibbs and Tillett. Mr and Mrs Tillett took a kind interest in me and suggested that, although I was unknown in England, it might be worthwhile for me to take an audition the BBC was holding the following week. So, on my return from Dublin, I took the chance and played for the BBC.

What did you play?

The Bach C major Suite – that is my *cheval de bataille*. I thought I should include a French piece and chose Ravel's *Habanera*, and I also offered something more unusual: a cello transcription of the *Moto Perpetuo* by Paganini. There was no one else in the room – nothing but a microphone. Only afterwards, when I was in the corridor, was I greeted by a man with a little beard. 'Mr Tortelier,' he said, 'when you next plan to come to London, just drop me a line.' That was all; I didn't know what it implied. When Mrs Tillett asked how the audition had gone, I replied, 'I'm pleased with the way I played, but all I can tell you is that when I went out I met this man . . .' 'What sort of man?' 'A short, plump man with a little beard.' 'That was the music director, Julian Herbage, and what did he say?' 'He only said, "When you next plan to come to London, just drop me a line."' 'Oh, marvellous,' she exclaimed. 'He couldn't have given you a more encouraging reaction.'

You were introduced to English understatement.

Voilà! These casual words meant a lot. So I had one more hope. While I was in London, I took my meals at a restaurant in Sloane Square called 'Cinderella'. I had come to know the owner of this restaurant, Miss Lily Frieland, on the suggestion of a mutual friend in France who thought Miss Frieland might be helpful to me in England, as indeed she proved to be. She was a rather mysterious person, a most distinguished lady, an aristocrat from Vienna who had had some difficulty in her life, perhaps a financial disaster. In any case circumstances had made it necessary for her to open this restaurant. Miss Frieland was always most charming and kind to me, and fed me as if I were a king.

One day at lunch she asked me how things were going. 'Just hope . . . and more hope,' I sighed. And I told her the story of Van Beinum and of Beecham. 'Young man,' she replied, 'you must help fate along. You must telephone Sir Thomas Beecham.' 'What are you saying?' I protested. 'He would never come to the phone for me.' But she was adamant: 'You must telephone him, and you must do it now.' She took me to the call box in the corner of the restaurant. I dialled the great man's number with a shaking hand. A cold voice greeted me on the other end. 'Who is speaking?' It was not Sir Thomas. 'Who is speaking, please?' 'Paul Tortelier.' 'Who? Doctor Telier?' For some reason my name becomes Doc-torTelier for those who don't know me. It shows how weak our hearing is. We always think we are so clever, but when we don't know something in advance we are very stupid. So, as he could not get my name right, I just said, 'The French cellist who played with Sir Thomas in Amsterdam.' 'Well then, just wait a minute.' I waited one minute; I waited two minutes and was on the point of hanging up, when the familiar drawl greeted me. 'Hello, my boy! Where are you? You are just the man I wanted to talk to.' And a date was fixed there and then for the concert. I shall never be grateful enough to Miss Frieland for having given me the courage to make that telephone call.

So that is how I was engaged to make my London début with the Royal Philharmonic Orchestra performing *Don Quixote*. Before the London date, we played the programme in Southampton as a sort of general rehearsal. Afterwards, Beecham called me to his dressing room. 'My boy,' he said, 'You will be successful in England because you have temperament and that is what they want.'

His words were prophetic.

In any case, the London concert was a great success. It was given at Drury Lane, a very fashionable old theatre. Beecham was in splendid form. The upper crust of London's musical society was there. Strauss himself attended. He was then in a difficult financial situation and Beecham wanted to help him.

Within ten days of my début with Sir Thomas, I gave a recital in Wigmore Hall with Gerald Moore, I played for the BBC on the choice programme of the week called the Friday Recital, and I recorded *Don Quixote* for HMV. Everything came at once to make a big impact. I know many young artists who make their début in a big city. Yet, as we say in French, *'Il n'y a pas de lendemain* – there is no tomorrow. If you play only once a year, it may take many years to be recognized. But to perform four times within a few days had as much effect as giving ten concerts spread over ten years. I was launched in England.

And the English public is most faithful.

I cannot tell you how many times I have played in England over thirty-five years. In London alone I play several times a year. The immigration officers know me at sight. When they see me coming with my cello they just wave me straight through. I was recently told, 'You know, you are an institution in England.' Well, if one must be an institution, that's the best place for it to be.

Fate or chance? Again, the strands had come together and it is difficult to know what determined their course. Had I not played *Don Quixote* with Strauss in Monte Carlo ten years before, Beecham might not have engaged me. That's why he took the risk, little knowing that I wasn't the star he assumed me to be.

Had Martinon not engaged me for Dublin I would not have passed through London, met Mrs Tillett, and auditioned for the BBC. And it was fortunate indeed that I lunched that day at Miss Frieland's restaurant.

Not inappropriately called 'Cinderella'.

X
The Children

When I was a little boy my father used to tell me that in fifteen or twenty years' time I would become a father myself and find it wonderful to have a boy of my own. I opened my big eyes, because he presented it as a marvellous event – the coming of a child within your family.

This idea – to instil in youngsters a sense of wonder that they themselves will one day become parents – probably originated with my grandfather. Both my father and grandfather were humanists – not in an abstract way, but in tangible ways, and my father's love for his children was an expression of this.

When were your children born?

Now, now, now . . .

All right; I won't ask for the exact dates. But in what order were they born?

My first child was Anne, the daughter of my first marriage. Owing to my divorce, and the fact that Anne was raised by her mother's parents, I did not have the opportunity to see her as often as I would have liked. However, from her sixth year she regularly went on holiday with us, and at the age of 15 she came to live with us in Paris. She stayed with us for four years, and during that time she and Maud developed a warm relationship. Anne is now happily married, and living in Paris. She is very friendly with her half-brother and half-sisters.

My son Pascal was born a little over a year after Maud and I were married. Pau came three years later, and Pomone nine years afterwards.

Was there any special reason why you and Maud gave your children names beginning with the letter 'P'.

That really came about more or less unintentionally. We called our son 'Pascal' because it was the name Maud had given her favourite doll as a child; she preserved the name for her real son. And Pau was named after Casals; her full name is Maria de la Pau. In Catalan Pau means 'Peace' as well as 'Pablo'. When Pomone was born I happened to be away on tour; Maud was in a quandary about the name, as she had planned on having a boy. At first she could imagine no other name for the baby than 'Maud', but during the night she recalled our first rendezvous during which we had listened enraptured to the beautiful aria of Pomone from Bach's Cantata No. 205, *Der zufriedengestellte Aeolus*. Moved by this memory she chose the name Pomone, which I love too, for our last child. Pomone was, by the way, the Roman goddess of fruit and trees.

When did you think that your children would become musicians?

One day, when Pascal was four, Maud and I decided that he should play the cello. We persuaded ourselves that our reason for this choice was to make it possible for him to benefit from our cellistic experience, but it may have been only lack of imagination. Whatever it was, my father-in-law disagreed with our project. 'There are already enough well-known cellists in the Tortelier family,' he declared. 'Let him play the violin.' In this, my father-in-law was also perhaps a little biased, as he himself was a violinist. We did take his point, however, and Pascal began to study the violin with André Proffit, an excellent teacher; at the same time he took piano lessons. When Pau began to study music she seemed, like her brother, equally gifted for both the piano and violin. As Pascal was three years older than she, he was the first to enter the Paris Conservatoire. It so happened that the entrance competition for the violin preceded that for the piano, and Pascal succeeded in being admitted as a violin student. We then told Pau, 'Your brother will now be devoting his time to the violin, and we would like you to concentrate on the piano.' She did not object, and it proved a good choice for both. Pascal progressed beautifully. When he was 14 he won the first prize in the class of René Benedetti, and went on to study with Dominique Hoppenot. The following year he made his English début, performing the Brahms Double Concerto with me in both Chester Cathedral and the Royal Albert Hall. The Double Concerto is a formidable challenge for any artist. You are not at ease as you are when playing a solo concerto. It is at one and the same time a solo concerto and a piece of chamber music and requires great control and fine musicianship. Nor is it ideally written for the violin; certain arpeggio passages in the Finale are more pianistic than violinistic. Pascal's performance of this work is outstanding. He could also have conducted it when he was fifteen.

Jean Gallon was by then too old to teach Pascal harmony, but he did once come to our home to test him. Afterwards he confided that the boy was so talented that '*Il ne faut pas le louper*' – 'he mustn't get out of it'. We did not want to take advantage of Gallon's visit to ask him to test Pau as well. However, he gave her a glance and told us *mezza voce*, 'The future Miss Europe'. Such was Jean Gallon. If Pascal could not have the benefit of Gallon's help, he did have the good fortune to study harmony privately with Nadia Boulanger for several years, and counter-point and fugue with Henri Challan. He once performed part of Hindemith's *Ludus Tonalis* at the piano for the composer himself and received warm encouragement. For five years Pascal was leader of the Orchestre du Capitol de Toulouse, but he has been increasingly drawn to conducting in which field he's beginning to make an international career. On the personal side, he has a lovely family with two children.

Pau also showed prodigious talent at an early age, did she not? Those who knew her when she was 12 remember her ability to play at sight such a score as the Shostakovich Cello Concerto, much as other children read comics.

Yes, she is a remarkable sight-reader; in fact, she received the first medal in sight-reading from the Conservatoire when she was 13. Her piano teachers were Jeanne-Marie Darré, Lélia

Gousseau, and Detlef Kraus. She began to give concerts at an early age. For instance, when she was 12 she gave a series of recitals in England with Jacqueline du Pré who was then 18. Pau has not only an innate musicality, but an unusual power of communication.

I felt this at once when she played Mozart's C major Concerto (K. 467) with my Orchestre Symphonique Genevois. It was a performance of rare beauty.

Pomone, arriving on the scene nearly a decade later, complements the musical activities of the family. She began by studying the piano from the age of 6 to 11. I hoped that she would become a cellist so that we could create a trio of Tortelier juniors. She showed promise for the instrument, but rebelled against the plan I had chosen for her, thought of studying medicine, and eventually at the age of 16 came back to music by way of the flute. Within two years she succeeded in entering Jean-Pierre Rampal's class at the Paris Conservatoire and obtained her prize four years later. She is now also studying singing.

Did your children practise their instruments more willingly than you did as a child?

Pascal needed more looking after than Pau. It's hard to convince eager and energetic children that they have to devote a certain number of hours each day to practising.

The Torteliers were staying at the home of Mr. and Mrs. Travers Symons in London. Paul and Maud had to go out, but left strict instructions with the children to practise. After a while Mrs. Symons took pity on them and sat them both down with lemon squashes in front of the television. Their pleasure was intense, but short-lived. Maud suddenly returned sooner than expected and was shocked at the scene which confronted her. The children were immediately ordered back to their instruments.

I'm afraid Pascal followed the same pattern I had followed thirty-three years before. He was talented but lazy, just as I used to be, and I had to urge him along just as my mother urged me. On occasion, I would lose my temper just as she lost hers. In fact one day, in a moment of rage, I broke a superb Peccatte bow, something my mother would never have been able to afford to do. Given the choice I would prefer to break a bow than hit a child, and, as I recall, this happened more than once. It was, I must say, a very costly proposition. Another time, when Pascal and I were working on the Brahms Double Concerto, I reached a point of desperation and threw my cello on the floor.

Not the Guarnerius, I hope.

I don't remember, but luckily the floor was carpeted.

Pau and Pascal recall the bicycle tours the family took together in Brittany as being among the happiest memories of their childhood.

They were among the happiest experiences for Maud and me, too. From 1953 we spent our summers in a house we owned on the island of Noirmoutier off the Atlantic coast of France just south of Brittany. We adored the house and were always overjoyed to go there.

> On one occasion when departing from the Gare Montparnasse for a holiday on Noirmoutier, the children were informed that their father would not be able to come with the family because of his concert commitments. Maud, Pascal and Pau said goodbye sadly to Papa as they boarded the train. After it pulled out, the children spent half an hour running about the corridors before returning to the compartment to join their mother. There was now a strange man sitting opposite them whose face was entirely covered by the newspaper he was reading. The newspaper was suddenly whisked aside. It was – Papa! – who had boarded the train secretly at the last moment before it left.

We would use Noirmoutier as a base for the summer and set out on *randonnées* – what you might call bicycle rambles – for a week at a time. It was wonderful for the children's health, not to mention the adults. We all developed very strong legs. As we never made any reservations in hotels, there was always a chance that we might have to sleep in the fields. Once, when we toured along the Atlantic coast, we did in fact spend the night on the beach.

We all adore cycling. I think the bicycle is the finest of man's inventions. It provides just the right speed for discovering the countryside – not too slow, not too fast. You have just the proper length of time to see the landscape without it becoming monotonous.

Although Noirmoutier has now been joined to the mainland by a cause-
way, it was at that time a real island. For six-hour periods it would be cut
off by the tide. The Tortelier family had planned to depart the following
morning on a bicycle tour. The children consulted the time of the tides
and discovered that there would be low tide from midnight to 6.0 a.m.
after which time they could not leave until noon. The parents agreed to
depart at midnight. The children's excitement could not be imagined.
The hour struck and they set out on their journey. As they rode through
silent, sleeping villages in the dead of night, Papa would sing folk songs
or imitate military fanfares to wake up the local inhabitants. Morning
finally came and they arrived in Nantes, a tired but happy foursome.

Even the fiercest rainstorm didn't stop us. It was on such a day
that we descended the long steep hill that leads to the old Breton
town of Quimper. One of the tyres on Pau's bicycle had a
puncture. So I had to take Pau, who was then 7 or 8 on my own
bike and hold hers with one hand. It was terribly slippery, and if
something had happened I wouldn't have been able to stop. We
went round a turn and I felt I was about to fall. At that moment a
car came by. I threw Pau's bicycle to the side of the road, and just
avoided an accident. We arrived in Quimper absolutely soaked
through like four people who had just come from a swim fully
clothed, and found refuge in a very poor, typically old café. We
had to take off all our clothes, which the *patronne* dried for us by
the stove in the main *salle*. I can't imagine what people thought
of us.

We made trips to various parts of Brittany: to Carnac to see
the dolmens and menhirs, to Belle-Île, and to Mont-Saint-
Michel. We have always continued to cycle, and do it even now.
I even manage to get up the hill to my house in Nice. Maud
and I recently made an excursion, but this time we spoiled
ourselves and chose a flat terrain: the Camargue in the south
of France.

*The Tortelier name is now not only associated with solo playing,
but also with the highest level of chamber music playing. When did
your children begin to perform with you?*

We began with chamber music at home when the children
were quite young. I think it's important to introduce chamber
music as early as possible. They first played in public with me
when they were 13 or 14. Pau and I have given innumerable

recitals all over the world, and Pascal has often joined us to give trio concerts or to play Beethoven's Triple Concerto. I must stress as well that both Pau and Pascal have established independent careers on their respective instruments.

Could you tell us something of the musical interaction that takes place between you and your children when you perform together?

When Pau plays the piano one senses that she once played a stringed instrument. She has such a natural sense of line that she seems almost to be playing with a bow. Our artistic rapport is so complete that sometimes when she is playing I think I myself am at the piano. When I perform with my son I feel that I am being enriched, because he is just a little different from me. For instance, he has more sense of regularity of tempo than Pau or I. The two of us sometimes lose tempo a little; we like to take liberties. Of course, in Beethoven, for example, there are places where it is natural to have a slight modification of tempo, as in the second subject of the Finale of the A major Cello Sonata. But, generally speaking, it is important to maintain a unity of tempo. And Pascal has this in his blood.

When not giving concerts do you and your family often play music together at home?

I wish I could answer 'yes'. But it's a family of professional musicians and none of us has much free time to make music 'for pleasure'. As we live in different places, it's difficult for us to co-ordinate our schedules. But when we do meet to prepare for concerts it's a great joy for all of us.

Children of well-known musicians who eventually develop their own musical careers sometimes feel handicapped, as it were, by the fame of the family name.

This has perhaps been something more of a problem for Pascal who, like his father, plays a stringed instrument. Pau as a pianist cannot easily be compared to a cellist. However, the situation is now becoming reversed. It is I who must be careful to measure up to the strength and vitality of my children's playing.

When you work together, do you lead the rehearsals?

Not nowadays. Both Pau and Pascal are complete artists. When we rehearse, we all share in making suggestions. And, of course, interpretation must never stand still.

One learns all one's life. I have learned from my wife and from my children, and now I am learning from my grandchildren.

XI

Casals

Of all interpreters I have heard, Pablo Casals has moved me the most. I first met him when at the age of 15 or 16 I took part in a concert given in his honour by fifty French cellists at the Théâtre des Champs-Elysées. Charles Kiesgen introduced me to Casals and told him that I could play Paganini's *Moto Perpetuo* on the cello. And Casals replied that he also used to play it to brush up his technique when he was young. Shortly afterwards Casals gave a recital at the Salle Pleyel; the programme included Bach's D Minor Suite. I remember being impressed by his simplicity and dedication, by the way the entire work unfolded as a unity. I was still too young to appreciate fully the extraordinary means by which he achieved that simplicity. My next experience of Casals was through recordings.

Which ones in particular?

The Intermezzo from *Goyescas* by Granados, Bach's Adagio in A minor, and eventually the Dvořák Concerto. I don't think I had any others, but these were enough for me to realize his greatness. It wasn't until after the war that I heard him play again in person, and had the opportunity to become fully acquainted with his art.

Did you ever actually study with him?

No, I didn't.

Yet many characteristics of your playing have struck me as being in the tradition of Casals, though expressed in accordance with your

99

own temperament and technique. For instance your variety and taste in the use of vibrato, or the spontaneity and subtlety of your rubato. You must have been influenced by his playing.

I was influenced, I was enlightened. For me it was the moment of truth.

Could you describe his playing?

The music that came out of his cello was the ideal. His sonority was unique. How can I express it? I somehow associate it with a fruit. It had a quality that was mild and yet with a touch of lemon. It was like a mixture of all the best fruits: juicy, yet not too sweet. I'm sorry to make a gastronomic comparison, but it is, I suppose, as good as any other. Casals's sonority was really indefinable; it was something spiritual. It so fitted the music that the sonority didn't seem important in itself. The same applied to his vibrato. Young virtuosi, beware: if someone compliments you on your 'exceptionally beautiful vibrato' it probably means that you've been seduced by the irrelevant. One never thought that Casals was playing the 'cello'; he was playing music.

As for his rubato – that was sheer poetry. Again, it seemed so natural as to be inevitable. Such a rubato is done almost against one's will. It is not studied, not planned. It is the intuitive awareness of the relativity of notes in every direction: vertical, horizontal, diagonal. You feel in the moment of performance that one note should be given a little more time than another. This feeling is, I think, very much influenced by the study of composition, and Casals was, of course, a composer.

The fact that you are to a large extent self-taught is reminiscent of Casals who also developed his own technique.

It's true that Casals broke away from many aspects of the traditional cello technique of his time. One of his most important innovations was the development of the articulative power of the left hand. I once asked Jean Gallon, who greatly admired Casals, to tell me what he found to be most extraordinary in his playing. Gallon responded by tapping percussively upon the table with his fingers. It was by means of such articulation that

Casals could put the string into immediate vibration, and this had a profound influence upon the style of his playing. It gave more freedom to the bow which was no longer solely responsible for clear articulation. Casals was also probably the first cellist to use his left hand in the manner of a pianist – that is, by normally placing only one finger on the string at a time, rather than keeping all the fingers clamped down. This allowed the fingers to vibrate freely. Carl Flesch, the famous violinist and teacher, once wrote an article in *The Strad* in which he said that even violinists were influenced by the revolution Casals brought to bear on cello fingering. Not only did he open out the hand and increase its reach, but he shifted position in accordance with musical rather than technical considerations. Another major contribution to the art of string playing was his use of 'expressive intonation' – the subtle, but vitalizing, sharpening or flattening of notes in accordance with their melodic or harmonic tendencies. Well, these are some of the things Casals worked out for himself, and we have reaped the benefit.

When did you first play for Casals?

That was an important day in my life. It was Bastille Day, 14 July 1945; Casals was visiting Paris for the first time since the end of the war. Charles Kiesgen arranged for me to visit Casals at the Asile San Fernando in Neuilly where he was staying. I remember his room as if I had been there yesterday. It was as simple as could be – more like a cell than a room. The walls were completely white. It was awe-inspiring to be in the presence of this great man whose simplicity of manner matched his surroundings. I played some of my own works: the Prelude from my Suite for Solo Cello which I had recently composed in tribute to my father, and one of my virtuoso pieces, *Spirales*. When I had finished playing I waited for Casals to make a comment, but he didn't say anything. He just sat opposite me deep in meditation. Absolute silence. I felt embarrassed, so I got up and put my cello in its case. I was on the verge of leaving, but summoned the courage to say, 'Before I go, *Maître*, I would be grateful to have your criticism – to know at least the most important things you would wish to tell me.' More silence. He reached for his pipe, filled it with tobacco, lit it, and took a few puffs. Never did the lighting of a pipe seem to last so long. Finally, he looked up at me. 'My criticism?' he asked. 'My criticism is that you have conquered me.' So I had wings forever.

My first long-term encounter with Casals came in 1950 when I had the good fortune to be selected to lead the cello section during the first Prades Festival, devoted entirely to the music of Bach. By then I had given up all orchestra playing, but I felt privileged indeed to play in that orchestra under Casals's direction. This festival was a major event, not only for me personally, but for the music world as a whole. Since 1939 Casals had been living as an exile from Fascist Spain in the village of Prades in the foothills of the Pyrenees close to his native Catalonia. During the war years he gave his chief attention to helping the hundreds of thousands of Spanish refugees living in destitute conditions in France. After the war, when it became clear that the Allies would continue to tolerate the Franco regime, Casals withdrew from the concert stage and retired once more to Prades to protest against the triumph of political expediency over morality.

The first Prades Festival was more than a celebration of the bicentenary of the death of Bach. It was a tribute to Casals for his greatness as an interpreter of Bach's music, for his stature as a human being. The musicians – about thirty of us – came from America and Europe to the village of Prades as if on a pilgrimage. And for Casals it was a great and deep joy, after four years of seclusion, to have this group of fine, dedicated musicians come to his place of exile to make music with him. In later years there were so many visitors that the atmosphere in Prades was, comparatively speaking, a little spoiled – though Casals himself was never spoiled. But at that time the atmosphere was pure. We arrived a month before the first concert – a month to be devoted entirely to rehearsing Bach. A few posters were the only sign that a festival was to take place. Otherwise the village was as peaceful as it always had been, nestling in its quiet valley at the foot of Mount Canigou.

The practical aspects were not yet very well organized. The Abbey of Saint-Michel-de-Cuxa – later used for rehearsals and concerts – was not available to us. So we rehearsed in the dining-room of a girls' school. As we had plenty of time in which to work, there was no sense of extraneous stress at the rehearsals. Casals, who had devoted a lifetime to studying the Cello Suites, now brought these insights to bear upon Bach's orchestral music. He sought the distinctive mood of each piece, and worked with us again and again on the shape of the phrasing till the music seemed to breathe. It would take hours to describe his marvellous way with Bach.

We began our rehearsals with the First Brandenburg Concerto. I shall never forget the depth of feeling he brought to the slow movement, with its poignant dialogue in D minor between oboe and violin. Performing that movement with Casals was unutterably moving. It was, I think, the most beautiful moment of my musical life. This piece expresses the deepest sorrow, a total sorrow. One would expect that such intensity of grief would lead a man to despair. Yet, extraordinary as it may be, it is not so. Thanks to the music, this sorrow transforms itself, metamorphoses into a flower. You can weep, yes, but you feel a sort of happiness at the same time, happy to know that beauty exists, that beauty is not in vain, that beauty can reach such heights . . . the colour, the harmony . . . well, this cannot be put into words. I cried, we all cried, and I felt like kneeling before Casals who brought us so close to the spirit of Bach. I don't think I could hear the work again. I would prefer simply to read the score and imagine how it sounds. How Bach must have suffered! But what a power, when you suffer, to be able to give birth to a miracle.

The recordings from the Prades and Perpignan festivals are extra-ordinary. The roundness of phrasing is wonderfully integrated with the vitality of rhythm. One senses the orchestra's total dedication. True, the quality of recorded sound leaves something to be desired by today's standard – but the interpretations are none the less preserved for posterity.

Unfortunately, many people today are so spellbound by high fidelity that they don't hear in depth. They hear only the superficial truth, not the essential truth. It makes me happy that my son, who has heard so many of the latest recordings, says, 'Aha . . . the Casals recordings are a revelation.' After all, Pascal is of a different generation; his approach to music may be different in many ways, but he still recognizes that with Casals the spirit and true character are there.

As if to bring further wonderment to the festival, our daughter Maria de la Pau was born during the time of the rehearsals. My colleagues made a huge sign decorated with two cellos, representing Maud and myself, which they put up in the village, welcoming her birth.

It was during the festival that my son Pascal, then aged 3 made Casals' acquaintance. I don't know whether I'm proud or ashamed to say that Pascal followed the family tradition when it came to being introduced to famous people. I refer to the moment when I myself, at the age of 3, was asked to kiss Sarah Bernhardt and, repelled by her make-up, cried out '*Je ne peux pas, Sarah!*' Well, I held up Pascal to kiss Casals, but when he found the Maestro's cheek unshaven, he made a terrible grimace and shouted, '*Tu piques!*' – 'You're prickly!' Casals and everyone else present laughed. I was rather mortified and gave Pascal a scolding afterwards in the street.

One day some members of the Festival orchestra asked me to play for them an alternative Prelude which I had composed for my Suite for Solo Cello.* When I had finished I turned round, and was startled to see that Casals had come up behind me to listen. 'Excuse me, *Maître*,' I said, 'had I known you were there I wouldn't have played.' 'No, no!', he exclaimed, 'I was most interested and surprised as well, because you play your piece differently from the way I play it myself.' I had given him the music some time before and felt honoured that he had taken the time and trouble to study it. Such was my admiration for Casals' intuition that even though I had composed the music myself, I felt his interpretation must be better than mine.

Since then I have in fact changed my conception of this piece, and have probably come closer to the way he played it. I was not serene enough then. I was in my mid-thirties, and I think to play the piece properly I had to be older. Isn't that interesting?

*In my recording of the Suite (for EMI) this alternative Prelude is played as the second movement, replacing the original Allemande. Unfortunately this Prelude is not included in the edition published by Salabert (see Appendix I).

The creative process comes, in part, from a layer deeper than consciousness. The conscious personality sometimes needs time to assimilate and understand what has been produced.

That is true. There are works which I could not interpret to my satisfaction when I wrote them. I am more at ease in a sonata by Beethoven or Brahms than in my own Sonata. It was only last year that I succeeded in playing it in a way I feel to be right.

What contact did you have with Casals after 1950?

I returned three times to play in the festivals given in Perpignan or Prades.

It was in 1968 that Pierre René Honnens, then cellist of the Danish Quartet, happened to run into Paul Tortelier in Bucharest. They decided to give a private concert at the Danish Embassy, in which Paul would join the quartet to perform the Schubert C major Quintet. Honnens practised the second cello part in his hotel. But when they next met, Paul told him that he himself always played the second part and insisted that Honnens play the first. Honnens duly returned to his hotel to practise again. At the rehearsal Paul reminisced, 'When I last performed this work, the first cello part was played by Pablo Casals.' The quartet's first violinist, Arne Svendsen, found this most amusing. 'You'd better do very well, indeed,' he ribbed his cellist colleague. 'Ah, in that case,' Paul added, turning to Svendsen, 'I'd better tell you that the first violin part was played by Isaac Stern.'

The Perpignan Festival recording of the Schubert Quintet is incomparable – the sustained song of the Adagio, interrupted by the wild anguish of the middle section! I've loved that recording for thirty years.

It was wonderful to play chamber music with Casals. He was simplicity itself. At a later date I performed the Tchaikovsky *Rococo* Variations at the Casals Festival in Puerto Rico. I once paid a special visit to Prades to play a Bach suite for Casals. He seemed very happy with my interpretation. 'It is rare,' he said, 'to hear the Sarabande performed, as you do, in its proper tempo. Usually it's played too slowly, in six beats per bar, rather than three. It's a sublime piece of music – true – but it's nevertheless a dance, a sacred dance which is performed even today in the Cathedral of Seville.' A few years later, after a concert I had given in Zermatt, he paid me a great compliment. 'When you play,' he said, 'the music speaks.'

You told me that you once met Albert Schweitzer in Casals's presence. When was that?

In 1951, in Zürich, at a concert given by 120 cellists in tribute to Casals. Schweitzer struck one at once as being a most remarkable man. His eyes were unforgettable – the blue of those eyes under the forest of his eyebrows! One immediately felt a *force de la nature*. I met Casals briefly just after he had spent some time in conversation with Schweitzer. He was visibly moved. 'Do you know what he told me?' Casals asked. 'He said that I should go beyond Prades, to play again for the world – that it is better to create than to protest. But I am a human being first and a musician second. When I see how the world has abandoned my people, I must protest. I cannot play . . . I cannot play.'

At the time I was preparing a concert in New York honouring Albert Schweitzer's ninetieth birthday – Casals spoke to me of that conversation. He had, he said, responded to Schweitzer with some advice of his own. After the Doctor had told him, 'It is better to create than to protest,' Casals answered, 'I also have something to say to you. You speak so often on behalf of the suffering millions and they admire you and your wonderful work in Lambaréné. But, though you have written many books, you have not addressed any of your writings directly to the common man.' With a dash of satire Casals imitated how Schweitzer got up from his chair, shrugged his shoulders and said, 'Well, I have told you what I want to say.' Casals continued, 'I think my words were not lost on Dr. Schweitzer. In his declaration entitled Peace or Atomic War? *he eventually did speak directly to the peoples of the world.'*

I should add that for his part Casals found a way in which he could go out into the world to create without violating his principles. In his performances of his oratorio El Pessebre *he carried the message of peace wherever he could. It is interesting to see how these two men were able to influence one another.*

Some years later, when I was flying to Buenos Aires or Bogotá – I forget which – my plane was scheduled to stop for an hour in Puerto Rico to refuel. In fact it remained there two days. Never have an aeroplane's mechanical difficulties given a passenger more joy. Casals invited me to visit him at his home; at that time he lived in a house right by the sea. He did not look upon the delay of my flight as a mere coincidence, any more than he regarded it as a coincidence that his wife's mother had been born in Puerto Rico in the same house as his own mother sixty years previously.

He spoke at length of his mother, whose memory he cherished, recalling the sacrifice she once made when he was young by cutting and selling her beautiful hair in order to be able to pay their expenses. To understand what that represented one must bear in mind that at the end of the last century it was virtually unthinkable for a woman to cut her hair short.

More than any person I have known, Casals believed in the dignity of man – one could almost say the sanctity of man. He believed that man's nature should be trusted from the beginning, rather than despised. He told me how he had once been scandalized by the disrespectful way in which a customs officer had searched him, assuming that he must be carrying something fraudulent. This small incident, he said, was symbolic of man's distrust of man. Such things would not happen, Casals thought, if man were given confidence in himself – pride in the value of human life – during his earliest years, at home and at school. Though the concept of the ideal anarchist appealed to him, he was not sentimental in this regard. He believed in the necessity of giving a good kick to those who dare trespass upon another's rights. When we were walking on the beach together, he said, 'Am I free to walk on your feet? Freedom must not be misused.'

I have always believed that the supreme ideal is not liberty – but love. Love is unconditional, while liberty is limited. This applies to art as well. Think of the self-discipline required of a musician to achieve firm rhythm or good intonation!

When, as a student, I first met Casals and he learned that I was an aspiring conductor, he commented with a twinkle in his eye, 'Don't forget that in order to be a conductor, you must first be well-conducted.'

He knew how relative is the freedom we have, whether in music or in life. The musician who loves his art and his family, and cares about others, knows how to find infinite happiness within a very limited freedom.

All the same, Casals had a great love of liberty, as he demonstrated time and again throughout his life. Paradoxically, despite his opinion that religious beliefs should not be imposed on people, when Maria de la Pau was born he was most excited at the idea of being her godfather. And, though Maud and I are agnostics, we offered no opposition to having her baptized in a ceremony that brought Casals much joy.

Casals was not only a unique cellist, a unique artist. He was also the sort of person I think Bach must have been: a complete man whose life and art formed a whole.

XII

A Year on the Kibbutz

From the autumn of 1955 until the summer of 1956 you lived on the kibbutz of Maabaroth in Israel. For a concert artist with an international career, this was an unusual thing to do, all the more so as you are not Jewish. What were your reasons for this decision?

I would say that Maud and I had two reasons, the first being our idealism, the second, our affinity with the Jewish people. We had always wanted to live in a community in which social differences are not felt – one that might perhaps come close to my father's ideal of a life in which everyone shared equally both in the labour and the fruits of that labour. And the idealism my father passed on to me was to some degree inspired by his Jewish friends with whom he had so many long intellectual discussions. I feel there is a Jewish impact on my personality. Of course so many outstanding musicians – especially string players – are Jewish. Well, love for music is just a typical expression of the enthusiasm the Jewish people have for beauty, for ideals, for culture. No race has a deeper or more intimate feeling for music. My wife and I seem to attract Jewish people and we feel at one with them. Some people even think I look Jewish because of my nose.

Is it a Breton nose perhaps?

I cannot say, but it has a strong curve. We also call it *le nez bourbon*. The Bourbons were kings of France for over 200 years.

They had noses like that. No matter; I would support the common people against the nobility any day.

In any case, my going to Israel was in no way related to Zionist ideas. As a matter of fact, as a humanist I never think of segregating races or of making differences between men. I know that people have differing traits, but I love everyone in the world – as long as they behave in a civilized way towards their fellow men. In this respect I must say that I am deeply distressed that the Israeli government has as yet failed to recognize the needs of the Palestinian people. Without the intransigence that exists on both sides we might have seen a Switzerland of the Middle East, rather than the tragic situation which has developed.

I have often played in Israel. Perhaps the most significant of these concerts was the inauguration of the Frederic R. Mann Auditorium in 1957. For this occasion they invited four great Jewish artists to perform: Leonard Bernstein as conductor, Rubinstein, Stern, and Piatigorsky as soloists. But Piatigorsky fell ill and, rather than invite another Jewish cellist, they asked me to play. That was indeed a great honour. Moshe Atzmon, the Israeli conductor who now directs the Basel Symphony Orchestra, told me that what touched him most deeply on that historic occasion – beautiful as were the concertos of Mendelssohn and Beethoven played by Stern and Rubinstein – was Bloch's *Schelomo*. This work transcends a purely personal message; its notes seem to express Israel's longing for its lost temple. The phrases seem to rise from out of the past like a distant wail. All Israel heard it – not just those in the concert hall – but those listening to the radio, in the towns, in the kibbutzim. That night, when playing Bloch's work, I felt at one with the eternal soul of Israel.

> The evening of the historic concert, the manager of the Israel Philharmonic went to the Dan Hotel to fetch Arthur Rubinstein and Paul Tortelier. Rubinstein was ushered into the car, but Tortelier was nowhere to be found. His room was called, but there was no answer. A search was made everywhere – to no avail. Becoming increasingly worried, the manager ran out to the terrace. No one was to be seen – no one, that is, on land. Barely visible, far out in the ocean were what looked like two bobbing heads. He waved to these heads – and, to his amazement, they waved back. Paul and Maud, oblivious to the passage of time, swam ashore and were told that the concert was just about to begin. Soon they

were on their way to the hall with a police escort, arriving just in time for Paul to play. Maud, now elegantly dressed, looked on; only her wet hair, hanging limp and straight, told of her sea adventure.

When did you first have the idea of living on a kibbutz?

The idea was put to us by Isaac Stern's wife, Vera. Knowing of our ideals, she suggested that we visit a kibbutz, recommending in particular Maabaroth, midway between Tel Aviv and Haifa. The following year I toured with the Israel Philharmonic, and Maud and I decided to take the opportunity of visiting Maabaroth to see if the reality measured up to our expectations. I shall never forget our discovery of that kibbutz. We arrived at about 11.0 in the morning on an extremely hot day. As most of the people were still working in the fields it was nearly deserted. But we happened to find a couple, who later became our friends, who showed us around the kibbutz. It was so silent, so impressive, so beautiful that we fell in love with it at once. We stayed on for a day or two, and were able to see the people working without thought of money, just for the joy of building a community. In a way it was something like a monastery. But I'm not fond of monasteries because I have no special feeling for religion – for any religion, that is, except music. When we told them we wanted to return the following year to live there, they warned us against thinking of it in too romantic terms; we should consider it soberly. We insisted that we would return – and we did. Back in Paris, we prepared ourselves by taking Hebrew lessons two or three times a week, and I refused all engagements for the following year. At that time engagements were not made two years in advance as they are now. I remember the enthusiasm we felt while taking those Hebrew lessons. It was not only the discovery of a different language but of another culture, another heritage. I remember the day we left. It was a real expedition. In addition to our children – then aged 5 and 8 – my sister and mother came with us, as well as two of my students, both charming girls: Shirley Thompson from England and Suzanne Perrault from Canada. The voyage by sea lasted several days; it was a memorable time for us all.

I must say that when I disembarked at the port of Haifa, an immigrant on Israeli soil, I was immensely shaken. I felt a great power in the light of the sun, the great sun shining down upon this Middle-Eastern country. 'What am I doing here,' I asked myself, 'thousands of miles from home, in a completely foreign country threatened by enemies on all its borders?'

This thought was swept away by the joyous greeting we received from our new comrades – our *chaverim* as one says in Hebrew. We felt at once as if we were the best friends in the world. It was like a dream to be driven by my new brothers – I'd never had any before – from Haifa to Maabaroth. As our jeep roared at full speed through the heat and dust under the incandescent sun, music began to sing in my head. It was to become the Prelude to my Israel Symphony.

Upon arrival at Maabaroth we began a simple life: just love and work, and no waste of time. At Maabaroth the man who collected rubbish was on an equal status with a professor of science. Everyone wore the same clothes, ate the same food, and was treated equally. For a man like me who doesn't like to be bothered with material things, such a life is ideal. Nothing belongs to you, so you have nothing to worry about in that respect. And you have whatever you need because, after all, you don't need so much in life. We acquire a lot of unnecessary things, whether through fear, temptation or habit. The climate there was also a favourable factor. All I required was a shirt and hat to protect me from the sun. It was wonderful to experience a life of brotherly love and freedom. For me, freedom means a life in which you don't have to lose time on all the hundreds of meaningless obligations that one encounters in city life. And I call brotherly love the radiant contact between people who share daily the same love of nature, work, and beauty in complete equality and simplicity.

Did you do a lot of physical work?

Not very much. Normally you have to do what is needed, but the committee asked me what I preferred to do. I told them that I wished only to be an ordinary member and to share in the full life of the kibbutz, which means to take part in the manual work as well. They were, however, happy to have a musician of a certain reputation living among them and they insisted upon my carrying on with my musical activities. Thus I was assigned an extremely light workload, occasionally picking bananas and grapefruit.

How did you reconcile doing physical work with playing the cello?

I must say that physical work has never troubled me. When I have taken a shovel or picked fruit in the trees I have never worried about my fingers. It's not good to wrap yourself in cotton wool. It's better to take the minor risk of hurting a finger than to be too careful. However, to be honest, the women in my family – Maud, Geneviève and my mother – did more physical work than I. They worked daily for a few hours either in the laundry (*mahbessa*), in the fields or in the kitchen. I took my turn serving dinner once a week.

How did you manage?

I don't think I would have qualified as a waiter in a three-star French restaurant. But serving at Maabaroth was an easy matter; there's nothing to do but set things down in any order in any place, and I'm quite good at doing just that.

What were your musical activities?

They gave me time to do what I like best – above all to compose, then to play, then to teach. Within a period of four months I was able to complete the Israel Symphony. The slow movement was based upon a Biblical text, and I remember working on the Scherzo at night in the open air, in a little theatre used by the kibbutz on special occasions. Writing under the sparkling stars of an oriental night was a divine affair. And I think that some of that dancing light was infused into the Trio of this Scherzo – a movement that was particularly enjoyed when I performed the work with the Israel Philharmonic six months later.

Maud and I formed a trio with Geneviève at the piano, and we gave a few concerts. And, as I've said, I did some teaching. I also found time to help Pau and Pascal with their musical education, even if this wasn't quite within the rules of the kibbutz.

How did the children take to Maabaroth?

They seemed to be happy. I know that the practice of separating children from their parents has been criticized, possibly with justification. I feel the parents are necessary to the children, but the kibbutz system had some advantages too. At that time the children were allowed two hours each day after school to be with their parents. At 4.0 p.m. they were playing in the house of 'Mummy and Daddy' and it was a lovely picture to see the children together with their parents who were relaxing after having finished their work. Owing to the heat, one starts at 6.0 a.m. sometimes even earlier, and after midday one cannot work; it's too hot. So the parents have a siesta after lunch, and then at 4.0 p.m. take care of their children. In a way there seemed to me to be more family life on the kibbutz than in a modern city. We are supposed to live with our children, but in fact we are busy all day; they are busy too. When they return home they do their homework and we are tired out or pre-occupied, so we don't really spend much time with our children after all. But, of course, on the kibbutz the children took their meals separately from their parents, and had separate sleeping quarters. Yet during those two hours in the afternoon they could talk and play with us and make the necessary link.

One particularly happy experience was the visit paid us by my first daughter Anne – then 15 – who stayed with us for two months.

And what did your mother think of life on the kibbutz?

How could she, with her maternal instincts, accept the principle that children should be separated from their parents? Her ideas about raising children were always quite definite. When we lived in America it was the same; she didn't agree with the American way of raising children. She couldn't understand that it might be good for others. If she didn't like it, it wasn't good for anybody. Furthermore, she also felt that I had a musical mission which I could not fulfil while living on the kibbutz. On the other hand she admired the people living there, and, as usual, she never stopped working and being helpful from dawn to dusk.

While on the kibbutz were you aware of the armed tension in the area?

At first we thought very little about the sentry who patrolled Maabaroth nightly while we slept, nor about the military exercises in which some of our friends participated. However, the danger came home to us one night returning from a concert. As we drove near Wadi Ara we suddenly heard a burst of gunfire. This was no television movie; it was real, and directed against us. Our friend, Mehir, who was driving, was shot through the cheek, but miraculously no one else was hit. The extraordinary thing was that, rather than drive away as quickly as possible, Mehir stopped the car so abruptly that it nearly flew off of the road. And what for? To shoot back with the pistol he had at hand. That was an audacious tactic, which might have meant the end for all of us – but it worked. Our attackers apparently thought we were a military patrol, and they stopped shooting. In a twinkling Mehir had us on the road again, but now he was driving like a drunken man, the car swerving from side to side. At that moment my sister Geneviève proved herself to be the most courageous member of our family; she took over the wheel, and promptly drove to the hospital in Natanya where Mehir could be treated. It had been a narrow escape. We counted seven bullet holes in the windows. Maybe seven proved itself to be our lucky number.

I hate to think what an eighth bullet might have done.

That was the only episode to remind us of the ever present danger of which our *chaverim* were only too aware. Other than that, we passed our days in an extraordinary state of tranquillity. The only thing that worried me was that time went by so quickly. Every Sabbath seemed to come sooner than the preceding one. When life is dull it seems long, but when it's wonderful it seems short. It was some of our *chaverim* who suggested, in the summer of 1956, nearly a year after we had arrived, that I should not neglect my career as a soloist. They urged me to make a tour and then return. I was torn between my love for life on the kibbutz and love for the cello. Finally, after much soul-searching, I agreed, on condition that my fees as soloist would be sent to the kibbutz. It is interesting: when you don't work for yourself, you work with even greater pleasure and enthusiasm. It was a joy for me to think that I could help the kibbutz materially. So I accepted several concert engagements in Europe, fully planning to return. Maud and my mother flew with me to Paris while Geneviève stayed on the kibbutz with the children.

However, a short while after we arrived in Paris, the 1956 Sinai War broke out. We were terribly worried. Maabaroth is situated on a narrow strip of land not far from the Jordanian border, so it could easily have been taken. Even before our departure there had been a fear of war; shelters were being built for the children. Our friends on the kibbutz decided to send the children to us in France, as they didn't want to take responsibility in case something should happen. It was a great day when they arrived in Paris. We were, of course, immensely relieved. But now we were all gathered together in France – far from the kibbutz which we so loved. Just at that time I was offered the post of professor at the Paris Conservatoire, and I was also granted legal guardianship of my daughter, Anne. Owing to these factors, and the continued unrest in the Middle East, we decided to remain in Paris. I must say that it was difficult for Maud to reconcile herself to this. It seemed to her almost a betrayal not to have stayed in Israel.

Well, for better or for worse, I returned to my career. Had I delayed doing so, it's true that I might not have attained the recognition I have today. I know that reputation is not the essence of our mission as musicians, but all the same we must make a career. A monk need not concern himself with acquiring a public and filling a hall, but we musicians have to spread the message. To do so we have to be known.

For my mother, my appointment as professor at the Conservatoire was the realization of her dreams. Paradoxically, as my career developed, her hearing progressively deteriorated until she finally became completely deaf. Despite this affliction, she was the sort of woman who always kept her spirits high. And amazingly enough, her deafness did not obliterate her musical receptivity. Once, when she was entirely deaf, she came with my sister to a performance I was giving of the Haydn Concerto. My mother did not know that I was playing the traditional D major Concerto but the newly discovered one in C major. She watched the conductor give the upbeat to the orchestra and, turning at once to Geneviève, said, 'But this isn't the Haydn Concerto!'

On another occasion she attended a public performance of my students at the Conservatoire – perhaps twenty played. Afterwards she said in the most natural way, 'Oh, Number 6 plays best.' She said this so matter-of-factly that for a moment I forgot that she had heard nothing at all. And, you know, she was absolutely right. She had seen it, she had sensed it. That proves how right Casals was when he would say, 'Beautiful playing is beautiful to look at.' That is what my mother observed in Number 6 . . . the physical equilibrium, the emotional involvement. Perhaps she could really hear the piece inwardly. Isn't that marvellous?

It tells a great deal to a musician – that he is communicating not only with his sound but with his whole being. In fact there are times when a musician must communicate on stage when not even playing. Lotte Lehmann used to make the whole song an experience – the piano prelude and postlude – not just the voice part. By way of contrast, I once heard a famous string player perform a transcription of Wagner's song Träume. *During the whole of the piano prelude, which lasts about 50 seconds and in which Wagner delicately invokes a world of dreams, the virtuoso was fidgeting about perfectly bored. At the last moment he adopted a heroic pose and began to play with complete self-assurance, ignorant of the fact that the mood of the piece was utterly shattered. I wonder if music schools shouldn't provide examinations for performers to sit and feel the music without playing.*

And my mother would have been an ideal examiner.

She was an extraordinary woman. She died at the age of 84. Throughout her life she believed that moral suffering was something far more difficult to endure than any physical suffering. It was not until her last months that she had a severe illness; she knew then that both kinds of suffering can be terrible. Despite her distress, she died with a sense of fulfilment. Though not a musician herself, she was the founder of a musical family. Without her faith, her good sense, her sacrifices, the course of my life would have been entirely different.

Well, you see, I have had my career, but I have not returned to live again on the kibbutz as I had hoped. However, Geneviève, by then divorced, stayed on and lived at Maabaroth for another seven years. Each time I play in Israel I try to return to Maabaroth if only for a day. Last time I was there I went out again to help in the orchard. I have big hands; this is an advantage not only when playing the cello but when picking grapefruit.

XIII

A World Without Bar Lines

You are almost constantly on tour, often alone, going to strange cities and strange hotels. Yet you once told me, 'I am able to be happy wherever I am.' Would you like to comment on that?

Perhaps it's because I was accustomed to solitude right from the start. Having been born eight years after my sister, I grew up as virtually an only child. As you know, I was taken out of school when I was 11. I had very few playmates, and so I learned how to enjoy being by myself.

Nowadays I have the ability to abstract myself from my surroundings. When I'm absorbed in my work I forget where I am. And, as I've said, my mother taught me to use my time well. If there's a delay at an airport I can occupy myself with composing; the introduction to my *Offrande* was, in fact, written at Dublin airport. The Finale of my Double Concerto was written on my lap in trains.

A British Airways captain told me with some pride that you had recently flown on his plane and had practised during the flight.

There you are; I do manage to be happy wherever I am, though I must confess that I increasingly feel the need to have Maud with me when I travel. But aside from this question of love for my wife, I am never bored. As long as I have music paper and a pencil I am content.

One of the inestimable benefits of my profession is that it enables me to see the world – a world without bar lines, as I

119

would put it. I have played in forty-five countries. It has become a cliché to say that music is a universal language, but I have truly experienced that phenomenon as a remarkable fact, whether in Tunisia, Korea, Tasmania, Finland or Peru. For instance, when in 1980 Maud and I were invited to spend a month teaching at the Peking Conservatory, we were able to speak through the music of Bach and Beethoven without learning Chinese – which would have taken us years to do. Isn't it wonderful that one can communicate in this way?

What were your impressions of China?

My father always dreamt of going there. As an idealist he had great faith in Mao; I had the same faith, which was to a large extent borne out in what I was able to see during my visit. The greater part of the population has a hard life of course, but today's China is a far cry from the China of a few decades ago, when thousands of starving people slept on the pavement in the big cities. People are adequately fed and decently dressed. However, we must not forget the excesses of the Cultural Revolution. In fact, Maud visited China in 1967 as a tourist and experienced albeit to a small degree something of the repressive atmosphere that existed then. At 7.0 every morning after board-ing the sightseeing bus, the tourists were ordered to read out loud along with the guide a page from *The Little Red Book*. And when Maud wanted to speak with some members of the Shanghai Symphony Orchestra, Red Guards prevented her from doing so. Despite the effort to suppress all Western music, it was, luckily, not entirely abandoned; it was played privately. Now, of course, it is officially sanctioned and great progress is being made.

By Western standards Peking is an amazingly quiet city. As cars cannot be owned by private citizens, there is little motor traffic. The only disturbing noise is the little fanfare of honking horns as the few cars try to cut a path through an endless maze of bicycles. But this relative calm is only the external aspect of the serenity. What is most striking is the inner quality of the people. We experienced this time and again while there. Almost every-one in Peking wears a blue or green Mao jacket. Normally I don't like uniforms. They are stiff; they kill personality. However, I like seeing the Chinese women in this clothing because their faces and expressions stand out far more vividly than if they were wearing sophisticated dresses designed to catch your attention. The older women have a particular dignity and beauty dressed in this way.

In China I discovered a sincerity, a simplicity, a sort of peace of mind which is not readily found in the West.

I hope the Chinese will recognize that we in the West have not set the best example. Owing to the influence of our own Big Leap Forward into an over-industrialized, over-consuming society, commercial development is gradually influencing the taste of the masses, and the arts are suffering as a consequence. I told the Chinese whom I met that I hoped their country would be able to resist this dangerous tendency. It is difficult to speak to the Chinese in this way because they are still in a period when they have vital needs to cover; they must have production. But I expressed my view to them all the same.

Did you find the students receptive to your teaching?

We were most surprised and gratified by the warmth of their reaction. When we started our course, thirty or forty cellists were in attendance. By the end of the first week there were about 150 who had come from all parts of the country. Naturally, many of the students had a great deal to learn, both technically and interpretatively. However, everything we suggested was immediately understood and embraced with enthusiasm. They felt what we wanted to communicate. The Chinese eagerly want to take in hand our heritage of musical interpretation – a precious heritage which, in fact, we in the West are gradually abandoning. I believe they have the capacity to do this, because they are near to the spirit of Western music in the openness of their feelings.

I am proud to say that I was the first musician from the West to be designated Honorary Professor of the Conservatory of Peking, and I have a standing invitation to teach there. During my short visits, I hope I shall have established to some extent a basis for a tradition of cello teaching. But in addition to instrumental teachers, they need teachers for composition and teachers to help develop their understanding of Western rhythm. Their rhythm is Chinese! We see in this case how

closely rhythm is linked with language. Throughout Europe
there is a community of language. The accent may fall on any
syllable as in English, or on the last syllable as in French, but all
the same there are rhythmic patterns that are intimately related
to our music.

*For instance, Mozart's instrumental music, influenced as it is by
Italian vocal art, and thus by the natural accentuation of the Italian
language.*

That's precisely what I mean. The Chinese have a problem
in this respect because their language is absolutely different:
it is based upon monosyllables. Even when syllables are joined
together, each one retains its specific meaning. This makes it
difficult for the Chinese to adapt instinctively to the inflections
of Western rhythm.

On my return to France I received some wonderful letters from
Chinese cellists. One of them sent me poetry in English. It's
interesting to see how their language is permeated with images
of nature. In ancient China nature-deities were at the centre of
religious life: gods of the wind, of the river, of the sky. This
imagery is still very much alive in the way the Chinese express
themselves.

My heart is with the Chinese. They are a magnificent people. I
was sorry to leave. It is strange how you can be touched by
something seemingly insignificant. One day I visited the home
of a little boy of 10 who studies the cello, and there in his room I
saw a bust of Beethoven. It was no more than a simple piece of
alabaster, the sort you might find in a Viennese souvenir shop.
Yet I have never been more deeply moved in my life than upon
finding an image of Beethoven in that place.

Think of Beethoven who wrote the Ode to Joy *in deafness and
isolation. How moved and amazed he would have been!*

Voilà. If one ever wanted proof that music is a universal
language, it would be to see that little Chinese boy in love with
his god.

*Before we leave the subject of China, I would very much like to
quote a letter I received from one of your Chinese colleagues, Chŭän*

Ju Shih, professor of cello at the Peking Conservatory. With her permission I will reproduce it without 'improving' her English.

30 July, 1982

Dear David Blum

How are you?

I am very excited to received your letter. Because you are working with Our Beloved Prof. Tortelier on his biography . . . I think our thinking and working with one heart and one mind.

I am clumsy of speech and write. But my letter tells my innermost thoughts and feelings . . . In my life I have an ideal. It's to learn from the teaching of Casals and Tortelier and I'll give my gained back to our people. I know I gained not only music, but its invaluable treasure. I mean I have gained a person's Soul.

It's deeper than the ocean;

It's higher than the sky;

It's pure than the gold;

It's brighter than the light!

I think if everybody were like Casals and Tortelier, the Earth is in the Heaven!

Yours sincerely

A drop in the ocean –

Chừän Ju Shih

You have visited Russia, haven't you?

Yes, several times. One incident stands out from my first visit in 1971, when I appeared as soloist with l'Orchestre National de la Radiodiffusion Française under the direction of Jean Martinon. It relates to my friend Mstislav Rostropovich, whom I have always greatly admired both as man and artist.

When did you first meet him?

In Prague some twenty years ago at an international cello competition. Later, we both took part in a festival of Russian music given in Paris. I played the Shostakovich Concerto, he the Prokofiev, and we attended each other's performances. Afterwards, at a reception in the restaurant of the Eiffel Tower, Rostropovich said to everyone, 'I finished my studies by learning from Paul Tortelier.' That was a very moving compliment. It so happened that my first visit to Russia came just at the time when Rostropovich had taken Solzhenitsyn into his house, a most courageous thing for him to do. I decided to express my admiration for Rostropovich publicly, but, owing to the political climate, I had to make these preparations secretly. I had once written a miniature piece for two cellos called *Danse Triste,** which I now orchestrated so that it could be played by our whole cello section as an encore after my performance of the Saint-Saëns Concerto. I revealed to my cellist friends in the orchestra that I planned to announce the piece as a tribute to Rostropovich. Busy and tired as they were from all the touring, they enthusiastically gave of their free time to rehearse with me in my room. I asked my interpreter to teach me a little speech in Russian so that I could announce the encore myself. All musical Moscow turned out for this concert and, furthermore, it was broadcast. You can imagine the amazement of the audience when, after the performance of the Saint-Saëns Cello Concerto, I made an announcement in Russian stating that the work to follow was dedicated to Mstislav Rostropovich. There was complete silence for a few seconds; then the applause came like an avalanche. At that time Rostropovich was not showing himself in public, but he heard the performance over the radio, and was greatly moved. The next day he decided to pick me up at the hotel and bring me to the airport. What an extraordinary thing it was to be driven through Moscow by Rostropovich and to talk to him about what was happening to Solzhenitsyn while the whole world was wondering what was becoming of him. I remember his telling me, 'Had I not taken Solzhenitsyn into my house he would have had to sleep in the woods, since it was dangerous for him to stay in his own home, and his ex-wife would not have him in her flat.' He complained about the incompetence and stupidity of the bureaucrats who had control over musical affairs in Russia. Yet, despite his disagreements with the regime, he could still give credit where it was due, for instance to certain positive aspects of Russian education.

As to my encore, it had come as a surprise to our conductor, Jean Martinon. We had something of a problem about encores during the tour. The difficulties began, in fact, in Leningrad when, at the general rehearsal before our first concert, Martinon had taken away the time allotted to the Saint-Saëns Concerto and used it for his orchestra encores. He assured me that all would go well because we had rehearsed the piece in Paris. I was

*Miniature 1 in *How I Play, How I Teach*.

unhappy, to say the least. It was my first concert in Russia, and I was not even to be given a few minutes to test the acoustics in the hall, as well as my position on the podium. The musicians felt how unfair this was, and though they already had one foot off the stage they kindly agreed to rehearse with me. That night I made doubly sure to give my best in the Saint-Saëns – and, having enjoyed an enormous success, played two encores. From that moment, in each successive concert it was a battle of encores between Martinon and me. Finally, we had a talk and made a truce. I regretted this unpleasant incident for I had known and respected Jean Martinon for many years.

Concert tours mean constantly renewed adventure. Something unexpected may happen at any moment, and if the concert takes place in Portugal there may indeed be a series of surprises. It was such a day not long ago when I arrived in the town of Albufeira, and was pleased to learn that the Bach recital I was to give that evening was scheduled to begin at 8.0 p.m. As anyone who attends concerts there knows, concerts in Spain and Portugal usually begin just after the last lights of an English concert hall have been turned off. Wishing to warm up in advance, I arrived at 7.15 at the church where the concert was to be given, but as a religious service was in progress, I had to wait outside for half an hour. When I went on stage at 8.0, I noted with surprise that there were only twelve people in the church. After playing the First Bach Suite, I returned to the podium to acknowledge the applause of these devoted listeners, who did their best to convince me that quality is more important than quantity. At that point I found myself – for the first time in my career – trapped on stage. The door through which I was to return to fetch my cello had locked itself. So I took a seat in the church as the thirteenth listener until a key could be found that would unlock the mysterious door. The twelve applauded like a hundred when I appeared again on stage, cello in hand, to play the Second Bach Suite. When after the interval I returned to perform the Third Suite, I noticed that the public was beginning to multiply in a curious fashion. After the Prelude there were nearly forty listeners; after the Courante, a hundred; and by the time the Gigue was underway, the church was nearly full. At

9.25, when I had come to the triumphant conclusion of this glorious work, I received the explanation of this phenomenon. A man jumped onto the stage in a rather alarming way, but proceeded to calm everybody's anxiety by announcing in perfect English, 'Mr. Tortelier, we beg your pardon. The people who have just arrived thought that your recital was going to begin at the usual hour of 9.30, for they were not informed of the change of time – nor was I. We are terribly sorry.' I felt I had to perform something for these deprived music lovers, some of whom had driven fifty miles. So, expressing my regret at the misunderstanding, I announced that I would give five encores. After the last of these – the gigantic Prelude in D major – I was really exhausted. Yet, to my despair, more and more people kept crowding into the church. What was I to do? Just then the parish priest approached me. 'Please don't play any more,' he said. 'The people arriving now are coming for the 10.0 p.m. mass.'

It was in Portugal too that, after a recital Karl Engel and I had given, we were invited to dine at the home of Senhora Pedroso, a patroness of the arts, a charming elderly lady of immense wealth. At dinner I asked with my usual tactlessness, 'Senhora, you are a Christian. Is it in the spirit of Christ to keep such wealth to yourself?' 'Why, yes,' Senhora Pedroso said in the most natural way; 'after all, if there were no rich, who would help the poor?' Had I been my father or grandfather I would have pursued the question for the remainder of the afternoon, but, admiring the ease of manner with which my hostess had responded, and noticing that the other guests were already shocked enough, I refrained from further discussion of the matter. My discretion was apparently appreciated, as I was invited to return for lunch the next day when no less than three exiled kings would be present. I had to refuse the invitation, as I was scheduled to fly the next morning. However, I did in fact once dine in the presence of the King of Italy and various descendants of the Habsburgs. Ideal company for one whose family consists of republicans, atheists, anarchists and Marxists!

One of the benefits of my world travels is the opportunity it gives me to meet so many people, a number of whom have become close friends. I am often offered the hospitality of their homes and this adds a human dimension to my travelling, as I am sick to death of impersonal hotels. However, I should give my friends fair warning: I have a gift for doing just the wrong thing in a house. Normally I am told which doors not to open, and I try to remember. But Isabelle, the devoted Peruvian housekeeper of my San Francisco hosts, said nothing of doors when she left me alone in the big house for a few hours – alone, that is, except for a cat and dachshund who eyed me suspiciously as I went upstairs to practise the Fifth Bach Suite. Can you believe that in that tranquil setting I managed to set off not just one, but two burglar alarms, which rang continuously for two hours? Strangely, nobody seemed to notice.

America is the land of accidental burglar alarms. No one takes them seriously.

That may explain why it took the police so long to arrive. I would have traded an evening of Stockhausen for that infernal din.

There would have been no need for any sort of burglar alarm if, as Isabelle explained to me, our society followed the custom of her race, dating back to the Incas. When one Peruvian Indian takes leave of another, he says, as they shake hands, 'Don't lie, don't steal, don't be lazy.' And the other says, 'Don't you, either.' The idea is simple, but efficient. What is most important is that they follow these precepts.

My visits to Tokyo – often with my family – are always a delight, thanks to the hospitality of Sumiko Kurata and her lovable mother. Sumiko – who won the first prize in my class at the Paris Conservatoire – is now married to a tall clarinettist, and they have an amusing little boy. A traditional Japanese house seems like a toy to Europeans. Sumiko's house – in the suburb of Setagaya – is no exception. It has only five miniature rooms. Yet the Japanese have developed the art of living comfortably within a limited space. However, had this pocket house not had a sort of flexibility, I wonder how it could accommodate not only four Kuratas, but four Torteliers as well.

On my last visit to Japan I brought my daughter Pau to Kyoto as I wanted her to have an opportunity to see the beautiful Buddhist temples. As we were strolling through one of the most

remarkable of these buildings, I became increasingly enthusiastic in my desire to point out its splendours. Already when I
was four years old I was inclined to show off, doing different
tricks and then saying to my father, '*Sois tout épaté*' – 'Be quite
astonished'. 'Look here – and there,' I said to Pau, pulling her
to every corner. Before us loomed a colossal statue of Buddha,
whose story has always enchanted me. I felt drawn to this
statue, and, as we were alone, it seemed a propitious moment to
step over a rope that separated me from it. No sooner had I done
so than an alarm bell rang throughout the temple *fortissimo*.
From the far end of the main aisle a muscular, tunic-clad *bonze*
came flying towards me at Olympic speed. 'Who knows how
this will end?' I wondered, 'The whip perhaps . . . or worse?' The
bonze regarded me with horror, but, upon hearing my explanation, decided that I could leave without punishment. No doubt
Pau's soothing presence helped my case. By the way, she had
cautioned me that stepping over the rope might not be the right
thing to do.

Thanks to my friends the Kuratas, we have learned something
of traditional Japanese life, such as the ritual of taking a bath
before bedtime. The kind of fixtures installed in a bathroom
reveal much about the characteristics of a nation. We all know
that the English care less for physical comfort than do the French.
It therefore doesn't come as a surprise that the typical English
bathroom contains no such frivolity as a shower, while no
French *salle de bain* would be without its *douche*, nor would a
respectable German *Badezimmer* be without the latest in shower
gadgetry. Even if the French and Germans are more sophisticated
in this respect than the English, bathing remains a function for
them, while in Japan it is an art. For my Japanese friends, being
immersed in hot water at the end of the day is comparable to
eating a refined dessert at the end of a meal – a sort of *meringue à
la crème Chantilly*. After first taking showers, all the family
members bathe in the same water, one after the other, a heavy
wooden cover keeping the bath hot. The guests are invited to
bathe in the same way. Providing that nobody is so badly
educated as to stay in the tub more than ten minutes, all the
eight persons seated at the dinner table in a Japanese house can
find themselves bathed and in bed long before midnight. Now,

can you imagine a French or an English hostess giving a bath to seven persons plus herself after dinner, having to fill, empty and clean the bathtub eight times? The French *maîtresse de maison* would not join her husband (already asleep) in their double bed before 2.0 a.m., and the English hostess would not join her hot-water bottle (already cold) in her twin bed before 3.0 a.m.

XIV

My Best Friend

Have you ever thought what your life might have been without the cello?

I can't imagine it. My mother knew I was fated to play the cello. What was it that so moved her when she heard the instrument played by Francis Touche*? She had never heard the Bach suites, yet she sensed in the cello a majesty – a sovereign majesty matched by no other instrument. She had never heard *Don Quixote*, yet she sensed the cello's emotional range. What other instrument could bring Strauss's immortal hero to life?

Go on speaking in this way, and you'll win a lot of converts to the art of cello playing.

That wouldn't be a bad thing, because the cello brings out the best in us; it immediately stirs the heart. When I played for the silent films, if there was a tender moment on the screen – if there was a romance – the tune was given to me. The cello is the instrument of love . . .

Think of the beginning of Tristan und Isolde.

Wagner knew it too.

Tell us about the different cellos you have played.

Feuillard – my protector, my guardian angel – wanted me

*F. Touche and I played together in the concert given in Paris in 1930 by fifty cellists honouring Pablo Casals, as I recently discovered on finding the programme.

130

to have a fine Italian cello as early as possible. He was right; he knew that if you start playing an Italian cello when you are young, your tone is modelled by that instrument. You acquire a feeling for the Italian colour which you retain in your fingers and bow even if you eventually play a French or a German cello. It's a matter of taste, and difficult to express in words. So, when I was 13 or 14, as soon as I was ready for a full-sized instrument, Feuillard arranged that I should have a fine Italian cello made by Lorenzo Ventapane. In so doing, he proved once again his love for me and his concern for my musical future. It was a beautiful instrument with an aristocratic quality.

Was it a gift?

No, he did not give it to me outright. Feuillard was reasonable. I paid for my lessons; I paid for the cello. He didn't believe in charity. He was right; I don't either. But he selected this instrument for me with a sure knowledge of my needs. It's not enough just to acquire a cello. What is important is to acquire the right one, and to develop the feeling for quality and purity of tone. Many people think, 'Let's wait to buy a good instrument until the youngster is older, when we're sure he'll make a career.' For me it was different. Nothing was too good for me, whether from Feuillard, my mother or my father.

How long did you play on the Ventapane?

Until I received my first prize at the Conservatoire at 16, or perhaps a year or two longer. By then, lovely as my Ventapane was, I needed an instrument with a larger volume of sound. I had a choice between an excellent modern cello and an Italian instrument – a Pressenda – that belonged to Feuillard. It was difficult to make this decision. It's hard to judge the full quality of an instrument if you don't play it at a concert, and when I was 18 I had no such engagements. I felt that the Pressenda had a beautiful sonority and I also wanted it because it had belonged to my teacher. On the other hand I wished to develop my power. A critic once wrote that a cellist with a small tone is like Samson without his hair. As the modern cello had a very large tone – if less beautiful than the Pressenda – I was tempted to buy it. Luckily, I followed a colleague's suggestion and brought both instruments to a violin maker for his opinion. 'My dear young man,' he advised, 'you may be impressed by the volume of the modern cello, but I assure you that the Pressenda is an outstanding instrument with a quality which will carry further in the concert hall. Besides, within a decade the Italian cello will double its value, while the modern one will not.' So I bought the Pressenda – inexpensively, because Feuillard did not want to make a profit out of it.*

When Feuillard brought this instrument from Italy, he showed it to Chardon, at that time France's leading expert on stringed instruments. Feuillard had a case which opened from the top. Even before seeing the rest of the instrument Chardon identified it as a Pressenda from its distinctive scroll. Later, when I was in America, the excellent violin maker Simone Sacconi told me that he had never seen a more beautiful Pressenda. Well, one day, when I had returned to France, my bridge needed adjusting, and so I took the cello back to the violin maker who had originally recommended it to me. As I had not seen him for some years, he did not recognize me. While he examined the instrument I commented upon how fine an example it was of Pressenda's work. 'But this isn't a Pressenda,' he replied. No doubt he had another instrument which he wanted to sell me. I felt like taking him by the shoulders and shaking him, but, as I'm not that kind of man, I simply looked at him in a threatening way and said, 'Excuse me, I am Paul Tortelier. It was you who advised me to buy this Pressenda – an instrument which is well-known in Europe and America.' He quickly looked back at the instrument and said, 'Yes, I think you are right; I didn't examine it closely enough.' It is useful to know this story. I regret to say that another violin maker once tried a similar sort of trick on me. Luckily, the exceptions prove the rule. I am indebted to many violin makers for their trustworthy and invaluable help.

The next cello I acquired was a Guarnerius, a superb instrument made in 1706 – the work of 'Josephi Filius Andrea'. (It was Josephi's own son who came to be known as 'del Gesù', but 'del Gesù' seems never to have made a cello.) This instrument

---

*Pressenda (1777–1854) was one of the last of the great Italian violin makers. He studied in Cremona, and subsequently settled in Turin where he gradually gained recognition for the fine quality of his instruments.

had been owned by a cellist living in a provincial town in France, and I was able to obtain it through the help of an intermediary. When I first tried it out, I was rather disappointed with its tone. Fortunately this wasn't due to any fault in the cello itself. Georges Lanchy, the well-known bridge maker, fitted the instrument with a new bridge and the sound was utterly transformed. I had promised Feuillard that I would never sell the Pressenda, and indeed I would never do so even without having made that promise. I still love the Pressenda, and it is, in fact, the instrument which my wife plays.

During the past few years I have been playing on yet another instrument made in about 1850 by Charles Adolphe Maucotel, one of the finest of French violin makers. Maucotel, who was a pupil of Vuillaume, was an outstanding craftsman. He modelled his instruments on those of Stradavarius, and, in fact, mine looks very much like a Strad. It has a lovely light varnish; the back is particularly beautiful. No wonder one of Maucotel's cellos is kept on display in the museum of the Paris Conservatoire.

Where did you obtain the instrument?

It was owned by my childhood friend Georges Mondain who tragically died when in his forties. His sister offered to sell me his cello, which I bought rather as a gesture. One day I was thinking of the risk to which I was always exposing my Guarnerius when travelling, and wondered how the French instrument might sound in a concert hall. I tried it out, and found its tone to be so beautiful that I did indeed decide to take it with me on tour. It's an easy instrument to play. In a way it has an advantage over the Guarnerius in that it speaks even more readily. I really cannot tell you which cello sounds better; that is a question of taste.

One of your principal innovations in the art of cello playing has been your use of a new kind of end-pin which changes the angle at which the player holds the instrument. How did you develop this idea?

It came from an observation my son Pascal made when he was 10 years old. One day I was tuning his violin for him. As I did so I held the instrument between my knees, because it's difficult for me to hold a violin under my neck. Pascal – who even then had a perceptive ear – said, 'It's strange, Papa, but when you tune my violin between your knees it doesn't sound as good as when it's tuned under the chin.' I listened and I too noticed a difference. The tone of the violin was darker when it was held vertically rather than horizontally. I began to wonder whether there would be a difference in the sound of a cello if the instrument could somehow be held more horizontally. As you know, compared with other instruments, the cello is handicapped in power and brilliance. The cello is really an aristocrat: when he's alone his noble voice is heard; put the mob with him and he's easily covered. When we play the Brahms Double Concerto, it's always a fight for the cello to be heard; the violin has the more cutting quality, the greater acoustical impact. So I picked up the cello, held it on a more horizontal plane, and played several movements of Bach for the members of my family. We were at once struck by the increased power of projection. I made many tests. For instance, on several occasions I asked musicians to listen out in the hall as I played the cello in the two positions. They confirmed my findings. In the new position the sound waves are not projected immediately forward into the absorbing material of the hall, but are directed upwards into the free air like the violin which resonates upwards. Once, in Italy, a piano tuner told me, 'There is no comparison; in the new position the cello sounds more like a tenor than a baritone – but with no loss of warmth.'

I realized that the only way to hold the cello securely and comfortably on a more horizontal plane was to invent a special end-pin set at an angle. After some experimentation I found just the right degree of angle (see Plate facing p.174). Hence the Tortelier end-pin which I subsequently patented. A German violin maker tried to obtain a similar result by producing a very long, straight end-pin. The cello became more horizontal, but when the bow pressed upon the strings the instrument tended to sag, while with my end-pin, on the contrary, the cello seems almost to be buoyed up. When I introduced the end-pin into my concerts, it created a sort of scandal. How could I dare tamper with tradition? I would explain that it was indeed a sacrilege to put *any* kind of end-pin on a cello, for prior to Servais in the

1840s, none at all was used. So why not change the end-pin's shape if the tone is thereby improved?

You have sometimes spoken of other advantages which your end-pin provides.

Yes, there are several. In the new position the cello rests on a higher level, and its sides are not covered by the knees; thus there is less dampening of vibrations. The fact that the instrument is set on a more horizontal plane has three advantages: (1) It allows the bow to lie more naturally on the strings and cling better to them (in the manner of a violinist's bow); (2) It brings the higher positions into easier reach; and (3) It relieves the player of any possible tendency to bend forward when playing in the upper register; back problems can thus be avoided. (It is particularly recommended for players with long legs.) Furthermore, the greater horizontal inclination makes it easier to hold the left hand at right angles to the string, which is an important aspect of my technique.

Apparently all these factors are not enough for some people. Pascal once saw a cellist in the orchestra of Angers using a Tortelier end-pin. Without identifying himself, he asked the musician what Tortelier's purpose had been in inventing such a thing. 'The truth is,' came the reply, 'he invented it because he has heart disease.'

The end-pin's benefits are recognized widely, and it is now used by many cellists. Some years ago Maud attended a concert given by Rostropovich in the Salle Pleyel in Paris. I was away on tour at the time. When she greeted him after his performance, he said that he had heard about my end-pin and would like to learn more about it. They arranged to meet the next morning in the workshop of the well-known violin-maker Vatelot. When Rostropovich arrived he asked for a full explanation of why I had adopted the end-pin. She told him all that I have told you, and demonstrated how I play the cello in the new position. Rostropovich responded immediately, 'I want to play with it that way,' and told Mr. Vatelot to fit the end-pin on his own cello. On hearing that Rostropovich's next concert was to be the following day in Copenhagen, Maud said, 'It would be risky to put the end-pin on today because your left hand will

need time to adjust to its new placement in the first position.'
'Don't worry,' answered Rostropovich, 'I never play in the first
position.'

The end-pin has only one very minor drawback. Owing to
its angle, there's no room for it in the cello case. It must be
carried separately. That can create difficulties for a forgetful
person like me.

> On more than one occasion Raphael Sommer's telephone has rung.
> 'This is Paul. You must help me. I'm here in England to give some
> concerts and I've forgotten the bloody end-pin again. Please lend me
> yours.' Another time, for some reason the end-pin couldn't be removed
> from the cello, and the cello, therefore, wouldn't fit into its case. Paul
> took his dressing gown, hung it over the cello as if it were truly an
> aristocrat and brought it in this apparel first to a recording session at St
> John's Wood Hall, and then to the famous violin makers W. E. Hill &
> Sons, in Bond Street.

*You have also made an innovation in the construction of the
bridge. Before commenting on this, would you first explain the role
that the bridge plays in sound production?*

The bridge transmits the vibration of the strings into the
wood of the cello. It does this by vibrating laterally, like a man
rocking from one foot to another or, one could say, like the
rolling of a boat. The width, shape, and placement of the bridge
have a vital effect upon the sound. People believe that a
Stradivarius will automatically sound splendid. It won't if the
bridge is poor. My Guarnerius was a case in point. It's almost
better to play on a bad cello with a good bridge than on a good
cello with a bad bridge.

The design of my own bridge came about in the following
way. We know that on every stringed instrument the middle
strings sound weaker than the outer strings. I wondered whether
anything could be done about that. I experimented by ex-
changing the position of the highest string, the A, with that of
the next lowest string, the D. What happened? Unbelievable!
Anyone who tries it will have a shock. The A string which is so
glorious on the cello – in French we call it *la chanterelle*, 'the
singer' – becomes dull if placed in the centre of the bridge, while
if the D string is on the outside it becomes as bright as the A

string normally is. I then reversed the positions of the two lower strings, with similar results. I replaced the strings in their normal position and asked Maud to play. As she did so, I pinched the sides of the bridge, the two 'wings'. The outer strings again sounded as if they were muted. I understood that if the outer strings sound so well, it's because the wood at the edge of the bridge is flexible and vibrates more freely than it does at the centre. How then, I wondered, can one free the wood at the centre? I first contemplated using two bridges instead of one, with two strings on each bridge, but this proved too complicated and I abandoned the idea. Finally I solved the problem by having a small incision about 14 millimetres deep made in the centre of the bridge to allow the wood supporting the middle strings to be more supple. Georges Lanchy made an ideal bridge for me in this way. As a result, the G and D strings, though not yet quite so clear as the outer strings, have none the less gained considerably in brightness. I demonstrated my discovery at a violin makers' competition in Liège, and everyone could hear the difference. Since I have adopted this new kind of bridge, listeners often comment upon the equality of sonority of the four strings on my cello.

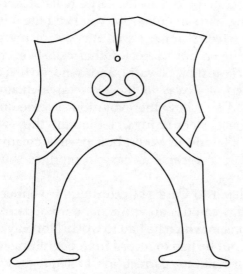

My bridge, made by Georges Lanchy
(drawn two-thirds of actual size).

I know that you use steel-wound strings. Did you ever play on gut strings?

I used to play on gut strings, and I gave them up only with great reluctance. The fibre of the gut has a slight unevenness of texture. This gives each string a warmth and individuality all its own. The player can put more of his personality into the sound he produces. If the gut string has the advantage of greater beauty, it has many technical disadvantages. The attack is problematic: the gut doesn't respond quickly to the bow and tends to be scratchy. It is also susceptible to changes in the weather, and intonation becomes variable. As the gut is supple, it will not resist the pressure of the bow beyond a certain degree, and so you must limit your power. Finally, in the high register, if the bow is not placed in precisely the correct position near the bridge, the sound will be lost. Now, the steel string has none of these disadvantages. It responds quickly, and, being firmer, it can withstand more bow pressure and keeps better in tune. It will respond in the upper register even if the bow placement isn't ideal. Its one drawback is a more neutral timbre.

Of course, for recording, what is required is perfection, absence of scratch. And in the large halls of today, especially when playing with an orchestra, you need the increased power afforded by steel strings. I was the last of my generation to change over from gut to steel. Other cellists such as Cassadó, Feuermann, Fournier, Navarra, and Gendron had done it before me. Attached as I was to the expressive quality of the gut strings, I had to follow the evolution. I remember that when I began to use steel strings, I thought they were too easy to play on. Playing my cello had been a creative battle, and then suddenly it became as easy to produce sound upon as a violin.

When I listen to Casals's recordings I wonder if any string player of today could achieve his standard of performance given the conditions in which he had to work. Not only did he play on gut strings, but he had to record from beginning to end without being able to make any corrections. Listen to the transcription of the Chopin Nocturne in E flat major which he recorded in 1920. The style is, of course, inimitable, and the sound is wonderful, even on the recording made over sixty years ago. Such a personal sound, very warm and pure at the same time!

You have spoken of your cellos, but what is Don Quixote without Sancho Panza? Could you say a few words about your bows?

It's rather difficult for anyone who doesn't play a stringed instrument to imagine that two bows which look almost identical, made of such simple material as wood and horsehair, can vary so drastically in quality. It's as hard to find a magnificent bow as it is to find a fine cello. The exact weight and balance are critical factors; the stick should neither be too resistant nor too supple. Not only does the cello vibrate; the bow vibrates also, and its vibrating capacity depends upon the cellular structure of the wood. The most famous and costly bows are those made by the French makers Tourte and Peccatte.

Some people are unlucky in love. Alas, I have been unlucky in bows. The beautiful Vigneron père that Feuillard gave me – it was his finest bow – was lost. How, I cannot say. Did I lend it to a student who never returned it, or did I leave it to be repaired by a bow-maker and forget to pick it up? This second hypothesis is not as improbable as it may seem, for only recently a violin maker reminded me that I had forgotten to collect a bow I'd left with him several months before.

I've been privileged to own three Peccatte bows. The first was broken when I left it on a bed and someone lay down on top of it. The second broke when I was rehearsing the Mozart Divertimento for Violin, Viola and Cello with Isaac Stern and William Primrose during the 1952 Casals Festival at Perpignan. I made a *forte* attack at the point with too much fervour – and *voilà*! The third – as I've already said – broke when I slammed it down in anger while teaching Pascal. It's almost as if a wicked fairy had put a perpetual curse on my bows.

Paul was giving a lesson one day in his flat on rue Léon-Cogniet when Pau, aged 5, entered the room. She was dragging one of Papa's finest bows along the floor. At that moment Pascal, aged 8, came running in, and, not seeing the bow, crushed it under his foot. Paul, who had been the helpless observer of this little family scene, exploded in rage – yet he would not hit the child. In his frustration he cried out, 'If you can break one bow like that – why not all the others?' He snatched two other fine

bows from where they were hanging on the wall and snapped them in
two. 'I am terrible,' Paul said later; 'When there's a catastrophe I like to
make it complete.'

The sorry saga of my bows must include the episode of my
Nürnberger père. While in Gothenburg to give a concert, I left
this highly valued bow with a colleague who kindly took it to a
violin maker to have it rehaired for me. When I got the bow
back, it felt sluggish in my hand; it seemed to have lost part of its
character, notably the superb resiliency of its springing action.
I became so upset over this as to convince myself that the bow
was, in fact, not mine, but another that had been substituted for
it. I went so far as to make some rather unpleasant accusations,
until the bow was examined by an expert and proved beyond
any doubt to be mine. Not only had I made a fool of myself, but,
to my undying regret, I had cast aspersions on the character of a
most honourable man. Better to have lost a hundred bows than
to have done that. This bow was indeed ill-fated. A few weeks
later, while I was both playing and conducting the C.P.E. Bach
Concerto with the London Mozart Players, at the moment I
whipped the Nürnberger père through the air to give the upbeat
to the orchestra, the head suddenly flew off – and fell pitifully to
the stage, followed by the mass of hair. The effect was so comical
that the entire audience burst out laughing.

Inside a stringed instrument is a small piece of wood that
nobody sees, but which is of vital importance to the quality of
tone. It connects the top and back of the instrument and also
compensates for the pressure of the bridge. It must be positioned
with enormous care; a change of only a few millimetres can alter
the quality of tone. Now, the English and Americans call this
'the soundpost' – an efficiently conceived word; the Germans
have a similar functional name for it, *der Stimmstock*. However,
the French and Italians think of it in another way; they call it,
respectively, 'l'âme' and 'l'anima' – which both mean 'the soul'.
Maybe it's due to my Latin temperament, but that's how I feel
about the cello. It's more than a piece of wood. As my mother
knew, it speaks with the voice of the soul.

XV

More than Chance?

Shortly after the war, I was engaged to give a concert tour in Morocco with Madame Dussol, a pianist from Perpignan. The concert organizer in Casablanca, a certain Mr Morette, had requested the name of my accompanist. I was as bad then as I am now at answering letters and I simply forgot to reply. Mr Morette renewed his request in a telegram, and when I went to the post office to send an answer, I suddenly couldn't recall Madame Dussol's Christian name except that it began with an A. So I wrote on the telegram 'Pianist: Annie Dussol,' hoping that I had guessed correctly. When we had completed our tour, we visited Mr Morette at his home in Casablanca. He was a teacher of English, and shared with his wife a love of music. After we had enjoyed a fine meal, he suggested that we take coffee on the verandah, adding, 'Please sit down because what I have to tell you might give you a shock and you might fall down.' This seemed intriguing, so we seated ourselves. 'You remember, Mr Tortelier, that I asked you to let me know the name of your accompanist.' I apologized for the delay. 'Yes,' he said, 'you were a naughty boy not to have answered sooner.' I was young, so he could call me a naughty boy. 'Well,' he continued, 'I could not wait any longer, and had no choice but to make up a name. That's not so easy to do as you would imagine. Any name you think of sounds odd. I considered Dupont or Durand – too common – and finally I hit upon "Madame Dussol". This very name was confirmed to me in your telegram which I received only the following day.' We were more than amazed at hearing this. 'But,' he said, 'that's not the end of the story. My dear Tortelier – I almost guessed her Christian name as well. I thought of Evelyne or Marcelle – too refined – and then decided to call her Andrée Dussol. When I saw the name Annie Dussol on your telegram I realized that I had even guessed the initial.' 'Excuse me, Mr Morette,' I interrupted. 'It is you who had better sit down now. I sent the wrong name on the telegram. Her real name is Andrée Dussol.'

What do you think of that, David? Can you make any sense of it?

Richard Wagner once went up to a roulette table in the Wiesbaden Casino and, without placing a bet himself, told a friend with quiet certainty that number 11 would win – and it did. Then, as if under a spell he predicted rightly that number 27 would turn up. When his astonished friend urged him to place a bet, Wagner said that if he were to introduce his own personal interest into the game his gift of prophecy would disappear at once. Does that story make any sense?

There seems to be some force at work here that we don't understand. I've already mentioned several significant events in my life which I can explain neither in terms of 'cause and effect', nor as coincidence. I could tell you another story of this sort, less startling perhaps than my previous one – yet, I think, of interest – in which the inner and outer seem related in an inexplicable way.

Please do.

About ten years ago I was rehearsing the Boccherini Concerto in Stuttgart with Claudio Abbado conducting. When I had finished with the Boccherini, I decided to listen to the rest of the rehearsal, as it would give me an opportunity to acquaint myself with Mahler's Sixth Symphony. I must be sincere. Aside from a few pieces such as the Adagietto from the Fifth Symphony and some of the Lieder, I am not very much enamoured of Mahler's music. I respect his great skill as an orchestrator but, for me, his symphonies lack sufficient unity of style and organic cohesion. For this reason I could never consider Mahler as one of the truly great masters in the same league as Beethoven, Mozart or

Large hands have uses
besides playing the cello.
Paul picking fruit on
the kibbutz, 1955.

With Maud, Pascal, and Pau in Israel, 1955.

With Maud and Arthur Rubinstein, at the inauguration of the Frederic R. Mann Auditorium, Tel-Aviv, 1957 (*Isaac Berez*).

Tortelier father and son in relaxed mood backstage. (*Bristol Evening Post*).

Paul and Maud playing his own Concerto for Two Cellos – 'communion of thought and feeling' – Zurich, 1974.

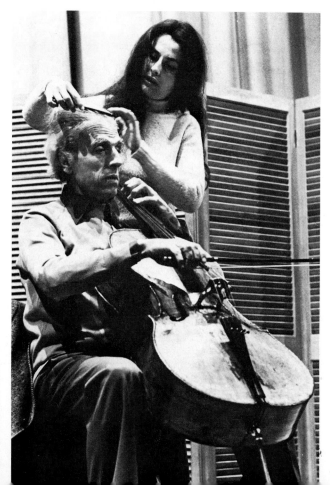

On tour, with Pau – 'How would I ever manage without the women in my family?'

Discussing the Dvořák Cello Concerto with André Previn in
preparation for a recording. (*EMI*)

With Yehudi Menuhin,
rehearsing Frederick
Delius's Concerto for
Violin and Cello. (*Clive
Barda/EMI*)

Schubert. But I thought that since almost everybody likes Mahler, I should take the trouble to listen to this work as objectively as possible. So I put myself into the best of spirits, and I must say I found much of the first movement to be quite beautiful, the second also, though I began to feel rather uneasy. But when the Finale came I just couldn't bring myself to like it. There were too many passages which seemed to be in bad taste – a pretentiousness, a vulgarity. All told it left a disturbing impression.

But isn't this element of the grotesque – the stridency of the outer world in conflict with the harmony of the spirit – isn't this an essential part of what Mahler is trying to express?

It is artistically perilous for a composer to insert all sorts of 'meanings' into his work. What counts is the result. For all its 'effectiveness' I found the work unconvincing as a whole. Well, afterwards I happened to meet Abbado in front of our hotel, and addressed him rather dramatically: 'Why do you play this symphony? It's not a good work. I implore you not to play bad music.' He told me that it takes years to understand Mahler fully: 'You should get to know his music better. Haven't you heard all his works?' And I replied, 'May God save me from such a thing.'

I had to play that evening, and so I took a nap after lunch, and during that nap I had a terrible nightmare: a young man in his mid-teens was terrifying his brother, a boy some years younger. He pretended that his face was a mask which he repeatedly threatened to tear off. When he finally did so, he removed the front of his face with it, exposing the inner part of his head – a half-shell, gaping and dark, with flames leaping up from within. Then the children's mother arrived; she herself was a horrifying vision, resembling a robot with fierce eyes. She scolded the little boy because he had been shouting, and shut him up in a coffin-like cupboard to punish him, just as if the older boy had done nothing wrong at all. At that point I awoke, shaken and perspiring, wondering why I should have had such an awful dream: I hardly ever have nightmares.

This dream remained a mystery to me for a long time. I only knew that it was intimately related to the unsettling effect the Mahler symphony had had upon me. It wasn't until some years later that I learned something of Mahler's life when his biography by de la Grange became available. I discovered that Mahler had suffered a severe depression when his younger brother Ernst died at the age of 14 after a lingering illness. As many writers attest, Mahler probably felt a sense of personal guilt. The experience left a mark upon his music. For instance, the text of *Das Klagende Lied*, written by Mahler himself, deals, with fratricide – the murder of a younger brother. And, when composing the *Kindertotenlieder*, Mahler may have been particularly drawn to Rückert's poems because the child in whose memory they had been written was named Ernst. Furthermore, another of Mahler's younger brothers, Otto, committed suicide at the age of 21. These memories always haunted him. Could they perhaps have played an unconscious role in his Sixth Symphony which he originally called 'The Tragic'? I don't want to draw any definite conclusions from all this, but I can't escape the eerie feeling that on hearing this music I had crept for a moment into the recesses of the composer's mind.

I find these stories fascinating. In our super-rational world many people poohpooh this sort of thing. But even if something can't be explained, it doesn't mean it's not real. Such happenings occur more frequently and in many more ways than we normally realize. We are trained intellectually in such a way that we don't always recognize them. In the Orient synchronistic events are taken for granted, as shown, for example, in the use of the I Ching as a book of wisdom.

I think the Chinese would appreciate the story I will tell you now. They believe in the affinity of nature and art.

Pau and I gave a recital at Marlborough College in Wiltshire on a particularly pleasant autumn evening. Already during the Brahms E minor Sonata, which opened the programme, I noticed a slight shadow that flickered from time to time across the brightly lit floor. And when I began playing my own Cello Sonata, I was aware of something coming towards me from above, then floating away again. It was there and yet not there, like an apparition. While playing, I had little time to give my attention to it, but by the time I reached the middle movement of my sonata I was able to identify my mysterious stage companion. It was a butterfly – a beautifully coloured, rather big butterfly. It began to circle around me and, as it did so, it seemed almost to be tracing arabesques to the music I was playing, its wings moving in harmony with my bow. The audience's attention had now been drawn to this wholly unrehearsed ballet. Closer and closer the butterfly would come, almost touch me, and then fly away. It was having a flirtation with me, or perhaps I with it. The slow movement of my sonata concludes quietly on a sustained harmonic. At that moment I closed my eyes, my bow barely moving on the string. I did not want to disturb the atmosphere of peace and calm. As I slowly drew the note to an end I opened my eyes again, and there, perched on my left hand, was the butterfly. It had alighted so gently that I hadn't even felt its presence. For a moment or two we looked at each other. It didn't move; I didn't move. It was so lovely, so ethereal that I couldn't bring myself to shake it off. It had chosen the ideal moment for repose, I thought, settling there at the end of the slow movement; it seemed not to want to fly away. What could I do? Almost without thinking, I slowly brought my hand, with the butterfly still perched on it, up to my lips. I was sure it would fly away, but it didn't. I kissed it very tenderly, but it still didn't move. Not everyone has been able to kiss a butterfly. I never thought I would do so, least of all on the concert stage. Finally I shook my hand very gently, and it floated off into the air. That was just before the interval. After the interval we played Beethoven's A major Sonata, and there was the butterfly again dancing all the way through, only coming down to rest from time to time on Pau's music as if wanting to have a look at what she was doing. The piece came to an end and the butterfly was nowhere to be seen. 'Aha,' I thought, 'it has left us to join the other butterflies in the fields.' Not at all. It was perched at my foot, and as the audience applauded it flapped its wings.

Who can judge what forces of spirit or nature guide our actions and bring harmony to seemingly disparate things? Such forces are there; that's all I need know. The audience that day knew it also. We had all lived a fairy tale.

XVI
Recreating

In Brittany, in the old days, there was a tradition of story-telling. The storytellers were not professional; they had other work to do during the day. But, as they were very poor, they would go to farms to tell stories after dinner. They weren't really paid, but they got a free bite to eat and a glass of cider, and they were content with that. The Celtic world is full of legends, and these men ensured the survival of these legends from generation to generation. As I've said, my grandfather was endowed with the gift of oratory. Storytelling is probably in the blood of the Torteliers.

I feel that the instrumentalist is a kind of musical storyteller. Music speaks from the great masters to the performer, and through the process of telling a story his playing becomes imbued with life and character.

Do you always have a definite picture in mind?

Not necessarily. That depends upon the piece. If I play *Don Quixote* or *Schelomo* I am telling an actual story – but other works may not strike my imagination in the form of a concrete image; it can be a feeling, an atmosphere, a mood. These moods are something like the colours in painting – the blue and yellow of Vermeer, the brown of Rembrandt. When I hear a piece of music I give my imagination free rein. However, I cannot stress sufficiently that the imagery comes out of my feeling for the music, and not vice versa. It's a matter of intuition, intimately connected with the work I'm playing.

Those who have heard you teach or speak about music in these
terms have been struck by just this intuitive ability to find verbal
imagery which suits a musical passage – in other words, to express
the inexpressible.

Nothing must be superimposed. When such a story comes to
me it seems to unfold of its own accord, much like Wagner's
impression – more beautiful than anything I could express – of a
day in Beethoven's life, based upon the C♯ minor String Quartet.
Op. 131.

Fortunately, we need not enter here into the delicate question of
programme music versus absolute music, the question of whether or
not music can succeed in representing something extra-musical.
What we are concerned with is the performer's relation to his own
imagination.

A purely subjective question. But the fact that it is subjective
in no way deprives it of value to the individual any more than a
dream is deprived of value because it is subjective. The question
is, how does the fantasy act upon the *interpreter*?

You wouldn't therefore necessarily expect your listeners to share
your specific imagery.

The imagery is not for the audience; it is for the performer. It's
not at all important whether or not the audience thinks of the
same image as I have in mind. What is important is that the
imagery helps *me*. Let me give you an example. For many years
I hesitated to play Bach's First Suite. The Prelude is so simple,
yet so difficult. Those things which are simple are sometimes
the most difficult.

I wasn't entirely convinced by any interpretation I heard, nor
is the manuscript of the suites in Anna Magdalena Bach's
hand very helpful; the slurs are indicated sparsely and incon-

sistently. If you follow this text to the letter, it sounds like an exercise.

Nowadays, however, I often play this suite, and the Prelude is actually my most successful encore. I don't think Bach would mind my playing it as an encore. People tell me that it provides a wonderful conclusion to a concert; the audience leaves the hall happy and refreshed. So I suppose that my interpretation has brought me in the right direction. But how did I achieve this? As long as I was only looking for bowings and fingerings I couldn't find a convincing way to interpret the piece. Then one day, while playing it through, an image sprang into my mind. It's as if it had been there all the time, only I had never been conscious of it. I saw a stream wending its way towards the sea where the water merged into the infinite. This image 'clicked'; I began to play the piece with joy.

It's difficult to find just the proper degree of intensity of expression for this Prelude. When I picture the water flowing before me, if I play with too much expression, if I play senti- mentally, it will not flow nicely; the water will not be refreshing. On the other hand, if I don't put enough expression into it the water will pass by without loveliness, without character. I finally found a middle way: I think not of the stream itself, but of the play of reflections upon its surface. In other words the water becomes limpid or dark according to the way it reflects the colours of the sky. If the water is blue, as at the beginning, it's because the sky is blue; if there are patches of darkness in this prelude – when the music passes into the minor – it's as if the stream were flowing under trees and reflecting the shade of the branches. At the end, when it is transformed into a river and merges into the sea, the waves glisten in radiant light. Needless to say, all this is highly personal, but I feel it has validity in that the texture, movement, and colour intrinsic to the music are well expressed in my imagery.

I believe that Bach would have found your conception quite natural. He himself thought in pictorial terms. We see this in his vivid musical depictions of the texts of his cantatas. And, as Schweitzer pointed out, he carries over this sort of pictorial language to his purely instrumental music. For instance, Bach responds to a mention of 'waves' in several cantatas by composing flowing musical patterns not dissimilar to that of the G major Prelude.

As you know, in German the word *Bach* means 'stream'. I will go so far as to state my belief that, in this movement which opens the set of six cello suites, Bach meant to sign his own name.

I once played this Prelude for Isabelle, the Peruvian housekeeper of my hosts in San Francisco, and asked her what she had felt when she heard it. She said that she had had a beautiful experience, as if she were soaring through the sky, driven by clouds. Then I told her of my wave imagery. Isn't it interesting that we both in our own ways felt carried by the motion of nature? The music had so impressed Isabelle that she asked me to play it for her relatives who were coming to visit her. The best audiences are not always sophisticated concert-goers.

Do you try to develop this sort of fantasizing in your students' approach to their playing?

Yes, whenever possible. Of course, the fact that this is my way of developing interpretation doesn't mean that it's everybody's way. Nevertheless, I find that most students have this potential even though it may be latent. They are often afraid to trust to the power of their imagination. As fantasizing is, after all, an irrational activity, they don't consider how truly relevant it can be. They seek security first and foremost in their technique, not realizing that it's just this 'irrational' activity which can help liberate the technique. One must learn to trust – to let the imagery come to one from the music, to follow it and play with it. If a student needs coaxing along these lines, I have to take the lead. Let me give you an example. I've had the pleasure of having Raphael Sommer among my students. The first time he came to play for me in my class in Paris he was 22 years old. I had a rather international class: American, Japanese, Israeli, French, German. There were about twelve all told, and Raphael performed for us the first movement of the Boccherini Concerto in B♭ major:

His exceptional gift was immediately apparent. He played with a lovely tone, pure intonation, good taste, and respect for the score. 'Bravo,' I told him with genuine enthusiasm. 'You are a fine cellist. However, I must say that, despite your exceptionally beautiful playing, I felt something lacking. The distinctive personality of the piece didn't speak to me.' I noticed from my students' expressions that they too seemed unmoved by what they had heard. At that moment I decided to make an experiment regarding the eternal question of subjectivity and objectivity, not in the philosophical sense of Descartes and Kant, but in the practical sense necessary for a performer. With all these youngsters present, of different backgrounds and from various parts of the world, it seemed the right moment; so I played the movement through without comment. When I finished I saw that their faces were lit up with pleasure, 'I don't play better than Raphael,' I told them, 'and my musical interpretation varies from his only very subtly – but do you none the less hear a difference?' They all answered immediately, using different words to express the same thought – that my performance had *communicated* in a way that the other had not. Raphael himself said, 'It's like night and day.' 'Well,' I continued, 'when you play this work, what does your imagination tell you?' And Raphael answered modestly, 'I'm busy enough thinking about my cello playing.' 'That's just the trouble,' I responded; 'the notes must be taken for granted. Do you know what I did to make it different? I told a story as I played.'

Raphael told me that your words came to him as a revelation. He had studied the cello for years and no one had ever said anything of the sort to him. He felt utterly deflated in five seconds, yet, at the same time, elated by the challenge which lay before him.

He was moved by what I said because it touched a potential not yet awakened within him.

He remembers the way you characterized the opening of the concerto: a knight returning from the wars, meeting his lady, describing his success in battle . . .

As with the Bach Prelude, the imagery came to me spontaneously; it seemed to step right out of the music. This knight is of proud, aristocratic bearing – one hears this in the vivacious upbeat, in the sweep of the opening phrase. Yet, as the subsequent bars tell us, behind his proud exterior he has a tender heart; one feels that in the lyrical contour. He says to his lady, 'You were in my thoughts while I was away. How I longed for you!' For a fleeting moment he even wondered if she had remained faithful – the music touches upon the minor – but his doubts were quickly dispelled. Naturally, this storytelling must be realized in purely musical terms. To delineate the character of each phrase requires a delicate rubato, a variety of nuance. But all this must be managed without distortion. The music should be characterized, not caricatured. One must have the impression that the music is telling its own story in a natural way. This piece has great poise and beauty of proportion; one must respect that. When I play Boccherini or Haydn, or conduct Mozart, I apply the following dictum: on the inside I am romantic; on the outside I am classic.

If in my teaching I often refer to imagery, it's not only because it helps to vivify our performance; it also helps us to think beyond our technique, to forget our problems. We practise so long and so hard that we tend to become obsessed by passages that are technically difficult. Such fixations easily lead to disaster. You will play more eloquently if you are not a cellist worried about your technique, but a knight worried about your lady's chastity.

If a student's imagery differs from yours, do you none the less value it?

Absolutely. If something is to be genuine it must be one's own. When a student says he feels something different from what I feel, I always take his view into consideration. If his manner of conceiving a passage seems vitally connected to the piece he is playing, I don't impose my view; I first see how his conception works for him.

While watching your master classes, I have thought that if I were your student I might sometimes approach a work with a different imagery in mind than yours – but I would never close the door to my feelings and imagination. That's the finest gift a teacher could give me.

And that's precisely what I try to offer a student. The important thing is not the image itself, but the *process* of using the imagination. Interpretation must neither be a servile copying, nor, of course, taking pride in being different just for the sake of being different. I say to my students, when they are sufficiently developed, that the best thing they can do is not to run after teachers and listen to recordings, but to seek their own way. Think of the artists *du bon vieux temps* (of the good old days) – Kreisler, Casals, Schnabel, Busch, Cortot, Thibaud – they had genuine personalities of the sort one rarely comes across in the concert hall today. Was it in part because they lived at the birth of the recording era and were not influenced by standardized performance?

Geoffrey Pratley, who has played a great many recitals with you, remembers how you once told him, 'One never plays Beethoven or Brahms; one gives birth to children conceived through a love affair between the recreator and the spirit of the composer. Each child is bound to be somewhat different from the others.' And Geoffrey said to me, 'When you think like that the whole performance comes to life. Every time I have played with Paul it has seemed absolutely brand new – not radically different – but none the less completely spontaneous.'

How kind of him to say that – and for my part let me say that it has always been a joy for me when Geoffrey's been at the piano. Yes, it's got to be *your* performance. The printed page is just a rough guide. You don't go on stage to play; you go on to recreate.

Over the last decades there has been a tendency towards

'authenticity', towards 'respect'. Sometimes a critic throws a brick at you for doing something that's not marked in the score or that's not orthodox. Well, some people can be blinded by respect. I think that love is more important than respect; in real love there is not only respect, but also something more, while in respect there is not necessarily love. We mustn't be too afraid of making the music ours. We should know that we are participants; otherwise there will always be a barrier between the composer and ourselves. If I play a Beethoven sonata, I have to feel his music as he felt it, or as I suppose he felt it. In a sense, during the time of the performance, I *become* Beethoven. That may sound incredibly egocentric, but in fact it's quite the opposite. You immerse yourself in the music so completely that for the time being you really forget your own identity. You are outside of yourself – in an *état second* as we say in French.

It may help the interpreter to recreate with greater under-standing if he is at least to some extent a composer himself. If you have been through the process of creation you will be more responsive to the process of recreation. What the composer has taken weeks or perhaps months to compose, you perform in twenty minutes; it's as if you yourself had been through these months of work and they are now reduced in time. Everyone knows how Beethoven sought to develop the shape of his music. You see in his sketchbooks when there is something important in the turn of his melody; a single transformation of an interval or rhythm can make all the difference. If you think merely instrumentally, it is easy to overlook the freshness, the ex-pressive message of these notes. But when you relive the miracle of creation, when you improvise along with the composer before the notes have been committed to paper, you will feel the tension of these details as they evolve into a masterpiece. Every per-formance will become a living experience. That's why I say you *become* the composer. You forget yourself and let the music act upon you spontaneously. One of the finest compliments I've ever received came from an Englishman who said, 'You don't play the music; the music plays you.' I felt this in a very special way when I performed the C major Suite in the Queen Elizabeth Hall just recently. During the Sarabande there came a moment when – how can I describe it? – my physical being seemed in complete harmony with my spiritual being. I felt I had no more conscious will. I played, but I was not aware of an effort in doing so. I felt as if I were floating on water, as if I were floating on the Dead Sea. The Dead Sea has so much salt that you can read a newspaper while you lie in the water; that's how relaxed I felt. You can never plan such a happening. It comes of itself after you have played many movements, when you're completely at one with what you're doing. Then everything comes with simplicity, perfect simplicity. Of course you cannot perform an entire suite in such a state; the quicker dance movements convey other moods. But such tranquillity suits a Sarabande – a moment of completeness, of serenity.

Directly related to the recreative process in performance is the question of rehearsal. I note that you don't insist upon having a great deal of rehearsal time. Wilhelm Furtwängler believed that it is almost as bad to rehearse too much as not enough. Do you share his view?

When I've not had much time to rehearse, it has usually been more the result of circumstances than planning. But I do agree that too much rehearsal can be a bad thing in that it can stultify a performance. I was recently asked how many rehearsals I wanted for a forthcoming concert with orchestra. As the programme was rather difficult, I asked for two rehearsals. I could have had more but I felt that if it couldn't go well in two, it wouldn't go well in ten. The main thing is whether or not you share the same feeling about the music with the pianist or the conductor. If you have that basic understanding with your fellow performers you don't need very many rehearsals and, as you say, you want to maintain the spontaneity of your playing.

'Fresh out of the Royal Academy of Music,' recalls Geoffrey Pratley, 'I received an engagement to accompany Paul Tortelier! I had no idea I would ever meet him, much less play for him. The contract was sent a year and a half in advance, and I expected the famous Tortelier to begin rehearsals months before the concert, to carve my playing into little bits and stick them together again. In fact Paul only arranged to meet me the day before the concert which, as I now realize, was quite a luxury. We plunged right into the deep end with Beethoven's Opus 69 – playing straight through the first movement. Paul then looked towards me and said, "You know, I'm sure we have not played together before . . ." "No, you're right, Monsieur," I replied timorously. "I'm sure I asked for someone I knew," he continued. Interminable pause – "But I must tell you that it feels as if we have played together for years. Let's go on to the next movement." First I thought I was going to be damned to hell, and the very next moment I felt ten feet tall.'

Many years ago in Puerto Rico I sat in on a chamber music rehearsal at Casals's home, in which he was joined by Stern and Arrau in a Brahms Trio. I expected to learn a great deal from what they said. In fact I learned more from what they didn't say. The performance seemed to shape itself from a mutual feeling of accord. Their reactions were so intuitive that they could adjust to one another while playing; they didn't need to stop more than a few times. It is interesting to note that Arrau valued the fact that I apparently managed to turn pages 'without breaking the mood'. He insisted that I should act as turner that evening. Unfortunately, I was assaulted by a giant tropical moth while trying not to break the mood during the concert, and consequently vowed never to turn pages again.

We have spoken of your students learning to trust to their imagination. It seems that you were able to envisage music in dramatic or poetic terms almost from the beginning.

That's true. My feelings were deep and strong and I trusted them. Where I have primarily developed over the years is in the artistic means of projecting my feelings. When, for example, as a young man I played the Haydn D major Concerto, I was stirred, as I am now, by the nuance of sadness in the middle of the first movement. But now my cello communicates more eloquently what I feel in this passage. My playing today more closely approximates my vision of a work.

I have learned that a soloist must articulate every phrase in such a way that it speaks directly to the heart of the public. Like an actor portraying Hamlet, he must be able to portray all gradations of emotion; he must have sufficient power of tone and clarity of enunciation to be understood in the very back of the hall. As we say in French, '*Il faut que cela passe la rampe.*'

During the past six years I have presented over fifty young soloists with my orchestra in Geneva. They are used to practising in their

rooms or playing for their teachers, but most have little idea of how to
take the measure of a concert hall. It would be helpful if students
sometimes took lessons in a large hall with their teachers seated in the
last row.

One difficulty is that the concept of purism, which often
prevails nowadays, paralyses the ability to project; the whole
expressive range tends to shrink.

Speaking of projection, I can tell you an amusing story. There
was once a trio consisting of three well-known musicians: the
violinist Ysaÿe, the pianist Pugno, and the cellist Joseph
Hollmann. Each of them weighed a hundred kilos. Ysaÿe was
enormous, and Pugno looked like Brahms. They couldn't take a
cab together; they had to take three. In keeping with his
physique, Hollmann produced a huge tone. Yet, like all cellists,
he was always worrying whether his sound carried. During a
rehearsal in the Albert Hall, he suddenly said to Ysaÿe, 'Since
we are in such a large hall, would you please go up to the top to
listen? Tell me how my cello sounds.' Ysaÿe was not very keen
on this, but as a favour to his colleague he took his gigantic
frame to the top of the vast hall. Hollmann then began to play
with his magnificent tone. After a few minutes he stopped and
shouted, 'Eugène, what do you think?' And Ysaÿe called down,
'I am waiting for you to start playing. Please begin.'

We cellists have special difficulties in communicating with the
public. It's not only a question of volume – although God knows
it's always a struggle to be heard, especially when playing with
instruments whose voices are higher than ours. But, as I've
mentioned, it's also a question of articulation. The cello strings
are long and thick and hard to put into immediate vibration. The
beginning of notes may all too easily sound fuzzy, and legato
passages may lack that inner articulation necessary to bring
them to life.

Casals was supreme in his power of articulation. He used
human speech as a model for clarifying and vivifying his playing,
and developed his left-hand and bow technique accordingly.
He could hear his own playing as if he were listening objectively
to himself from a distance.

So you see, the performer's task as medium between composer and listener is an arduous one. He begins by conceiving the work of art as if he were the composer; he must then find the means to communicate that conception to the listener. The circle is complete when both performer and listener participate in the process of recreation.

XVII
Bach

Pablo Casals used to say, 'First comes Bach – then all the others.' Despite my great love for many of the others – not least Beethoven and Mozart – I can only agree with Casals. Bach dominates the whole lot. I'll even go so far as to say that Bach has an advantage over God Himself. God may promise Paradise, but Bach already takes us there. When I conduct the Orchestra Suite in C major I truly experience jubilation; afterwards I feel thirty years younger. I have often thought that a temple should be erected to Bach – but where? In Eisenach, in Leipzig, in Jerusalem?

You've been building your own temple over a lifetime of performance.

We've already spoken briefly of one or two of the Cello Suites. Would you now discuss their interpretation in greater detail?

A book could be written on the subject. I shall have to content myself with a few general observations.

If I may somewhat extend the analogy of the temple, one could look at the Bach Suites as one would a cathedral, taking into consideration such aspects as the architectural, the aesthetic, the spiritual. Every Suite consists of a Prelude followed by five dances, each of which retains its basic rhythmic character. Many have a downright rustic quality; with Bach you are connected to the earth. It's a pity when performers sentimentalize this rhythmic element. Each dance also has its distinguishing tempo.

158

A Courante will be rapid, a Sarabande slow, though, as I've said, not so slow as to lose its three-beat-per-bar motion. By respecting the inherent nature of each dance, the interpreter will find the contrast of tempos which bring variety within the suite.

However, on the spiritual side Bach preserves an overall unity. The basic expressive characteristics set forth in the Prelude are carried over to the subsequent dances. For instance, all the movements of the G major Suite partake of the lovely, joyous colours of the Prelude, while the C minor Suite retains its foreboding, dramatic quality throughout. There are also several examples of melodic interrelationship from movement to movement within individual suites.

If the interpreter conveys the expressive cohesion of each suite properly, the final effect will not be that of a series of separate dances; it will be nearly symphonic in its total impact. A certain comparison can in fact be drawn between the form of the suite, especially as developed by Bach, and that of the symphony. One could, in broad terms, compare the first movement of the symphony (often with introduction) to the Prelude and Allemande of the suite, the slow movement to the Sarabande, the Minuet to the lighter dances which surround the Sarabande, and the Finale to the concluding Gigue. In fact quite a number of Haydn and Mozart Finales have a gigue-like rhythm.

Now if we turn our attention to the structure of the individual movements, we appreciate all the more the miracle that Bach has been able to achieve. Let us not forget that he is dealing with a stringed instrument producing a single melodic line from which, by normal definition, harmony and counterpoint are excluded. In spite of this he succeeds in constructing his melodic line in such a way that one feels – one hears – the underlying harmony, assuming of course that the interpreter gives it due attention. As to counterpoint, one often has the impression – again, given the interpreter's insight – that two voices are in dialogue. Let us take, for instance, the Prelude to the Fifth Suite in C minor. Bach has here created a piece which has all the characteristics of fugal style: an exposition in which the subject is set forth in four different registers, episodes alternating with statements of the subject, pedal points on the dominant and tonic, a coda. Not

only is it a great achievement in linear polyphony, but the whole
is formed into a powerful dramatic entity. It's typical of Bach's
greatness that his structural elements, though worked out in the
most sophisticated way, are integrated into a musical line which
never loses its freshness or spontaneity!

On the one hand it's the interpreter's task to articulate the
structural elements, to vary his colour with the modulations, to
delineate the contour of each phrase. On the other hand, with all
this attention to detail, one runs the risk of losing continuity.
We must not give the impression that we are looking into the
music *par le petit bout de la lorgnette*. Bach broken into fragments
ceases to be Bach. If the dances are to preserve their rhythmic
élan, the basic pulse must be maintained, and if the long lines of
the work are to be set forth, the melodic flow shouldn't be
interrupted. If, as I often say, the music must breathe, the art is
to let it do so without pulling apart the fabric. I've sometimes
suggested to a student that he should think of Bach's music as an
ocean of sound, and himself as a fish which doesn't need to put
its head out of the water; in other words, to breathe *inside* the
flow of music as a fish breathes inside the sea.

As well as looking for elements of differentiation, the player
should recognize elements of continuity – for instance a step-
wise pattern that requires emphasis:

or a scale of great length, disguised by leaps of a minor seventh:

In my edition of the Bach Suites I offer certain suggestions as
to how the moment-to-moment nuances can be seen in terms of
the longer musical line. For instance, I indicate the number of
bars which, in my opinion, comprise the longer melodic span; I
then show the smaller phrases within that larger grouping. I also
designate the relationship of one phrase to another: where a
clear break is desirable, or where continuity should be maintained. In some cases a single note may have the dual function of
ending one phrase and beginning another. I have tried to show
all this with signs which are clear and precise, but which don't
overload the page and confuse the performer.

In all these six suites Bach has left us no written indication of
tempo or nuance other than a few *f* and *p* markings in the D
major Prelude. It's therefore inevitable that in any performance
of this music subjective factors will play a role. If we join the
league of purists, with their respect for 'what is written' and
their passion for 'letting the music speak for itself', we might
have a heart attack when starting to play the very first Prelude in
G major. How fast should it be? Should we play *forte, mezzoforte,*
or *piano*? The ideal solution for members of the league would be
for both player and public to come to the concert hall with scores
in hand, and read them together in silence – because the moment
the performer begins to play Bach he must choose a tempo, and
that tempo cannot be anything other than his own.

I have already mentioned the limitations inherent in the bowings notated in Anna Magdalena's manuscript. As soon as you
begin to study the suites from the instrumental point of view
it becomes clear that these indications, though sometimes
helpful guides, are quite inadequate to the realization of the
full expressive range of these works. Searching for the ideal
bowings in each passage is a lifelong challenge for every cellist.
Paradoxically, though the right choice of bowing makes all the
difference to the expressive effect of the whole, the purists
hardly ever mention it.

A performance of Bach's music requires a balancing of many
factors. You must have both temperament and good taste. Finding the middle ground is more often a question of intuition than
of learning. Above all, I must pay homage to the achievement of
Pablo Casals who was the first to reveal to the world the true

spirit of these works. Today I may interpret a particular phrase or movement quite differently from Casals, but I feel, as so many musicians do, that I owe him an incalculable debt. Without him I might never have found what lies in these masterpieces.

In the preface to your edition of the Bach Suites and in the notes you wrote for your recording, you have refrained from giving your own imaginative impressions of these works.

As I have said, such impressions are for the performer rather than the listener.

Even so, would you describe some of the imagery which comes to mind when you play these pieces – not in order to fix a label on the music, but to bring the reader a little closer to a vital aspect of your recreative process?

If I do so, please remember that I am speaking of no more than subjective phenomena. All I can say is that the imagery is important to me personally.

I have already spoken of my impression of the Prelude to the First Suite; that, to me, is the 'stream' Prelude. In fact, I envisage the Preludes to the Third and Fourth Suites as also being nature pictures. I shall come to them in a minute.

In the Second Suite we enter into the sombre realm of D minor, far from the sunny and confident G major of the First Suite. The D minor Prelude seems to me a prayer; the rise and fall of the melodic line comes like a supplication.

When you implore, you join your hands together and reach upwards towards the sky. You fall back again, and the next time you reach out a little higher. Such is this Prelude with its ever more intense supplication, until at the end you can only accept the sorrow that is your lot, for there is no victory.

With the Prelude to the Third Suite I am again in nature. I dive into the depths of the ocean, and am then carried along by the currents and the surging waves. The colour of the music is also that of the sea; it's both dark and transparent. I imagine it a blue-green. Normally, I would not dare presume that Bach might have shared my fantasy, but I can't help wondering whether he too, when writing this Prelude, did not picture a flow of waves. The undulating semiquaver patterns, whether scale-like or arpeggiated, are highly similar to his depiction of waves in the cantata *Christ unser Herr zum Jordan kam* (Christ our Lord came to the River Jordan). Let's not forget that when Bach, at the age of 20, travelled from Arnstadt to Lübeck to study with Buxtehude, he did have a chance to see the sea. I have stood at the nearby harbour of Travemünde which Bach must have visited at least once during his long sojourn. The sea there is a powerful element; it must have made a great impression on him. Rather than stay in Lübeck four weeks as planned, he remained four months. And he didn't do so for Buxtehude's daughter who was supposed to be very ugly; he might have secured Buxtehude's post had he been willing to marry her. Did he stay on only to learn from Buxtehude, or did he perhaps also want to spend more time by the sea? That's my imagination working. But you're not an artist if you don't have imagination.

The Prelude to the Fourth Suite is, for me, the third nature picture. The colour is golden. It is noon on the mountains. All is bright and radiant. In their bold upward thrust of two octaves, the first notes seem to outline the peaks in their full dimension from foot to summit; then the contours are filled in.

Do you play this Prelude with separate bow strokes?

Yes; it has a grand, primitive quality and this should be preserved in the bowing. However, I always conceive it in melodic patterns. At the beginning I group four notes together, then twice two notes. In other words I give special emphasis to the first, third, and fourth crotchet beats of the bar.

Later on, however, we find a step-wise movement in the bass.
I then leave the listener's ear in temporary suspense by with-
holding the accent until the last quaver in the bar as it leads to
the first beat of the subsequent bar.

The Sarabande is divinely beautiful. You have come upon a
little chapel in the mountains. You arrive there and you are
alone. The snow which is never far away reflects a vibrant light.
You meditate on the miracle of happiness, why it exists and why
we can never possess it for long. After all, we experience real
happiness for only brief moments in our lives. And we experience it here when we reach this little chapel. All is as it
should be; you are at the centre of your being.

The concluding Gigue has the rustic quality of a Brueghel
painting. The peasants are dancing. In its jubilant 12/8 rhythm
and melodic contour it is reminiscent of the Finale of the Sixth
Brandenburg Concerto.

The mood changes radically with the Fifth Suite. The opening
is dark, almost violent.

It has the colour of a Goya. We can compare it to the Second
Suite in that neither is a nature picture, and both are in the
minor. But the C minor Prelude is quite different from the D
minor. It is less introspective – more tempestuous. I see a prophet
speaking – a prophet who has experienced injustice, who has
known deception – a man of God who yet expresses indignation
and anger. In choosing to begin with the most powerful notes,
the octave Cs in the cello's lowest register, Bach tells us that he

wants this music played forcefully. As nothing is marked in the score we can only go by such internal evidence.

We then come to the fugal section of the Prelude. Again I let my imagination speak. I see here the process of the creation of the world. The first two notes of the subject

represent the embryo – the origin of all life. How delicately it begins . . . gradually the cells multiply and life starts to germinate.

The Allemande is music of the greatest pain, the greatest anguish – an inner anguish that can sometimes only be spoken of in hushed tones. Could there be greater proof of what Casals has said, that 'Bach's art is not "abstract" but is the deepest expression of feeling'? Think of this Allemande and the sorrow it expresses, a sorrow one can well understand. Bach not only lost his first wife but also had to go to the cemetery to bury a baby or small child ten times. If that leaves a person cold, then he is a monster – and Bach was anything but that.

The Courante is a dramatic piece – turbulent and full of motion – not sentimental as one sometimes hears it played. For me this is one of the pieces in which Bach is medieval. I picture messengers arriving in agitation, speaking fearfully and bringing bad news. 'Hear us,' they tell their lord. 'We come from distant provinces. You must know that an army is gathering together to wage war upon you.' They are messengers announcing death.

The Sarabande comes as a prayer; it speaks in turn of sorrow and serenity. Has so much ever been expressed in so few notes?

The Gavotte and Gigue retain the dark coloration. I play the Gigue as a bold piece – not *grazioso*. I was once criticized in a newspaper for playing this movement too dramatically. The critic imagined that the piece is in E♭ major; he had taken the first six bars out of context, ignoring the seventh bar which clearly designates C minor. He not only mistook the key but failed to understand the continuity of expression throughout the work.

We come now to the Sixth Suite – the crowning work of the set. When I play the Prelude:

I have a vision before me. Bach has built a cathedral in the air. I see Chartres Cathedral as it appears from a distance in summertime, when the upper part can be seen rising above the wheatfields. It seems detached from the ground, floating over the golden wheat. The beginning of this monumental Prelude rings out like a carillon – forceful and joyous. How can I put it? Like a cathedral that flies in the sound of its own bells . . . This imagery is not as fanciful as it may seem. After all, making music is in fact making architecture in the air. The painter has a support in his canvas, the sculptor has the ground on which to rest his work, but our sound-waves are carried on the air.

Well, these are a few impressions — sketchy, incomplete and difficult to express. Heaven forbid that any purists should come upon these comments!

I think it would do them a world of good.

You have recently recorded the complete set of Bach Suites for the second time and are in the process of making a second written edition of these works for publication. What do you hope to achieve in these new versions?

To go further in Casals's direction than I have up to the present. More life! To speak of 'freedom' is dangerous – but more exaltation, more colour. In general I would say that I'm a little classical in my overall range of dynamics. I try to avoid extraneous effects and only rarely touch upon the dynamic extremes, but I feel that I could sometimes bring in more elements of contrast. I also think it's a good idea to vary the nuances during the repeats. Ideally, I would like to make an edition in which the repeats are written out in full, enabling me to suggest such possibilities. The publisher would probably not accept it, as it would result in far greater expense. However, the principle is a good one, and I hope that more performers will give thought to it.

When students and performers put your two editions – from the 1960s and 1980s – side by side, they will find many passages in which the bowings and nuances differ. I think much can be learned from that.

We must look at Bach's music in such a way that we evolve. We must be on our guard against routine. Once we have studied a work, there's a tendency to adopt a particular fingering or bowing permanently. What's true for physical gestures is true for our thinking process as well. My wife calls such thinking *prendre des plis* – a term the French use when something's been wrongly ironed and stays permanently creased.

Then a student might use your editions as a starting point, as a guide, to building his own interpretation.

Yes, as a starting point. My editions may help him find the beginning of the path; they will show him the kind of things I look for, the way I work. But it will then be up to him to follow the path to the end in his own way. However, far more important than a performer's choice of edition is his ability to bring to his interpretation a knowledge of harmony and counterpoint, as well as a natural feeling for the expressive nature of the music. Copying is not a very creative enterprise.

> What could be more dutiful than for a student to adopt his teacher's fingering? One can therefore imagine the shock received by a young cellist who had meticulously learnt the fingerings found in one of the Tortelier scores when he was asked by the self-same professor, 'Wherever did you get those fingerings? We'll certainly have to improve on them.' 'Why, *Maître*,' came the timid reply, 'they are from your own score.' 'Ah, but I have changed my fingerings since then. In fingerings, as in wine, there are good years and there are bad ones. You have chosen a bad year.'

I should like to make one final point. An all-important factor is our basic attitude towards Bach. Too many people, including performing musicians, still tend to place Bach on an unapproachable pedestal, as if his greatness would somehow be sullied by exposure to our humanity. The lack of written nuances in his music compounds the problem. The printed page cannot be brought to life by uncreative self-effacement. What's needed is active participation based on love. If we love someone we are not afraid to give of ourselves. Bach's music restores to us a sense of the full meaning of life – to those of us, at least, who have not been put off by unimaginative performances. Apropos of this, something amusing happened to me one day after a rehearsal at the Festival Hall. A charming lady, the wife of an English composer, came backstage to say a few words about the concerto I had performed. Somehow or other, the conversation turned to Bach. 'I don't like his music,' she said; 'I find it monotonous – in fact, irritating.' Sad to hear these words from a genuine music-lover, I asked if I could play her a piece by Bach there and then. She dutifully seated herself and obliged by listening to the Bourrée from the C major Suite. Lo and behold, she began inadvertently to nod with the rhythm; a smile began to play on her lips. When I had finished, I asked her how she had found it. With a touch of irony in her tone, as if to imply that I had somehow been cheating, she said, 'Well, of course it's not irritating if you play it like *that*!'

If, as Bach believed, there is a God who made the universe – who created the heaven and the earth – He was not merely a great mechanic. And Bach, whose whole art was dedicated to His glory, never wrote a note that is merely mechanical – never a scale passage or arpeggio, even in the simplest children's piece, that is not impregnated with beauty and feeling. How thankful we must be to have his music!

He speaks to us in our age of technology from his age of faith.

And restores our faith in all that's good and beautiful. So long as I can play my cello, I'll go on in my own way, as you say, David, building my temple to Bach.

XVIII

The Others

We have spoken of Bach, now let us speak of the others. But the cello literature has become extensive; we can't cover it all.

Perhaps we can, at least, touch upon some of the works which you have played throughout your career. Why not begin with Haydn? Do you have a preference between the two concertos?

I love them both. The Finale of the C major is irresistible, and the slow movement is extraordinary beautiful. On the other hand, the first movement of the D major concerto is richer in content than that of the C major. As you know, the authenticity of the D major concerto was doubted for many years, before Haydn's manuscript was found. I have seen it myself, through the kindness of Mrs Badura-Skoda who does research at the library in Vienna. Now this brings up an interesting question. Before the manuscript was discovered, it was fashionable for people to show off a little musical scholarship. 'No, no,' they would say, 'this is probably not by Haydn but by a pupil of Haydn named Kraft.' This reveals that they had absolutely no understanding of the miracle of creation. I would answer, 'If it isn't by Haydn it must be by Mozart. It's certainly not by Mr Kraft or Mr Smith. No student of Haydn, not even the best of his students, possessed the genius to write the beautiful things that are in this concerto.' We should trust to our spontaneous reactions and not think that we are cleverer than our feelings; then we would never take such beauty for granted.

You spoke just now of 'understanding the miracle of creation'. I think it's difficult for many people, whether performers or listeners, to imagine that there was a time when a particular well-known piece of music had not yet been created. We tend to see it too much in retrospect, and the academic way of dividing music, like cutting a pie, into 'classical', 'romantic', and 'modern' has a deadening effect. As an interpreter I've always fought against such artificial classification. You cannot confine Shakespeare to one of these categories; he is all three at once. One can say the same for the composers of the Salomon symphonies and of Don Giovanni. If you put yourself into the harmonic and formal context of the eighteenth century, so much of Haydn's and Mozart's music becomes revolutionary.

Ah, David, I couldn't agree more. Haydn and Mozart didn't know they were 'classic'. They were men who expressed in their music their suffering, their joy.

One aspect of Haydn's art which has always been of particular fascination to me is his way of using rhythm. He is more audacious than Mozart or even Beethoven in his variety of phrase lengths. For instance, the first movement of the *Eroica* is mostly constructed in groups of four or eight bars, but Haydn often alternates odd- and even-numbered bar groupings. And you don't feel it to be disconcerting because he does it in such a natural way. His rhythm is modern in this sense – not so far from Stravinsky or Bartók. Furthermore, in regard to vitality of rhythmic interest *within* the phrase Haydn is also a master. Unlike so much of the music of our time where rhythm exists in isolation – just rhythm for rhythm's sake – with Haydn rhythm and melody are indivisible; they seem to have sprung to life at one and the same moment. Sing a dozen of Haydn's tunes, and you will see how true this is. If you alter the rhythm, the music changes drastically.

Those who commercialize great classical melodies should take this into consideration. While in America, I heard a pop record in which the first theme of Tchaikovsky's B♭ minor Piano Concerto was taken out of its 3/4 metre and forced into a 4/4 pattern. I won't comment on the lack of elementary respect, the prostitution of values that this reveals; but I will say that those involved in this dirty business would have even more success if they respected the basic rhythmic structure of such pieces, because the listeners associate the rhythm with the melody as an almost biological necessity.

Well, let us return to the happier subject of the cello repertoire.

Would you share with us some of your thoughts about the Beethoven Cello Sonatas?

What a world of development there is in those five works! They range over nearly two decades, the first two sonatas dating from 1796, the third sonata from 1808, and the last two from 1815. When I hear the Allegro theme from the opening movement of the First Sonata:

a portrait comes to my mind of Beethoven as a young man arriving in Vienna ready to conquer the city. While one instrument sings a gay, carefree song, the other seems almost to provide the accompaniment of a guitar.

And when I play the first theme of the Third Sonata in A major:

I am reminded of a self-portrait of Rembrandt, one from the middle of the painter's life. I feel the weight, the texture of a Rembrandt; I feel the goodness, the nobility. I admire men like Beethoven and Rembrandt who had the saddest experiences in life and yet gave the best of themselves and expressed their faith in mankind. This opening passage has the perfect proportions of a Greek statue, but without the coldness. In this one phrase you have the head, the body, the limbs. Isn't it wonderfully balanced? Because it's marked *piano* one sometimes hears it played in a delicate, tentative way. But this *piano* must have substance. Beethoven has also marked *dolce* which, as is the case with Brahms, does not mean sweetly, but *expressively*. The sonata begins in a manly way. We should immediately feel that we are in the presence of the great composer who did not bow to the nobility, who considered himself, as man and musician, no less an aristocrat than they.

When we come to the last two sonatas we enter into yet another spiritual dimension. It was a period of alienation, one of the bleakest in Beethoven's life, the time of the crisis surrounding his nephew Karl. He wrote very few works during those years, one of them being the *Hammerklavier* Sonata, Op. 106. The musical language of the two Cello Sonatas Op. 102 has become more terse than in the earlier sonatas. He says what he wishes to say in a very few bars. One moment he is fierce and uncompromising, the next he is gentle and tender. These works are dedicated to Countess von Erdödy. She and Beethoven had a deep affection for one another. The fourth sonata begins with a benediction:

In this music of such infinite tenderness, I believe he is speaking to the Countess.

By way of contrast, when I begin the Fifth Sonata I feel like Siegfried – it seems to speak of a hero!

If you were to play this passage without imagination, what would come out of it? Nothing but an exercise.

It's interesting that you should mention Siegfried. These notes have a marked resemblance to Wagner's 'Sword motive' from the Ring.

You see the way the great composers could bring significance to such a simple thing as an arpeggio based upon a tonic triad.

At the beginning of the slow movement of this sonata the hero turns his gaze inwards. It is a chorale:

Beethoven kept on his table a quotation he had copied from Schiller's account of the religions of Egypt: 'I am that which is. I am all that is, that was and that shall be. No mortal man has ever lifted my veil.' I feel that in this music Beethoven approaches the very mystery of life. In the A minor passage

one senses a deep longing for happiness. Despite the sorrow you so often find in Beethoven's life and art, you feel that his credo is joy. You find this in the *Heiligenstadt Testament* where he cries out, 'O Providence – may I once be granted a single day of pure joy . . . in the temple of Nature and of Mankind!'

Beethoven expresses everything so fully, and yet so simply! One says that he was the greatest revolutionary in music. In some ways he was – but he was not a proponent of liberty for liberty's sake. That is the province of the modern avant-gardist. Beethoven was conservative in many ways. Despite his marvellous modulations he remains, as Ernest Ansermet said, 'the champion of tonality'. It's instructive to see how the great masters were able to create harmonic tension and suspense within the tonal system. Mozart was also audacious in this respect. Take, for instance, the opening theme of his C minor Piano Concerto with

its mysterious chromaticism and ambiguous tonal implications.
And Bach is no less adventurous. On occasion he's not only
polyphonic but polytonal. One finds passages in the Overtures
to the First and Third Orchestra Suites where the parts, if read
independently, seem to be in different keys; each part is pulling
towards a different centre.

And, of course, there is no greater master of modulation than
Schubert. It's a pity we haven't more cello works from him.
However, the *Arpeggione* Sonata is one of the loveliest pieces in
our repertoire. When I play it I hear Schubert's voice speaking to
us. I can picture him in his little room, alone, perhaps having
been betrayed by a woman. He was, as we know, unhappy in
his love affairs. The piece begins simply; it is soft and plaintive.

Soon, however, the music passes over into the major. I can
imagine the moment when he decides to go to meet his friends
at Bogner's Coffee House, have a good time, and forget his
sorrow.

That is the alternation which comes throughout this movement:
melancholy transformed into gaiety. When I play this music
Schubert becomes absolutely alive for me; I am with him in
Vienna. We musicians truly have the power to resurrect. Please
don't accuse me of sacrilege or megalomania if I say that just as
Christ raised Lazarus from the grave, we can bring Beethoven or
Schubert to life. In fact they cannot live without us!

*One of your performances which confirms this power of recreation
is that of the Schumann Concerto. Is it your favourite cello concerto?*

I love both the Schumann and Dvořák about equally.

Rehearsing for the Dvořák Cello Concerto recording. This photograph shows the slanted 'Tortelier' end-pin, which breaks with tradition in providing a more horizontal position for the cello. (*EMI*)

A family scene in Nice, *l.* to *r.*: Pau, Pascal, Pomone, Paul and Maud at their instruments.

Paul as painted by June Mendoza in 1983.

Paul with Professor Chúän Ju Shih, while teaching in China.

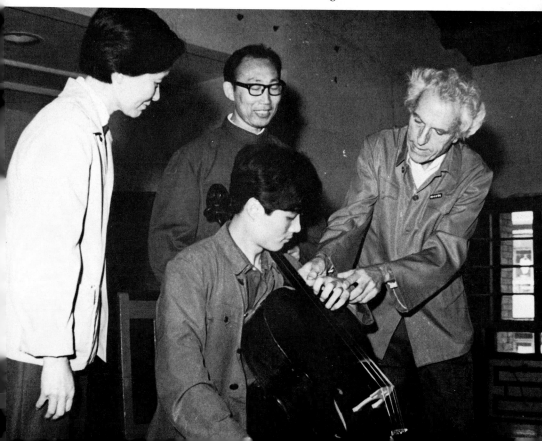

Paul in rehearsal. (*Clive Barda/EMI*)

They are quite different in character.

Very much so. The Dvořák is more expansive, while the Schumann is more concentrated, more human and intimate; it is a self-portrait of the composer at a time when he was close to the borderline of sanity. The work is terribly dramatic in that sense; it is, as it were, a window into the composer's soul. More than any other work I have played, it lends itself to something of an improvisational approach. Like life itself, it seems always to be changing, and can be felt in different ways at different times. For instance, if I feel a little tired or sad I will play it with a more melancholy quality. The work retains its basic character, but, depending on my mood, the nuances may be a little darker or lighter.

If this concerto has not always met with universal appreciation, the difficulty has, I think, been due to the Finale which, if played without imagination, can too easily sound like a dry virtuoso piece. The art of playing the Finale consists not only in singing the broad melodies – that's not so difficult to do – but in singing the quick passages. This is essential if one is to communicate its beauty. Furthermore, Schumann persistently reiterates the same basic rhythmic motif:

The idea obsesses him; it's like a spectre constantly flitting before us.

Exactly. Now, if this motif is always played at the same level of intensity, the repetitions will become monotonous. A successful performance depends upon finding the shades of colour which reflect the melodic and harmonic variety with which Schumann treats this motif. Then we discover the Finale's true character; it becomes something capricious, full of fantasy.

The strength of the real artist is to have a scale of accentuation, above all in his bow technique, which enables him to render the diversity of nuance required by the melodic shape, the harmonic process, and the rhythmic structure. Now, these elements may sometimes make conflicting demands. For instance, the harmonic and melodic accents may fall in different places. There is such a passage in the first movement of the Schumann concerto:

The melodic accent falls here on the highest note, the G ♮; the harmonic accent, however, falls on the first note of the bar – the G♯ which clashes with the G♮ in the bass. If we favour the harmonic aspect we emphasize the dissonance and leave the high G♮ in the air without special inflection. But if we see it from a singer's point of view, we will take advantage of the beautiful interval, the rise of the seventh, and sing out, as a Prima Donna would, on the high note.

Both interpretations are valid. Luckily, the phrase comes twice in succession. The first time I play it melodically and favour the high note; the second time I give more intensity to the G♯ and let the high note come almost as an echo. This gives a lovely contrast.

When the concerto is played, as it was by Casals, with all the variety of nuance, it is absolutely captivating.

Another element which, in your performance, adds to the effect of the whole, is the cadenza you've written for the concerto. It seems an integral part of the work. In bringing back the impassioned lyrical theme from the first movement a unity is established which lends deeper meaning to the 'capriciousness' of the finale.

A cadenza is a delicate matter. It should convey an improvisatory feeling, yet it must have good proportions. One has to be a little inspired while at the same time sharing one's spirit with the composer, penetrating into his world. Incidentally, I use in this cadenza the harmonic clash I mentioned before – the C♯ against the G♮ in the bass. It has great expressive force here, almost more so than when it is heard in the concerto itself, as both notes are produced by the cello. As you know, a dissonance

between instruments of different timbres is less noticed than
between instruments of the same timbre.

Now, the Dvořák Concerto seems to me to be a less intimate
work than the Schumann. It's not the drama of a person concerned with his own problems, but that of a man of action, a
man fighting for the independence of his country. I imagine that
I am portraying the life of a Czech hero. The cello's opening
theme comes like a call to arms:

A cello teacher instructing a master class, or a cavalry officer preparing for
battle? As Professor Tortelier sang the first phrases for his students he
cupped his hand to his brow, surveying the battlefield on both sides. He
then sprang to his feet. Trotting up and down the stage as if on horseback,
he passionately sang the subsequent dotted rhythm like a clarion call to
victory.

Finding the character is everything, and this influences all
that follows. I once had a student – a talented girl – who played
the beginning with great vitality, but when she arrived a few
bars later at the following passage:

she began to play in a dainty, graceful way. It was pretty in
itself, but the effect was that of a sudden enervation. 'What do
you see in that passage?' I asked her. 'Oh,' she responded, 'I
imagine I'm taking a little walk in a flower garden.' As I've said,
I like to give my students a chance to show that their conception
may be convincing even if it differs from mine, and I gave her
such a chance – though, I must say, not for very long.

Was she perhaps over-reacting to the fact that piano *appears in
the score?*

Undoubtedly. It's sometimes difficult for a student to realize
that there can be a concentration of energy in a *piano* as well as in

a *forte*. Furthermore, when one practises a passage in isolation hundreds of times, one tends to forget its relation to the whole. In any case, I think I succeeded in convincing her that this passage should be seen in the overall heroic context. Continuity of feeling – that's the important thing!

In Dvořák the colours are brilliant and the writing for the cello most effective. In Brahms the colour is comparatively lacking in brilliance, but it is nevertheless a most beautiful colour. It's hard for me to express what I feel when I begin Brahms's E minor Sonata, but I know that this music would not be what it is if the composer had been born in Naples rather than Hamburg. It has nothing of the Mediterranean sky. It's a beautiful grey – as one finds in Hindemith and also in many paintings by Manet. You know that in France we have not understood Brahms very well because he has mastered his passion. We prefer Schumann, the dreamer. Brahms is a philosopher. He brings security; he has the most wonderful domination over everything. He has courage, patience, faith. Joy too is present, but it's not an excited joy. That's why it suits the English better than the French.

There's a point I'd like to mention in regard to the interpretation of Brahms's Double Concerto. The theme of the Andante is usually slurred by string players in two equal groups of three quavers, so as to have an equal distribution of the bow:

This bowing, however has several disadvantages. It breaks the melodic curve; it implies a 6/8 rhythm rather than 3/4, and it ignores the fact that the theme is a development of the motif built upon the interval of a fourth, played by the woodwind in the introductory bars:

I would therefore suggest the following slurring. (The bow change should be imperceptible, and the distribution of bow handled skilfully.)

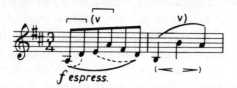

Brahms himself subsequently indicates that he conceives the notes in groups of four quavers:

Among the many outstanding violinists with whom I've played the Brahms Double Concerto, I should like to single out those two great artists: Yehudi Menuhin and Isaac Stern. I hope I may one day have the privilege of playing the work with another violinist for whom I have the greatest admiration: Oscar Shumsky.

It's always most interesting to see how Brahms develops his thematic material. I've mentioned his patience; that's one of the reasons he's able to handle large forms more successfully than Schumann. Schumann is quick to say what he has to say, while Brahms is a man who needs time to set himself in motion. Sometimes he begins almost passively – as in the opening of the Second Symphony – and develops his treasure slowly. Well, that's a difference in temperament.

One composer whose music is sometimes felt to be too fragmentary is Debussy. This is a misconception. He does have a long melodic line, but it is often developed from a series of short phrases. His Cello Sonata is a characteristic example.

It's the interpreter's task to gather these fragments into a melodic continuity, weaving the strands together into one fabric. Whether in Bach or in Debussy, it's always better if you see music in long lines rather than short lines – just as when Picasso draws a long line he knows from the beginning where he is going. Debussy unwittingly complicated matters in the Cello Sonata by utilizing a sign which his interpreters have frequently misunderstood, and with disastrous results. He tried to avoid ambiguity as to the duration of such indications as *Cédez, Retenu,* etc, by inserting two small diagonal dashes: //. These marks create a kind of visual reflex; they stop the flow. But they're not meant to be taken as caesuras. (When he does in fact want a caesura he inserts a comma: ' .) The piece already has more than enough indications of tempo modification, and it's a great pity that a misunderstanding over the signs results in a further fragmentation of line in a work which requires maximum continuity.

I must say that I adore the music of Debussy. He avoids the pitfall of a somewhat academic approach to harmony which one finds in much French music. He was of course a highly cerebral composer; the harmonic world he created could only have come from a subtle mind. Yet he made the indispensable bridge between intellect and feeling. His music is a mystery; it seems to have been born right out of nature.

When I hear *La Mer* I not only have an external picture of the ocean, but I feel I am also seeing it from inside. Sometimes I can even smell the sea! Wilhelm Kempff has said that when he stands before the ocean, he shuts his eyes, listens to *La Mer* in his imagination, and finds Debussy's sea more evocative of the sea than the sea itself. When we lived on Noirmoutier we would often go to a lonely beach to watch the waves. It was wild; but if you want to be close to nature you have to be alone with it. There was an hour during the day when the sunlight would flash upon the sea so that it would almost hurt your eyes. Now that's the glorious moment in *La Mer* when the cello section takes up the great sweep of melody.

I recall one of your televised classes when you were teaching the Debussy Sonata and telling your student, 'Forget about everything and just be a man in nature . . . Be aware of the sensations of your body when you play the cello. Feel that you are naked . . . Once in one's life one should have a swim in the sea wearing nothing at all in order to feel what it is to go completely back to nature.'

I fear I might have shocked the BBC a little with that . . .

Paul was touring with Geoffrey Pratley in southwest England. One afternoon they were driving from Plymouth towards Dillington House, Somerset, where a concert was scheduled for the evening. On the way, Geoffrey took Paul to meet his father who lived near Bigbury-on-Sea in Devon, and who, like Paul's father, was a cabinet-maker. After a pleasant visit, it was time to be getting on, when Paul suddenly asked how far away the sea was. As it was only a few miles down the road, they drove to the beach. After one look at the sparkling waves, Paul announced, 'I cannot resist the attraction of the sea!' Oblivious to the brisk spring weather he disappeared behind a rock, tore off everything except his underwear, and a moment later was submerged in the ocean. Some minutes later, as he was drying himself with his vest, he proclaimed, 'Ah, I feel like a new man!' Quite late now, they set off at top speed, allowing only the briefest stop to satisfy their hunger at a Wimpy Bar. Arriving at Dillington House at the stroke of eight, pianist and cellist stepped on to the stage, the latter without undergarments.

With its deep beauty of tone, the cello – more than any other instrument – seems designed to portray nobility of character. We need only think of Strauss's *Don Quixote* or of Bloch's depiction of Solomon in *Schelomo*. It's therefore not far-fetched if, when speaking of the cello literature, I often refer to knights and heroes. For instance, when I play the introduction to the Lalo Concerto I feel as if the cello is the voice of a prophet, and the orchestra that of a king – Daniel, perhaps, confronting Nebuchadnezzar: 'You must obey, my King, even though you are lord of the land.' The king responds in fury, shouting, 'No!'

'You shall heed my words,' continues the prophet. 'Monarch you may be, but you are also a human being, and you shall die like everyone else.' But the king continues to refuse. It's really violent.

The cello takes on another kind of aristocratic role in Tchaikovsky's *Variations on a Rococo Theme*. However, here I am not telling a story; I am dancing a story. It seems to me to be a ballet from beginning to end. The lovely melody:

is sometimes played sentimentally, but for me it has a touch of irony mingled with its tenderness. We are at a château; a courtly etiquette prevails. A man and a woman, each of the nobility, take part in the dance. They are in love, yet each is married, so they must keep their love hidden. As the phrase mounts, there is a certain sadness, a feeling of regret that their love cannot evolve. And as the man passes close to the woman, he whispers, 'Goodbye, my dearest . . .'

A musician has to be something of a dancer — even if he can't dance in the formal sense – for music not only sings; it speaks and it dances. If a student has no rhythm I will dance with him; it's really the only way to bring a sense of rhythm into someone's body. Rhythm is something physical; it's not enough to merely appreciate it cerebrally.

> When teaching the *Variations on a Rococo Theme* to his master class in Portugal, at one point Professor Tortelier asked the pianist to play the melody line. He then took up his cello and partnered it as if it were the Prima Ballerina Assoluta of the *Royal Ballet*. So tender were his gestures that the instrument seemed to become the woman he imagined it to be, yielding lovingly to his embrace. In one particularly graceful phrase, he raised her in lyrical suspension above his head. The variation drew near its close. 'The ballerina should really complete the dance by herself,' explained the Professor, 'but – alas – she is incapable of doing that.'

Another Russian work with which you are closely associated is the First Shostakovich Concerto.

I admire it greatly. The terse motif with which the first movement opens seems almost to pose a question: 'What will happen?'

When observing the use to which Shostakovich puts this motif we see how economical great music can be. It is reminiscent of Beethoven – for instance the first movements of his Fifth, Sixth or Ninth Symphonies. There's a joke about this – a little unfair to Shostakovich: a young composer in Russia is commissioned to write a symphony for an official celebration. He finds himself, however, devoid of ideas and, as the concert date draws near, becomes increasingly desperate. 'There's no problem,' a friend tells him. 'You need only take the score of a Shostakovich symphony, copy it backwards from last note to first, and you'll have a great modern work, suitable for the occasion.' The young man does just that and hurriedly sends the music off to the orchestra without reading it. He arrives at the general rehearsal at the very moment the orchestra begins to play his piece. And

what does he hear?

In case anyone thinks, after reading this terrible story, that I am disrespectful of Shostakovich, let me say that I've taken more trouble in the preparation of his Cello Concerto than of any piece I've ever played. That's because I decided to conduct it myself while performing it. As my hands were constantly occupied with the cello, I had to conduct with my head. Pau helped me greatly by playing a transcription of the orchestral score so that I could prepare my reactions. What's most difficult is to train the head to move to the left when the bow goes to the right, and vice versa. As well as developing the independence of different parts of the body, it required a complete relaxation of the neck muscles. Often, while playing, we have a tendency to become tense somewhere without realizing it. So it was a worthwhile challenge and excellent training. Before performing the piece – in Rennes, the town of my ancestors – I was a little anxious about it. Unlike, say, a Vivaldi concerto, I couldn't leave off conducting and let the orchestra follow on its own; the work is too rhythmically complicated for that. Luckily, all went well. Strangely enough, the most difficult moment came during the cadenza when, playing alone, I had to *stop* beating time with my head.

The slow movement has great evocative power. When I play it I feel lost in a vastness of open space – like the great steppes of Russia. But I think that every listener will sense something like that without needing a specially developed imagination.

The listeners may be able to sense it, but not every interpreter is able to convey it. Few cellists would dare use so little vibrato. The way you play the melody is disarmingly simple; it communicates this sense of solitude in nature.

The sense of solitude seems particularly acute in an extraordinary moment at the beginning of the cadenza. I sometimes like to be alone, but to experience solitude for an eternity – as one feels it in this passage – would be terrifying.

To turn to another major cello work – the Elgar Concerto – it is interesting to compare two equally beautiful but quite different interpretations of the Moderato 9/8 *theme: yours and that of Casals. While Casals played it as a series of sighs, with a rise and fall of nuance and expressively judged* glissandi, *you create an entirely different atmosphere, one that is calm and ethereal.*

Each artist's conception will be different, but the main thing is to *have* a conception and to convey it. From the spirit you easily reach the shape. In the transitional passage which links the opening bars to this melody, I feel that one is searching for something, searching more and more as the music rises. Finally you grasp that something – but what you grasp is a dream, and this dream is the theme . . .

The dream begins as if suspended in space and only gradually, as it descends towards the bass, does it move towards certainty, towards reality. That, at any rate, is my conception.

I would like to offer a suggestion to interpreters of this work. In the recitative–like passage which precedes the second movement, there is a phrase which comes several times, consisting of a bar of semiquavers followed by chords in *pizzicato*. Each time it occurs Elgar has varied his tempo and dynamic indications in such a way that if they are scrupulously observed, the effect will be one of spontaneity. If you add further *ritardandos* of your own, you risk losing the sense of the unexpected – just like Pau who, as a child, used to tell me, 'Papa, I am going to give you a surprise.'

The Elgar Concerto is a work of intense inner concentration. Think of the slow movement which says so much in so short a time. The end of the concerto – one of the most moving pages in all music – sums up a whole life. Like the endings of *Don Quixote* and of the Dvořák Concerto, it says farewell – but in its own poignant and tragic way. I've played the Elgar Concerto for over fifty years; it's become a part of me.

I must not forget to include the Hindemith Concerto (1940) in this discussion. It is, in my opinion, a masterpiece, one of the most important works written for the cello since the concertos of Dvořák and Saint-Saëns. I once had the privilege of playing it with Hindemith himself conducting.

What sort of man was he?

A most amiable person with a fine sense of humour. He was a roundish, bald little man. His mobile face, fair in complexion,

was illuminated by a pair of sensitive blue eyes. Hindemith was
the ideal conductor for his own music. His gestures were relaxed
and supple. He had a light touch, avoiding excessively slow
tempos and this helped bring the necessary fluidity and clarity
to his complex orchestral textures. Objecting to the slow, heavy-
handed way in which one of my colleagues had performed his
Cello Concerto, he said, 'He turns it into a tragedy – which it is
not!'

We have spoken of the art of 'recreating'. Well, when playing
the Hindemith Concerto under the composer's baton, there
was one moment when I was a little afraid to play the music as I
felt I should. This was towards the end of the work when the
cello takes over the lyrical theme for the last time. *Mezzo forte* is
indicated here; I would have liked to let myself go, and bring the
theme to a glorious and passionate conclusion but I restrained
myself. Afterwards, in her husband's presence, Mrs. Hindemith
praised my performance in general, only expressing some reser-
vation about my reticence to play out in this particular passage. I
said that I had wanted to play out more fully, but had felt obliged
to respect the *mf* in the score. *Qui ne dit mot consent* – 'Silence
gives consent' – for Hindemith's only response was a significant
smile.*

*Even a man so respectful of the score as Toscanini pointed out
that the letter does not invariably reflect the spirit. I'm sure you
remember that there is a passage for four solo cellos in the first act
of* Otello. *Well, it seems that one day at a rehearsal the La Scala
cello section, of which the young Toscanini was a member, was
taking particular care to observe the difference between the written
indications* pp *and* ppp. *Verdi himself was present and suddenly
stopped the orchestra. 'Who is the second cellist?' he demanded.
Toscanini stood up; 'I, Maestro,' he said, abashed. 'Well then,' the
composer continued, 'play your notes a little louder.' He wanted a
natural singing tone.*

*It's worthwhile mentioning that neither Hindemith nor Richard Strauss
made any objection to my changing the printed bowing slurs in the Cello
Concerto of 1940 and *Don Quixote* respectively when I played these works
under their batons. They appreciated the fact that many such small alterations
of bowing (virtually unnoticeable when skilfully executed) bring enhanced
vitality by improving the articulation of detail within the phrase.

That reminds me of another beautiful anecdote. Jacques Thibaud was performing Saint-Saëns's lovely work for the violin, *La Havanaise*, at a general rehearsal. As you know, general rehearsals were then open to the public, and indeed, the composer himself was present. When Thibaud finished, just before the audience could begin to applaud, the shrill, nasal voice of Saint-Saëns rose sharply from the hall: 'That's not at all what I wanted. That's not at all what I wanted.' Thibaud began to get worried, to say the least. Saint-Saëns then came nearer the stage and added, 'But it's much better.'

XIX
View from the Platform

Have you ever suffered from stage fright?

Blessedly, not very much. It's torture for a string player to suffer from it. The first thing that happens is that the bow begins to tremble. On one occasion when I was young I became exceedingly nervous. I've never forgotten it. I was perspiring so profusely that I lost control of my playing. I thought then that if the problem were to persist I would have to stop playing altogether – as have so many musicians, including some great artists I've known. Luckily it only happened once. Generally, I am fairly calm before I play. Should I become a little tense, I counteract it by breathing quietly and deeply. The key to overcoming stage fright is, of course, to harness your concentration. What does make me nervous is to play a modern work which I don't know well, where my memory might play me tricks.

Do you always play from memory?

Generally yes, with the exception of some sonatas which I don't play often and a couple of modern concertos. I do, however, play about a dozen important modern concertos from memory, among them the Hindemith, Prokofiev, Shostakovich and Khachaturyan – so you see I am not too lazy. The first time I played the Shostakovich E♭ major Concerto – it was at a Promenade Concert in the Albert Hall – I was rather worried that I might have a memory slip during the extraordinary long solo cadenza. Sure enough, I forgot to play a certain passage. Basil

188

Cameron, who was conducting, was even more worried than I, trying to find out where I had jumped to, and wondering if he would be able to bring the orchestra in with me at the end.

Are there any particular annoyances which tend to affect your concentration during concerts?

If you look out into the hall you may easily find something which could disturb you: someone yawning, or someone looking at his watch. That's enough to ruin your concentration.

I recall when Myra Hess stopped in the middle of a Beethoven sonata and told the audience that she could not continue to play if the coughing persisted.

A similar thing has happened to me on more than one occasion. I was once playing a Bach Suite for a fashionable chamber music society in Paris. No sooner had I begun the Sarabande – which is like a prayer – than a man, elegantly dressed, entered from the back of the hall and walked in the most casual way all the way down to the first row where he crossed over a dozen legs before seating himself right in front of me. I stopped playing and said, 'Do you realize what you have done, Monsieur? In the middle of a work by Bach you have disturbed everyone.' It turned out to be the president of the society! On another occasion the same thing happened, only in reverse. A dilettantish Parisian musician was attending my concert because he was a friend of the lady who had engaged me; he was sitting at the very front. Once again I was playing a beautiful slow movement when he suddenly stood up, turned his back to me, disturbed the entire row to make his exit, and walked up the central aisle to the distraction of the whole audience. As I don't play with my eyes closed, I saw all that. When he had reached the middle of the hall I stopped playing and said 'Au revoir, Monsieur'. His back stiffened as if I had put a knife into it. I regretted what I had done, but it was too late. However, I don't think he would have made such an ostentatious departure if he hadn't been aware of the effect it would have on me and on the public.

As a conductor I have an advantage in not having to face the audience. In fact, I often forget that it's there, and am startled by the

*applause. There can, however, be distractions within an orchestra,
such as the time a key fell off the cor anglais just as the player was
about to intone the plaintive echoes of 'Salce' in the 'Willow Song'
from* Otello.

*Dare I ask if your absent-mindedness has created any complications
for you on the concert stage?*

I've had some close calls. In my teens my English tutor used to
tell me, ' It's a good thing your head is fixed to your shoulders;
otherwise you'd be sure to lose it.' My family is always ex-
asperated with me before a concert. They say I'm always forgetting something – my glasses, my music, my tie, my tails, my
end-pin – always something. Luckily I know most of my music
by heart, so that when I forget the score it's not a catastrophe.
There was, however, an occasion when I did risk a catastrophe.
That was in Toulon about forty years ago when I played a recital
programme with the gifted pianist-composer Jean Hubeau. Just
as we were about to go on stage to play Fauré's Second Cello
Sonata – a work I didn't know by heart – I realized that I had left
the cello part in Paris. Without explaining why, we announced
that the Fauré would be played second on the programme, and
while we performed the other sonata, the concert organizer
rushed to the home of an amateur cellist to try to find a copy of the
missing music. I still remember with what anxiety I played that
first piece, how we purposely took very leisurely tempi, and how
I went out of my way to tune at length between movements. Just
as we finished and went off stage, the concert organizer returned,
breathless, and – thank God – holding the music in his hand.
   Sometimes I've arrived in a city having been mistaken about
the concerto I was going to play. Once, in Basel, I had prepared
the D major Haydn Concerto, only to discover at the rehearsal
that it was supposed to be the C major. Another time – I think it
was in Wiesbaden – I was seated on stage for the rehearsal,
waiting for the orchestra to play the long tutti that begins the
Dvořák Concerto. I looked at the conductor; he looked at me. 'I
am waiting for you,' he said. 'But I don't begin,' I answered; 'I
enter after the orchestral tutti.' 'What orchestral tutti?' he asked,
perplexed. 'We have only one chord to play' – and he showed me
the score of the Saint-Saëns Concerto! Well, such things happen

if you have a memory like mine and you have to play a hundred concerts in a year. Luckily, all these concertos are in my fingers, and I could make the change on the spur of the moment.

On occasion I have begun a sonata recital with the wrong piece. If I begin with the Vivaldi E minor Sonata when the Frescobaldi Toccata is listed first on the programme, it can prove disconcerting to the pianist.

There are times, however, when the fault is not mine; a piece I'm not scheduled to play is printed on the programme. When that happens I find it rather unprofessional to announce a change. I prefer to meet the challenge if I can. One challenge I might have had difficulty meeting was avoided when my manager urgently requested clarification of a telex she had received from me which read: *PROGRAMME MONTREAL 500 SONATES*. The telex operator had taken *Saint-Saëns Sonate* to be *cinq cents sonates!*)

It sometimes happens that I arrive only at the last minute before a recital. I know I am to play a Solo Bach Suite, but I forget which one. In such cases I have asked the public which suite I am supposed to perform. I can do that in England where people have a fine sense of humour and accept me as I am.

Once, as a young man – I must have been about 20 – I had been promised a good fee to play for a funeral in the church of St-Philippe du Roule in Paris. A few minutes before the service was due to begin I took out my bow and, with a shock, realized that I had forgotten my rosin. What made the discovery so dramatic was that my bow had just been rehaired the previous day. As all string players know, an unrosined, newly haired bow will produce no sound whatever when drawn across the string. I was in despair, especially as the *Maître de Chapelle* who had engaged me was none other than my revered teacher Jean Gallon. I tried to play. No rosin – no sound. I looked about in the hope that some musician might have left his rosin on a music stand. No such luck. Then I spied a double bass in the corner. Fortunately, it was very dirty, the top of the instrument being covered with a thin layer of dust mixed with rosin powder. I desperately rubbed my bow against it and managed to get a tiny bit of the precious material to stick to the hair, just enough to enable me to play, albeit with the faintest wheezing tone. Those listening to the service that day must truly have thought that a musical voice was speaking to them from the other world.

My inability to come properly equipped does not apply only to the concert stage. I don't have time to make preparations. I cannot be like those people who arrive at a ski resort wearing full regalia. I have none of the right costumes. I do my jogging in regular shoes. In fact, sometimes I do it in full evening dress. The other night before playing the Shostakovich Concerto in Manchester I felt I needed some fresh air, and so I went out and jogged a bit.

I hope without your cello.

It stayed behind that time. Once, out for a walk near Harrogate, I was jumping from rock to rock. It had been raining and, of course, I wasn't wearing the proper shoes, so I fell. I was bleeding so much that a friend who was with me had to take off his shirt and wrap it around my head. I needed six stitches. So, the next day I arrived in Amsterdam with my head completely bandaged. My Double Concerto was on the programme, and I explained to the audience that the Finale was inspired by Pirandello's play *Henry IV*, in which a man, masquerading as the medieval German king, falls from his horse on to his head and goes mad. They must have wondered if I were telling my own story.

Well, as you see, I can be a little chaotic, but I somehow manage all the same.

I think this is an appropriate moment to quote your Swiss manager Pio Chessini: 'Since I first worked with Paul in 1948 he has never missed a concert and has always played superbly. Temperamental he may be, but his temperament has never been a cause of disturbance. He's too true and serious an artist to give sudden surprises. Of all the musicians I've known, he's the most reliable.'

It's only natural that one should do the best one can. An artist has a responsibility towards his public.

Have you ever played under extremely disagreeable physical conditions?

Not long after the war I played in Berlin with Celibidache conducting the Berlin Philharmonic. They had no concert hall, as Berlin had been devastated. The whole city seemed to be nothing but scattered stones. At that time Berlin was divided into four zones, and the French authorities had invited us to play in a cinema in the French zone. It was winter and bitterly cold. The hall was absolutely freezing. I'm sorry to mention it, but somebody spat, and it immediately turned to ice. I rehearsed with my coat and gloves on. Man's capacity to adapt during times of war is extraordinary. I remember when we spent every winter in Paris without heating. I often think of the beggars who must sleep in the cold. When, at 14, I used to take the last Métro home from the cinema in which I played, arriving at the rue Marcadet at midnight, there would be some thirty beggars sleeping on the steps leading up to the street. I had to climb over them as there was almost no free space in which to walk. I shall never forget how they were, huddled together in the cold.

You have often played for poor or deprived people.

Yes, whenever possible. During many years, for instance, I took my family each season to play for the inmates of Melun, one of France's high security prisons. The audience was always most attentive. Recently, while we were on holiday in Corsica, a man came up to us to say how much our performances had meant to him which he had heard twenty years before when he had been a prisoner at Melun.

We have played in hospitals, and, on several occasions for peasants, for example in Picardy near our house in Novillers-les-Caillous. I give an annual festival, organized by my friend Patrick Chatelin, in Melle, a small village in Poitou. Of all the music I play for 'unsophisticated' listeners, Bach proves to be the most popular. The vitality of his dances makes a direct contact. Since I face my listeners when I play, I often notice that people like music when they can catch the rhythm. This doesn't mean that it has to be a march, but they have to be able to feel the beat. Ernest Lush, the superb accompanist with whom I played concerts over many years once told me that when listening to string players performing Bach solo suites he was often uneasy, as he couldn't discern the pulse of the music. In an orchestral concert, the conductor's gesture will indicate where the strong beat falls, but in an unaccompanied work by Bach you might try to be too refined, and lose the elemental rhythmic sense.

I've heard many stories about workers for whom you've given impromptu performances – of electricians for whom you played your piece The Great Flag, *of plumbers who came to install a shower being treated to a Prokofiev march . . . Do you remember the time during the Perpignan Festival when you lived on the Mediterranean coast next to a fisherman's house and entertained his family on Bastille Day by giving a little concert in their garden? Apparently it made quite an impact on the villagers, especially when Maud accompanied you in* La Marseillaise.

I do remember that I used to meet the fisherman at dawn when he returned with his catch, though I've forgotten the concert. But after all, the cello is there to be played – and not only in concert halls. People are hungry for good music, and it's my job to provide it for them if I can.

> Paul always enjoys playing at La Coûme, a school near Prades in which students and teachers share an extraordinary sense of communal life. He likes to compare the shape of Bach's music to the majestic outline of the distant Pyrenees. When during a snowstorm the electricity failed, he played sonatas by the flickering candlelight. On one visit he heard that the boy who would have most appreciated the concert – a young cellist – had broken his leg the previous day and was in hospital. 'Don't worry,' said Paul, 'I'll go to Perpignan to play for him.' Sure enough, the next day he appeared with his cello in the boy's hospital room. The young man's bed was wheeled out into the corridor, where Paul gave him a concert – the other patients in the ward and the nurses looking on.

Many years ago I had a most interesting experience in giving a series of recitals in schools throughout Holland. These concerts were called 'Een Uur Muziek' and were organized by Franz Aufrecht. I was fortunate in having the artistic collaboration of Willem Hielkema. Not only is he a fine pianist (with whom I have since played in many countries), but he is specially gifted in communicating ideas about music to children — by means of a few well-chosen words and many gestures. I learned much from him in this respect. Over a period of two months, we gave

about 100 concerts, travelling to every corner of the country. I
know Holland better than most Dutch people do.

*Willem Hielkema told me of an occasion when, substituting for
another pianist, he had to rush to Lübeck to play a recital with you.
'At the end of a long day's travel,' he recalls, 'I finally arrived at
the house in which Paul was staying. As I stepped out of the car I
thought I heard from far away the strains of the Dutch National
Anthem. I could hardly believe my ears, but the sounds came closer
and closer. Then I saw Paul somehow managing to play his cello
while striding up the street. "Am I right?" he cried out upon seeing
me. "Is it your anthem?" He was right, and only he could have
thought of such an original welcome.'*
*It's certainly characteristic of you that you don't always perform
on concert platforms. But when you do play in halls, do you have a
particular favourite?*

Most modern halls are aesthetically satisfying but the acoustics
can leave much to be desired. The builders don't seem to know
the essentials: that there should be a sufficiently high ceiling,
that absorbent materials should not be used on the floor or on
the seats, that wood should be used abundantly, that the hall
should not be too wide or tone will be lost at the side. Many
modern halls are too big. Yet you have to have big halls because
so many people want to attend concerts. It's a problem for which
I see no solution.

For the sheer pleasure of playing, I would single out the
concert hall of the Biblioteca Luís Angel Arango in Bogotá. It's
the most satisfying hall acoustically and, in this case, aesthetically as well. The interior is constructed almost entirely of a
beautiful wood, and is shaped like a fan or shell. The quality of
sound is influenced by the special structure of the ceiling. Above
it there's an empty space, and then another ceiling also made
of wood, thus providing an additional source of resonance. I
played the Debussy Sonata in that hall, and I shall be lucky
if I hear it again as I heard it there with those extraordinary
acoustics. The colours I could find in that setting were wonderful.
After the concert I asked the architect, Rafael Esguerra, who was
in the audience, to take a bow on stage. I recently played there

again with the Tortelier Trio, and Pascal and Pau were able to
share my pleasure.

Since then I've made another happy discovery: the magnificent
Concert Hall of Oslo.

*When speaking of your early years you described several con-
ductors with whom you played. Are there others you would like to
tell us about?*

One whom I admired was Willem Mengelberg. I was indirectly
influenced by him when I was only 15 through my teacher
Gérard Hekking who had been solo cellist in the Concertgebouw
Orchestra under Mengelberg's direction. Hekking had a particularly vital rhythmic sense, and this was also the case with
Mengelberg whose tempos for Beethoven symphonies I found
more convincing than those of Toscanini.

I greatly respected Dimitri Mitropoulos. In the days when
conductors of major American orchestras lived in luxury and
behaved like princes, Mitropoulos's attitude was most refreshing. He was concerned with social justice and equality, and acted
according to his convictions. When he was appointed director of
the New York Philharmonic, he continued to live very simply. I
liked him for this trait and for his natural sense of generosity. He
was always ready to lend a helping hand to his colleagues. He
always made you feel you were his equal.

Mitropoulos caused quite a stir in Paris about 1935 when he
introduced the custom of playing the piano and conducting at
the same time. I first met him when he came as guest conductor
to Monte Carlo. Judging by appearances, it would be hard to
guess that he was a musician. In Latin countries in particular,
an artist is supposed to have an excess of flowing hair. But
compared to Mitropoulos, Pablo Casals could have been an
advertisement for shampoo. Mitropoulos's face had an ascetic,
mystical quality – a modern-day Diogenes. But there was no
doubting his greatness as a musician when he stood before an
orchestra. Like Nadia Boulanger, he conducted without a baton,
but while Nadia's hands always remained dignified, his rather
resembled those of Muhammed Ali fighting for the world title.
Once, in Monte Carlo, while conducting a particularly intense

passage, he dug his nails so far into the palms of his hands that blood could be seen dripping on to the stage.

Like Toscanini and Karajan, Mitropoulos had an amazing memory. I attended several of his rehearsals. He never used a score, having memorized not only the notes but the rehearsal letters as well.

Have you ever performed with Karajan?

I played *Don Quixote* with him in Vienna in about 1950. The performance of the Vienna Philharmonic under his direction was superb. I felt that he perhaps allowed the melody of the wonderful lyric variation in F♯ just a little too much time to sing – just a bit too slow – but it was extraordinarily fine all the same. I remember with delight his performance of Schumann's Fourth Symphony; it was the most beautiful I have ever heard. And his performance of Ravel's *Boléro* was unique. He gave value to every note in the accompaniment; yet the piece had at the same time a great dimension, an overall sweep.

I don't believe that any conductor – especially in music from Beethoven's time to the present – has achieved a greater sense of architectural line and emotional concentration. I've experienced this time and again over thirty years, hearing Karajan conduct virtually all the main symphonic and operatic repertoire. To have been present at his performances of Tristan *or* Parsifal *– with every note in expressive continuity from first to last – was an overwhelming experience.*

I wish I had attended those performances.

Playing the Dvořák Concerto with George Szell was another memorable moment for me. To this day one of my favourite recordings is that made by Casals of this concerto under Szell's direction, in Prague in 1937.

I somehow always associate Szell's appearance – serious and intellectual – with that of Stravinsky. I first met Szell at Mrs. Leventritt's apartment in New York. During the dinner party the lady seated next to me whispered in my ear, 'Just look at him – he's anything but sexy.' This remark embarrassed me terribly because the object of her remark was sitting just opposite us, and I was shocked that a lady could use such words when speaking to a man she had only just met for the first time. In those years – it was about 1955 – the word 'sex' still had impact.

Centuries of Christian morality had made it an emotive word
and one could not use it without provoking a reaction. So much
has been said and written about sex since then, that now the
word makes no impression at all. I was struck not only by Szell's
remarkable control over the orchestra, but by his ability to read
at the piano the most difficult scores without making mistakes.
He played my first Cello Concerto at sight as if he had studied it
for years. During the rehearsal of the Dvořák, in the middle of
the second theme of the first movement:

he asked with great courtesy, 'Do you play a French or a German
triplet?' I asked him what he meant. 'The German is played
evenly, while the French is played with rubato.' 'My own way,' I
replied, 'is rather Franco-Allemand.'

Sir Adrian Boult was always a pleasure to work with. He was
invariably cordial and charming to me, the epitome of an English
gentleman. And of course he was always musical in whatever he
did. I was very pleased with the recording of the Elgar Concerto
we made together. I also had a fine rapport with Rudolf Kempe;
we never had any problems whatsoever. He was an outstanding
musician and his early death was a great loss to music.

*How did you respond to Beecham, with his inimitable style of
music-making?*

As you know, when I first performed with him I was making
my English début. I was, as we say in French, *dans mes petits
souliers* – in my little shoes. I was so preoccupied with my own
performance that it was difficult for me to give attention to the
orchestra. So I couldn't appreciate Beecham as I would today. I
can only say that he had great vitality and spirit. I know of
course that he was very witty and most elegant. However, I
cannot judge his emotional side.

*The wit and elegance were a part of his personality he revealed
to the public; his warmth – and an intense warmth it was – went*

directly into his interpretations. Whether conducting Mozart, Schubert, or Delius, the music had a special radiance. Beecham was one of the rare conductors who had the courage and imagination to shape the phrase. The music sang in arcs – never in straight lines. Not only did it sing, it danced. Even on those occasions when Beecham took a slower tempo than anyone else – and he did so with relish – he maintained an irresistible rhythmic lilt.

Such qualities are found rarely nowadays. They're the sort of qualities one also heard in the interpretations of Casals, Kreisler, Enesco, Schnabel and Edwin Fischer.

Another favourite of mine was Barbirolli. He also had that kind of rare gift for interpretation.

I surely agree. I first heard him when he was director of the New York Philharmonic in the late 1930s. However, I had only one occasion to work with him – when I played the Dvořák Concerto with the Hallé Orchestra. Unfortunately, Barbirolli was already ill at the time; all the same his performance was remarkable.

Piatigorsky told me that, of all the conductors he had played with as a soloist, the one who provided the best accompaniment was Barbirolli.

Barbirolli – like Kempe and Sir Malcolm Sargent – had the flexibility to follow. Not every conductor of strong personality has that ability. Indeed, conductors who have strong personalities are not always ideal accompanists. A conductor must be ready to accept and support an interpretation which may differ from his own.

There are two types of difficult conductors; one will be inflexible because of his strong artistic convictions; the other will be inflexible because he's not happy that his orchestra should see that a soloist may have stronger artistic convictions than he.

What do you do when you don't see eye-to-eye with the conductor?

I always try to be pleasant and reasonable. But when all else fails, I have to put my foot down. This can result in a rather painful situation.

I was present at one rehearsal when the conductor took a tempo in the Dvořák Concerto that was entirely different from yours; when you objected, he proceeded to argue the point. You then simply turned to the orchestra members, sang them your tempo, and conducted them yourself. I agree: it was a painful situation. I hope the conductor's ego has recovered by now.

Luckily, such confrontations are the exception. One advantage of my having played in orchestras for eighteen years, and being a conductor myself, is that I understand the needs of the orchestra and always try to make it easy for the conductor to accompany me. That's not to say that I would give in on important questions of tempo or nuance, but I know what sort of freedom I can take without getting into trouble. It also helps that I have a good rhythmic sense. We can normally prepare a concerto in a single rehearsal, and not a very long one at that. And I think that conductors are, in general, happy with me.

You yourself conduct fairly frequently. At what point in your career did you begin?

I had my first opportunity in my early twenties when I conducted an orchestra in the casino of Biarritz. However, it's mostly been since 1956 – when I conducted my *Israel* Symphony with the Israel Philharmonic – that I've often been invited to perform as a guest conductor.

How do you feel about conducting?

I find it stimulating and rewarding to dig into the big repertoire – a Beethoven or a Tchaikovsky symphony; it opens many windows on interpretation. However, I'm not 'hooked' on conducting as are some instrumentalists who take it up. Studying scores requires an enormous amount of time, and if I steal time away from my cello I prefer to give it over to composing. I must say that though I appreciate the rich palette of orchestral sound, I am not fascinated by colour *per se*. I approach this question from what I believe to have been Bach's point of view. If we take Bach's music – although he was not insensitive to instrumental colour as we find, for instance, in the Brandenburg Concertos – his chief concern was for the intrinsic expressive quality of the

musical substance; the melodic line, the harmony, the counterpoint are more important than the instrumentation.

One handicap the guest conductor often faces is a lack of
adequate rehearsal time. Under such circumstances I find it
difficult when conducting to attain a comparable depth of interpretation to what I might achieve when playing the cello. When
you do something by yourself, you can do just exactly what you
want.

*During recent years the televising of your master classes has made
it possible for a vast public to become acquainted not only with your
playing, but with your teaching. These classes have created a new
and wide appreciation for the cello and its literature, and have given
many people who have never attended a concert the feeling that
classical music is something they can enjoy. When we were together
in Paris and in London it was interesting to see how many people
would come up to you on the street or in a restaurant to express their
gratitude.*

It's true that in some places I'm well known. But in others I'm
not known at all, and then the mysterious cello case strapped to
my shoulder is viewed with considerable suspicion. When I *am*
recognized it's gratifying of course, not only for myself, but for
the sake of classical music which, as you say, is not very much in
the limelight.

One day Geoffrey Pratley and Paul were seated in the restaurant car of an
English train. They noticed an elderly gentleman looking at them from
time to time. Finally, he leaned over to Geoffrey and asked in a whisper,
'Is that . . . is that . . . Pierre Fournier?' 'No,' Geoffrey whispered back,
'it's Paul Tortelier.' 'Yes, that's right,' said the gentleman; 'I'd know him
anywhere. He's my wife's hero.'

XX

The Indirect Traveller

Given all the travel difficulties which can beset an artist who tours as much as you, have there been a number of times when you've had to cancel concerts?

I hate to cancel concerts and have hardly ever done so. Some musicians are well-known for cancelling frequently. It becomes part of their publicity. It's said that the manager of one such artist let it be known that 'Mr X will be available in the second half of February for a series of cancellations'. On the other hand you have an artist like Segovia who is legendary for never missing engagements. If this has almost been my case as well, I must thank my good health and sometimes incredible luck. 'Always try,' Lord Zetland once told me; 'Keep on moving,' Mrs Tillett advised when I had suffered a slipped disc. Despite all odds – external and internal – I seem to have the ability to arrive at my destination, though sometimes in an indirect way.

On one occasion I was scheduled to fly to Berlin so as to arrive the day before a concert I was to give with the Berlin Philharmonic. If there had been a direct flight from Paris this would have posed no problem. Unfortunately, for some reason, I had to make a triangular flight: Paris–London–Berlin. Just after my plane landed at Gatwick, the airport closed. An impenetrable fog had settled over London, the worst I have seen in thirty-five years. A cardinal rule: when there's a delay, don't lose time by waiting, but switch immediately to an alternative form of transport. After queuing for half an hour at the telephone box, I finally reached Mrs. Tillett, who assured me that by the time I arrived at her office she would have found another way for me to reach Berlin within twenty-four hours. Sure enough, when I emerged from the Oxford Circus tube station into a world of grey, and groped my way – luggage in hand, instrument on shoulder – to 24 Wigmore Street, good news awaited me. I would be able to reach Berlin the next afternoon, and the orchestra had agreed to rehearse the Schumann Concerto just before the concert. All I had to do was: walk back to Oxford Circus; take the tube to Liverpool Street Station; take the train to Harwich; take the boat to Hook of Holland; and then take the train to Berlin. This journey progressed well, and once I was in the compartment of the train to Berlin the next morning, I began to feel very confident. Alas, this was no ordinary train; it had two special talents: crawling and stopping. And when we came to the East German border, military police paid lengthy visits to each carriage. Evening was coming on, and I began to wonder if I had not been travelling two days and one night with my cello for no other purpose than to provide a *raison d'être* for European transport. Still, Lord Zetland's exhortation rang in my ears. So I went into the lavatory and changed into my evening dress, as if everything was bound to turn out right. At last we came to Potsdam; Berlin could not be far away. And finally, at 8.0 p.m. exactly we arrived at the station. The train was still in motion when I leapt out and ran for a taxi. No queue, thank God! Ten minutes later we were at the concert hall. I shot through the artists' entrance and met Wolfgang Schneiderhan who, violin in hand, was about to go on stage to perform the Beethoven Violin Concerto as a substitute for my Schumann. While the conductor and I hurriedly looked over some points in the score, Mrs Adler, my German impresario, arrived from the railway station where, owing to my escape, she had failed to find me. I shall never forget her expression when she saw me in the artists' room. She looked up at the ceiling to see through which hole I had fallen.

How did the performance go?

Splendidly!
During the course of my career I have taken wrong trains, wrong buses, a wrong suitcase, and even a wrong ship.

Not an ocean liner, I hope.

Luckily it was a somewhat shorter trip: a voyage from England to the Continent. We were already in the middle of the Channel and I was sunning myself on the upper deck, when I was asked for my ticket. The steward looked at me in alarm: 'But we are not sailing to Calais!' 'Where *are* we sailing to?' I asked. Helsinki or Istanbul flashed through my mind. So, when the man replied 'Ostend' I could have embraced him. The moral: when approaching two ships berthed side by side, take care to follow the right queue. In Ostend I had just enough money to take a taxi to the railway station, buy my ticket, telephone Maud and explain how I happened to be in Belgium.

Taking the wrong bus is what every foreigner has experienced in London, and I do it myself regularly. But it's even easier to take the wrong tube, especially when travelling from Camden Town to Parsons Green. There's nothing original in spending half an afternoon trying to find one's way through the labyrinth of London's Underground, with a multitude of trains coming out of the blue and going God knows where. The only originality lies in moving amid the anonymous crowds with a cello in hand instead of the *Daily Mirror*.

Speaking of originality, I did considerably better in Morocco some years ago when I took a wrong train from Rabat at 7.0 a.m. one morning. I had to get off at the next station, Salé, some miles away, and walk all the way back. This took me through an Arab medina. I happened to be wearing the full evening dress in which I had given my recital the night before. The local inhabitants found my appearance as puzzling as if they had seen Muhammed riding a cello instead of a donkey.

Nowadays, I travel mostly by plane.

You're almost sure to be on the right line; one goes through so many controls before departure.

Indeed! There are, however, two unpleasant moments for me when I am in an airport. The first is *before* flying when I check in, because of this maddening cello I carry with me; the second is *after* flying when I am waiting at the 'Baggage Claim'. I don't know why, but my suitcase always seems to be the last to appear, and sometimes it doesn't turn up at all. Now, it so happened that once, upon arrival in London, my suitcase was the first to arrive on the conveyor belt. I couldn't believe my eyes. As a matter of fact, I shouldn't have believed them, because the suitcase I picked up was not mine. It belonged to a lady – a discovery I made that night, only half an hour before my concert in Leeds. I had to play the Elgar Concerto in my yellow suit (it was either that or in a décolleté evening gown), while Sir Adrian, in his elegant concert apparel, seemed more distinguished than ever. The funny thing is that he was more embarrassed for me than I was for myself. Ever since then, each time I've performed with him he has asked me anxiously after the rehearsal, 'How must I dress tonight – in yellow?'

A brief tale: The Wrong Underwear.
'Will this do for Canada?' As Major and Mrs Kirkwood turned towards the guest-room door in their London flat, there stood Paul Tortelier fitted from head to toe in white woollen underwear. 'They call them "long johns",' Paul continued. 'I must wear them because it will be very cold in Canada.' His hosts begged him to remove them for the flight, at least; otherwise he would feel much too hot. But he refused to consider such a thing and departed for the West London Air Terminal with the long johns resolutely under his suit, proud of his secret status as man in sheep's clothing. Yet, as the saying goes, there is no armour against fate. Upon arrival at the air terminal he was asked for his vaccination certificate. Consternation. He had none. It was arranged for a doctor to stand by for his arrival at Heathrow. As Paul entered the coach, Mrs Kirkwood called after him, 'Don't forget to have the vaccination done on your leg; an inflamed arm could cause problems when you play!' Later Paul telephoned from the airport: 'Yes, it was done; they did it on my left leg. But it was an embarrassing moment, because I had to take off my whole sheep's suit.' Incidentally, although the plane headed for Canada, owing to poor landing conditions in Montreal, it was diverted to New York.

It's indispensable for the truly absent-minded traveller at least once in his life to follow the wrong funeral cortège. A distant relative of advanced age had died. Maud and I were supposed to meet a green car on the outskirts of Paris and continue on to the church where the service was to be held, a distance of eighty kilometres. Arriving at the meeting place, we saw the green car and the hearse and began to follow them. After about fifty kilometres, the green car suddenly disappeared from view – had it turned down a side road? – and only the hearse remained.

We pulled alongside it, expecting to see our relatives, but were amazed to discover it filled with women dressed in black and wearing the traditional Breton *coiffe*. We took out a map, cut across country lanes, and finally arrived at the right funeral halfway through the service. My sister was furious that we had come late; however, when I explained why, she couldn't help but giggle. Word of our misadventure was quickly passed around the church, creating an effect not entirely in keeping with the solemnity of the occasion.

You give a great many concerts each year in England. Have you had any difficult travel experiences there?

Normally it's been a blissfully unproblematic affair. I owe this to the English qualities of courtesy and efficiency, and I seem to have a mystical arrangement whereby I remain untouched by strikes. However, on one occasion, Raphael Sommer, my family and I were driving along the M1 when our hired minibus broke down. Our combined mechanical efforts – meagre at the best of times – failed to improve matters. As I had to fly that afternoon to another concert engagement, I had no choice but to leave the others in charge of the minibus, and to hitchhike along the motorway. It's actually against the law, but I got away with it.

Perhaps the driver who picked you up took pity on the cello.

Ah, the cello . . . my ever-demanding companion! Can you believe that in sixty years I have only forgotten it once? (True, on one occasion I took Maud's cello rather than my own – but I don't count that.) If an exception proves the rule, this represents a veritable triumph of mind over matter.

What was the exception?

I was once driving to Cambridge with Geoffrey Pratley for a recital, and was deeply engrossed in a copy of Shostakovich's First Cello Concerto when, almost halfway there, it suddenly dawned on us that there was a large empty space on the back seat of the car where the cello ought to have been. We tore back to Geoffrey's house, snatched up the damned instrument and raced up to Cambridge, arriving with only minutes to spare.

All the factors seemed to be working out ideally one day when

I arrived at Orly Airport ready to fly to Vienna. I had the right instrument, the right ticket for the right flight, and it was the right date – I had checked that. Nothing could go wrong. Nothing, that is, except for the fact – as I realized just before boarding – that it was the wrong *year*. I had consulted the wrong diary; I was one year too soon. It's clear that modern concert scheduling, with its planning of engagements two or even three years in advance, poses certain problems for me.

XXI

Teaching

Your mention of Sherlock Holmes inspired me to do a bit of detective work. I've found out the secret nicknames the cello students at the Paris Conservatoire in the 1950s gave their teachers. I must say that these nicknames did not always maintain a strictly reverential tone. You were let off comparatively lightly with 'Paul, le fou'.

It suits me well. In any case, 'Paul the mad' is more flattering than 'Paul the sane.'

When did you begin to teach?

I gave my first lesson when I was 14. Feuillard wanted me to be able to substitute for him when he was ill, but before entrusting me with this responsibility on a regular basis he asked me to give a lesson in his presence to one of his young students. As it was the first time I had taught, Feuillard was a little apprehensive as to what might happen. He was, indeed, surprised to see how severe I was. Perhaps I wanted to show off a little. The way I insisted upon the boy obtaining the result I had in mind might have proved discouraging.

Did the boy give up the cello?

I don't recall, but it wouldn't have been a bad idea. In fact it can be a kindness to discourage an ungifted student before he's gone too far, though one must of course break the news gently. When I taught privately in Paris, parents would bring their children to me for auditions, their hopes often exceeding their offspring's potential. In such cases I would bid them *au revoir* with the words, *'Votre enfant n'est pas sans manquer de talent'* – 'Your child is not without a lack of talent'. They would be some distance away before they grasped the full implication.

I have had the pleasure of speaking with several of your former students, many of whom are now well-known performers. They all agree that studying with you was the decisive event in their artistic development. But they concur that it wasn't easy. Hard work was demanded: 'Better one good bar than two bad bars!' You never counted the hours and were relentless in pursuing your ideal. Total dedication to the musical goals was expected. Those who succeeded in attaining those goals felt inspired and liberated. On the other hand, those who could not attain them quickly enough felt that they were placed under a great strain.

Knowing my own character, I can well believe it.

'Fantasy with order' was Casals' way of expressing a well-balanced rubato. And Paul was trying in every way to convey this concept to a student. Alas, the young man could not grasp the fact that his lack of rhythmic discipline was quite different from the subtle rubato of a mature artist. 'What you are playing is not rubato,' Paul remonstrated; 'It's disorder.' 'What do you mean by disorder?' persisted the student. A high pile of music lay neatly stacked on the piano. In a moment it was lifted into the air and dashed to the floor. Paul pointed to the mass of paper now scattered in every direction: *'Voilà, le désordre!'*

Of course, the main thing which a student must decide if he comes to study with me is, 'Do I want to learn from Monsieur Tortelier, or do I not?' If he wishes to persist in his old ways, there's no reason for him to study with me in the first place.

If a student comes to you who is already advanced, but whose technique differs in certain respects from yours, do you ask him to alter his approach if he's comfortable in his own way?

He must make a choice. If he keeps his technique he keeps his style. I cannot help a student develop without conveying my style, and my style is at one with my technique. If a student comes to me – not just to play a Popper *étude* or *The Flight of the Bumblebee* more quickly – but for the sake of colour, articulation, variety in vibrato, I must help him develop his techinque so that he will have all these skills at his command.

During a master class, when you know you won't be able to supervise a student's work afterwards, will you overlook a differing technique in order to convey your interpretative ideas?

All I can do is to speak of the character of the music as I see it, and then try to explain the way to attain the best result with the minimum of work in the minimum of time. I think one advantage of youth is the ability to remain open to development; indeed that is how one stays young.

> One began to wonder why the young German cellist had bothered to come all the way to Portugal to attend a Tortelier master class if he was unwilling to accept the ideas Paul offered. The more creative Paul's teaching became, the less receptive seemed the student. The situation was becoming tense; no one could predict the outcome, least of all that the cello lesson was about to become an Olympic training session. Suddenly Paul leapt up from his chair and began doing a series of callisthenics – push-ups, knee-bends – springing about as if he were half a century younger than his 67 years. He paused without being in the least out of breath, and told his bewildered student, 'I stay young, while you are already growing old. I am young not only because I do gymnastics, but because I accept new ideas. You are already old because your mind is closed to new ideas.'

What are some of the basic principles of your technique which you convey in your teaching?

This of course depends to a great extent upon the student. I must see what his strengths and weaknesses are. However, I would say that, in general, I put much emphasis on the position of the left hand. Cellists generally tend to place the left hand at a slight diagonal slant. I find this to be disadvantageous in that it draws the little finger away from the strings. In contrast, my hand is placed at right angles to the strings, just as a pianist's hands are at right angles to the keyboard. This makes it easier for the little finger to cross over to the lower strings, and – of special importance – allows the use of the little finger in the upper register. (When playing on the A string in the thumb positions I keep my thumb down on only one string rather than two, thereby facilitating the perpendicular hand placement.)

This hand position also allows me to vibrate in the middle of the flesh of the finger rather than on the side, and the vibrato (of course always variable) therefore becomes richer and freer. To help my students understand my technique, I ask them to stand at the end of a piano keyboard so that they will have a side view of my hand position as I play. We then apply the same principle to the placement of the left hand on the cello strings.

Add to this the fact that when playing in the upper register I sometimes keep my thumb *under* the fingerboard, and you can understand how surprised some of my colleagues are when they see me doing such unorthodox things. Some are even scandalized. A prominent Swiss cellist who attended a concert I gave in Basel commented, 'Tortelier plays in an illegal way.'

I once had a student who, coming to me with a left hand position that I didn't care for, was able to adopt my position completely from one lesson to another. It was quite an accomplishment, but she was a vivacious and determined young lady. This was the excellent English cellist Jennifer Ward Clarke.

That year the cellists at the Paris Conservatoire were given an examination piece called *Concerto Ibérique* by Bousquet. It was very poor music indeed, a sort of pseudo-Spanish confection. Jenny wondered why she was obliged by the Paris Conservatoire to prepare such a third-rate work when there's so much fine music to be had. I agreed with her, lamenting that we had to waste weeks on this composition. Well, she had a lot of spunk, and went with me to the director to make a complaint. She told him in no uncertain terms what she thought of this piece. One doesn't do that sort of thing at the Paris Conservatoire, an institution run along Napoleonic lines. The director was quite taken aback and insisted that it was not for her to criticize the choice of music. She replied in her charming English accent, *'Mais Monsieur, ce n'est pas de la musique.'*

In fact, one of my main reasons for resigning from the Paris Conservatoire, after twelve years of teaching there, was the inferior music repeatedly assigned for examinations. I recalled

Bach's dictum about Time, and decided that I could use my time more profitably elsewhere.

My next six years were spent in Essen where – between concert tours – I taught at the Folkwang Hochschule für Musik. I certainly didn't go to live in Essen as an epicure, nor did I go for the climate; but the teaching was a rewarding experience.

I settled in Nice in 1975 and taught chamber music at the Conservatoire there until 1979. Since then I have given up teaching in institutions except for the occasional master class. In my book *How I Play, How I Teach* I have set down my technical principles in some detail. I hope it will make up, in part, for my near-retirement from active teaching. While I think most of the concepts described in that book have general validity, I must stress that there are no absolute rules. Certain aspects of cello technique will depend on how you are built physically. For example, the size of the hand may influence such matters as extensions. My wife's hands are smaller than mine; when there's a large interval she makes her finger leap to the note rather than stretch towards it, and in this way retains her suppleness. Due to the greater size of my hand, I make both extensions and leaps. The bow arm, too, is influenced by such considerations. If a string player has short arms he may be more inclined – like Milstein – to direct most of the bow's movements from the whole arm.

You often describe the bow as the continuation of the arm.

Ah yes, that's the ideal: when you feel no separation between the arm and bow. The bow is a magnificent tool. Many people don't realize what training is needed to manipulate it. It's no easy matter, for instance, for string players to attain the rhythmic exactitude of the woodwind. The action of the tongue is direct and rhythmical, as it is when we speak; but the production of rhythm by means of a wooden bow strung with horsehair can be clumsy and delayed. I had an advantage in being brought up among woodwind players; I was always trying to imitate their sounds.

I could speak at length of the different functions of the left and right hands, but this is not the place for a detailed explanation.

I can, however, refer the reader to an ideal representation of a cellist's hands as they appear in a great work of art. I am thinking of *The Return of the Prodigal Son* by Rembrandt, which is in the Hermitage Museum in Leningrad. In this painting the son has turned his back to us as he kneels before his father to ask for forgiveness. We see the old man's gentle, compassionate face as he places his hands on his son's back to give his blessing. Those hands of the father are exactly like a cellist's hands because they are not identical. The left hand is a little larger and more tense, while the right hand has a calm, almost spiritual quality. Now, although I am right-handed, my left hand is in fact larger; it is in immediate contact with the strings, and is more tense and energetic because of the physical activity required for articulation and vibrato. My right hand is less developed physically because the fingers have less individual effort to make; its movements come primarily from the ensemble of the arm. How Rembrandt came to paint these hands in this way I cannot say. But there they are, just as if a cellist had modelled for them. One hand is that of a workman, while the other is that of a priest.

If I may return to the subject of your students, didn't you at one time teach Jacqueline du Pré?

Oh yes. She stands out not only for the radiance of her playing, but for her personal radiance as well. I first met her at the Dartington Summer School in England where I gave a series of master classes. I've never met a more ardent young musician. One night, after a recital I had given, she asked me if I would help her with Bloch's *Schelomo*. 'Why not?' I replied, 'but when?' 'Why not now?' she replied. As there had been a dinner after the concert, it was already past midnight. I protested that people were sleeping. 'We needn't worry about that,' she persisted; 'there's a room where we can work without disturbing anyone.' I thought it strange to give a lesson in the dead of night, but when she begged you like that you couldn't resist. She began to play and I began to explain, and in our enthusiasm the lesson lasted a good two hours, so that at 2.30 we were still playing and discussing *Schelomo*. When I returned to my home in Paris,

Maud told me that one night she had dreamt that I had been unfaithful to her. This was most extraordinary, because the dream had occurred on the very night I had given Jacqueline her lesson.

Jacqueline later spent some months studying with me at the Paris Conservatoire. I think it was very brave of her to do this because she was already a brilliant instrumentalist. I remember my artistic association with her with the greatest pleasure. She was an outstanding cellist, and, as everyone knows, she is a remarkable and courageous human being.

The year Jacqueline du Pré studied with me in Paris I was exceptionally lucky in having another extremely gifted student, Arto Noras.* Then 20 years old, Arto was already well known in Finland. He had fine musical intuition and a highly developed technique – but a small tone. Recently, over lunch at the Finnish ambassador's residence in Paris, he recalled his early lessons with me. I had found his bow hand stiff, the fingers being held artificially high. He said that in order to correct this ingrained habit, he had had to work eight hours a day for several months. I was terribly moved by this revelation. I knew that he had worked hard, but I never realized how much. Once you've found your position on the instrument, it's difficult to start all over again; you're like a beginner and have no control at all. What faith he must have had to make this enormous effort! By the time he left the Paris Conservatoire he not only had a marvellous big tone, but had developed into an artist of the highest calibre.

Arto Noras speaks of your teaching as representing a complete 'school' of cello technique, in the sense of the schools that have existed in violin pedagogy over the last two centuries, but which have been largely absent from the cello tradition. You specify everything; you keep no secrets to yourself.

Not since I was 16 and kept my Elgar Concerto fingering a secret.

*Among my many gifted students have been Daniel Domb, Renaud Fontanarosa, Walter Goedde, Rainer Hochmuth, Akiko Kanamaru, Aage Kvalbein, Aleth Lamasse, and Frieder Lenz.

To quote Noras, 'Most players have no more than a vague, general image of the sound they want, but Tortelier has a precise image. He seeks the purest sonority. He is not the servant of his hands; his hands are the servant of the music. His technique is advanced to the point where he avoids all mannerisms. He doesn't have peculiarities of technique which impose the "trademark" of the performer upon his playing. His hands can express each piece of music in its own right. We hear Beethoven or Debussy – and not Tortelier as such.'

Mannerisms resulting from technical limitations are certainly negative. However, when an interpreter can transcend such problems through a highly developed technique, he will still reveal something of his own personality in his performance, though of course, in a far more positive and creative way. It's a complex question. You must seek the character of the music, but your performance also carries your own character. One is both objective and subjective at the same time. We want to express as best we can what we think Beethoven meant in this Allegro or Adagio – but it will always be felt through our own temperament. That's the limitation and yet the value of our humanity. We are not machines. Everyone has something of his own sense of style, and, as I've said, the technique is at one with style. It's the same as physical and mental health which are intimately interrelated. Technique and interpretation react upon one another.

I have noticed that musicians will often resist a change in interpretation – even if they agree to the validity of the change – when it upsets their habitual technical approach. But in many cases the problem is not in the technique as such; the problem is that their musical conviction isn't strong enough; they don't will themselves to do it.

So you think that initially it's the musical conception that directs the technique.

I think that the musical conception moulds a real technique, because if you don't have the conception, you don't try to shape the music meaningfully.

All the same, I have noticed that when some of my students succeed in correcting poor technical habits, there is a change in their interpretation. They become aware that their interpretation has been mediocre as well as their technique. Sometimes you really don't know in which sphere the fault has originated.

What sort of technical material do you give your students?

In *How I Play, How I Teach* I have written numerous exercises which none the less have some musicality in them. Like Feuillard, I like to avoid the mental boredom of nothing but technique for technique's sake.

I also advise my students to think about their music when away from the cello. When you're on a bus or in the tube you can go through a Bach suite in your mind, and it will get into your hand without your even practising. I have sometimes asked a student to memorize a work before beginning to play it.

Do you emphasize scale practice?

Oh yes. I like to improve on Shakespeare: if music be the food of love, scales be the food of music! I begin my own practising with scales, playing them slowly, but not so slowly as to become static. I use very little vibrato, listening carefully for intonation. Poor intonation is Public Enemy No. 1 for us!

> The lesson in intonation was becoming more than she had bargained for. The young lady had already played the opening bars of Haydn's D major Concerto out of tune three times, and her professor was visibly approaching boiling point. The same mistake made for the fourth time proved fatal. He snatched up the nearest object and smashed it across his knee. Held aloft, one half in each hand, the two portions were being shaken furiously in the air. A few moments later Paul became aware of his students staring at his hands. He too looked to see what they contained, and discovered the remnants of what had once been Arto Noras's bow. Paul turned imperiously to the young lady now cowering behind her cello, and said, 'A bow can always be replaced – but the notes you have played out of tune can never be brought back again.' The bow was replaced, and handsomely too. This story teaches many things: play in tune at all times; watch out for your bow; look before you break; and finally, always rise to the occasion.

It is also useful to practise with the left hand alone for the sake of articulation.

One of your friends told me that when you stayed at his house he saw the light on in your room at 4.0 a.m., and heard the faint plucking of left-hand pizzicato.

. . . an excellent method for developing the technique without becoming an unwelcome guest.

In the light of your own experience, how much practising do you advise?

When I was young I practised a great deal. I would normally do two hours of scales, arpeggios and exercises before having the pleasure of working on a concerto. Of course, the quality of practice is more important than the quantity. Four hours were usually enough, though I sometimes did five or six. I did eight hours at the time I was preparing for my first recording, but that was exceptional. During periods when I've been busy composing, my time for the cello has been drastically reduced. None the less I always have to be ready to perform at my best. Paradoxically, having a limited time at my disposal has contributed to the development of my technique. I had to be sure of my technical principles, and sharpen the effectiveness of my exercises.

As you told me once, 'The proof of a good technique is that you don't have to practise long and that you can play when you become old.'

C'est ça. Think of Casals, who played until he was 96.

While we are on the subject of musical education, it seems an appropriate moment to discuss a special contribution you have made in this field, namely the system of solfège *which you have invented. Let me first state that one of my pet dislikes is the traditional French* solfège *which is an* idée fixe *in the country of its origin. Obviously the system of naming every note – do, ré, mi, fa, sol, la, si – has a value in training the ear and the eye. Yet at the same time it can have a negative influence in that it runs counter to a natural way of singing a melody. Take, for example, the opening theme of Mozart's G minor Symphony. When you recite a syllable to each note, it takes a real effort not to cut the melody to fragments.*

*After all, this is a theme which flows in a lyrical line. The quavers
are slurred, not articulated individually. Furthermore, the Eb and Bb
have a dark colour in the minor key. In fact, a sensitive string player
will subtly alter the intonation of the Eb, drawing it a little closer to
the D, to emphasize this feeling of minor. The bright vowel sound mi
is therefore inappropriate.*

While I believe your comments are entirely valid, I would like
to mention some positive aspects of *solfège*. From the technical
point of view, I think it is helpful to do exercises giving names to
the notes in the same way as we do exercises to strengthen the
articulation of the fingers – exercises which we don't actually use
when we play. It's good to know that Paul is not Peter – that *ré* is
not *fa*. I have noticed that musicians who have had this training
are particularly astute in recognizing intervals. It also has the
advantage of getting the student to sing – which is better than
not singing at all. On the other hand, if singing were exclusively
this, it would indeed be something dry and mechanical. So,
on the expressive side I agree with your criticism. Hindemith
voiced a similar view to me some years ago, and this led me to
see if some amelioration of the French system might be possible.
I therefore invented a *solfège* of my own which has been published in France under the title *Solmisation contemporaine*. It
works as follows: unaltered notes (white notes on the piano)
carry the vocal sound 'ah'. Starting with C, you would have *da,
ra, ma, fa, sal* (alternatively *tal*), *la, sa*. Each flattened note has a
darker vowel sound: 'oh' – *do, ro,* etc., while each sharpened
note has a brighter vowel sound: 'eh' – *dé, ré,* etc.*

The chief advantage of this method is that the intervals have a
colour more suitable to their harmonic tendency. In the Mozart
phrase you mention, a dark timbre will be preserved:

*Double sharps sound: 'ee' – *di, ri,* etc. Double flats sound: 'oo' – *dou,
rou,* etc.

mo ra ra

A further advantage is that every note has its individual name. Take, for instance, the following notes which, in the traditional system, would all be referred to as *ré*:

Although my *Solmisation contemporaine* has been looked at with interest by certain music teachers, it has not been generally adopted. The traditional *solfège* is too deeply ingrained in the French educational system. While I think my method is a useful step in the right direction, I can't stress often enough that every instrumentalist should also learn to sing expressively, and that no intellectual concept should interfere with his natural feeling for the phrase.

I'm sure we agree on the importance of aural training, harmony and counterpoint in musical education. Would you also recommend the study of the lives, letters and historical background of the composers? You often speak of these things in your teaching.

Obviously they're important. However, youngsters are easily distracted by the vast amount they have to learn. When I was young the emphasis was on my playing the cello. I was led to the lives of the composers through curiosity, and that came about in a natural way.

On the other hand, the average musician upon leaving a conservatory will probably never have read a single letter of any composer; that's an astonishing cultural omission.

Well, that helps confirm the old adage: 'Musicians are stupid, painters are dirty, and architects are wicked.'

Before leaving our discussion of the teacher-student relationship, I would like to mention a most refreshing attitude on your part: your willingness to take advice from others.

But of course one must. I ask people all the time if they have any suggestions to make about my performance. I don't have a monopoly of the recreative process. Some of my students have been very helpful to me in this respect. It's not difficult to be a teacher. The difficulty is to find the right students. Then I make progress.

XXII

Composing

For me, composing is an adventure far greater than any travel. When a blank sheet of music-paper lies on your desk, you have a world of discovery before you. Then everything is possible.

When did you begin to compose?

I began by writing some short pieces in the third year of Jean Gallon's class. Gallon sensed my desire to compose something more substantial but, knowing that I was rather hesitant about it, decided to approach the subject in a roundabout way. One day he said, 'Why don't you try your hand at writing a cello concerto rather that an opera, if that's what you have in mind?' Compose an opera – I had never dreamt of such a thing. A ballet, yes. My *Trois p'tits tours* for cello and piano lend themselves well to a ballet for marionettes.

Well, I took on the challenge by composing a cello concerto, which I performed with l'Orchestre Lamoureux, and eventually with the Radio Orchestra of Hilversum conducted by Erich Leinsdorf. A second cello concerto followed, but I still prefer the first. I was gratified that Gallon was able to attend the first performance of my Concerto for Two Cellos which I performed with Maud and l'Orchestre de la Radiodiffusion Nationale under the direction of André Cluytens. The press spoke kindly of the slow movement as *'une des plus belles pages de la musique moderne française'* and – more important – Gallon paid me some fine compliments, but expressed some reservations about the third

221

movement. These were justified and I have subsequently made a number of revisions in this movement.

I have already spoken of the Suite for Solo Cello I wrote in memory of my father. I have written a Cello Sonata, a Piano Concerto, a Violin Concerto, my *Israel* Symphony and a great number of shorter cello pieces.

One of the most satisfying events of my artistic life was the week-long Tortelier Festival organized in 1977 by Gordon Clark. Concerts were given by the Hallé Orchestra in several English cities. Maud and I performed my Double Concerto and Pau shared performances of my Piano Concerto with Tania Heidsieck. It was a moving experience for me, and I have the impression that it was a great success with the public.

How would you describe the musical idiom in which you compose?

When I began I was certainly influenced by French composers. You will find a French flavour in my Cello Sonata and in my virtuoso pieces such as *Spirale, Elégie, Toccata* and *Trois P'tits Tours*. However, my style has evolved since then. Khachaturyan once asked Maud in what idiom I compose, and she replied with some hesitation, *'Il fait du Hindemith chaud'* – 'he writes warm Hindemith'. This isn't to say that Hindemith's music is cold – that's just the way she put it. Writing in the *Guardian* about the Finale of my *Israel* Symphony, Edward Greenfield said, 'It was intriguing to find that Tortelier as creator writes music such as Hindemith might have composed had he been a Frenchman.' In fact, during the period I wrote the symphony I had been studying Hindemith's music closely. I'm fascinated by his way of manipulating chords, and I consider him a master of counterpoint.

As my composing progressed I became more and more interested in the possibilities of counterpoint. I finally took Stravinsky's advice to study it seriously, taking off a whole sabbatical year for that purpose when I was 57.

Did you do it on your own?

Not entirely. I had the help of Noël Gallon, Jean's brother. When I was younger I had written counterpoint in four voices; now I composed for up to eight voices.

In addition to my own compositions, I have made some harmonizations of the keyboard parts of old Italian cello sonatas – Sammartini, Valentini – and this is not so easy as one might think. Such harmonization is a test for any knowledgeable musician. After all, the composer has left us nothing but the bass line. If our realization of the harmony is too simple, it is dull; if too ornate, it interferes with the solo line. It requires imagination, and yet it must remain within the style of the period.

> Passers-by on the rue de Madrid were surprised one day to find confetti showered upon them from an upper storey of the Conservatoire de Musique. What was the happy occasion? It wasn't the 14th of July. Professor Tortelier had just torn the keyboard part of a certain edition of a Valentini sonata into little pieces and thrown them out of the window. The unstylistic harmonies still burned in his ears and tears welled in his eyes. Editors: remember the words of Jean Gallon! Face powder is not to be applied during mass.

There are still places in my own editions where I am not entirely satisfied.

It's strange that the purists, who complain so much when they hear a baroque sonata played on the piano rather than the harpsichord, will generally not notice a poor realization of the bass. They pay attention to the more superficial question, that of timbre, because they are often not sufficiently educated, musically speaking, to recognize lapses of taste in harmony.

I have also composed a number of cadenzas – for the concertos of C. P. E. Bach, Boccherini, Haydn (C major and D major) and Schumann – and I've transcribed for the cello various violin works, such as Sarasate's *Zapateado*, the piece that Maud heard me play before we met.

And you also wrote an encore to be played after Don Quixote.

Oh yes. That came about in the following way. I recently performed *Don Quixote* in Metz; my friend Bruno Pasquier had been specially invited to play the viola solo part which, as you know, depicts Sancho Panza. After the performance the audience wanted an encore, and I felt it wasn't fair to offer a movement of unaccompanied Bach, leaving my colleague offstage. As we were to perform the work again the following night, I decided to write an encore which could be played by the two of us. I composed it the next morning. It's set to a sad rhythm – a slow boléro – and the melody seems to sigh plaintively. I call it 'Sancho's Tears'.

Is it related melodically to the Strauss work?

Not really, but it has the same character. When we played it that night, not only did the public like it, but musicians from the orchestra told me that it sounded almost as if it had been written by Strauss himself. It would be interesting to know what Strauss would have thought of it. In Cervantes's time, and indeed in Strauss's, one didn't pay too much attention to the servants; the person who mattered most was Don Quixote. Today we give more thought to social equalities, and it's nice to be concerned with what happens to Sancho. My little encore reminds us of Sancho's existence and of his sadness that his master is gone.

Composing is a way of life for me; it's as essential to my musical being as playing the cello. I cannot judge what posterity may think of my works. But I do know that when the time comes that, for one reason or another, I shall not be able to carry on playing the cello, I shall not be depressed or nostalgic, for then at last I'll be able to devote all my time to composing.

I should like to add a word of advice to young composers: keep an eye on your manuscripts. Don't lose one – as I once did in Victoria Station. The entire station staff spent an hour helping me look for it, until it was finally found in the telephone call-box where I had left it. Aren't the English the most helpful people?

Just to be sure, why not try Waterloo Station next time?

Artur Schnabel felt about composing as you do. In fact, when he was 40 he said he would stop playing at 45 and devote all his time to composition; at 45 he made the same plans for 50. In past eras composer and performer were one and the same person. There was a natural synthesis of these two aspects which has now largely disappeared.

This was due in part to the fact that the performers had to make a virtue of necessity. In the seventeenth and eighteenth centuries there was much less music printed than there is today. For the most part the virtuosi played their own music. Think of Corelli, Tartini, Viotti. It was taken as a matter of course that if you were asked to play next Friday, you would bring not only your violin or your cello, but your music as well. Even as recently as the first part of our century, there were some famous virtuoso-composers: Paderewski, Busoni, Rachmaninov, Kreisler. Nowadays the need to produce one's own music no longer exists. This is a pity because many instrumentalists never give themselves a chance to study composition. However, if, for example, the Moscow International Competition were to announce that each competitor must perform a theme and variations of his own composition, then the situation would change immediately; you would have fifty composers. Perhaps you remember hearing my *Danse sur le mode gréco-chinois*. I wrote this because no music exists for the precise requirements of my family, namely, for flute, violin, two cellos and piano. There is of course chamber music which includes the flute – you have Mozart, what better? – but no music for just this combination. Necessity made me compose that piece, as was the case with my Concerto for Two Cellos, which is a musical love affair with my wife.

Now, I'm not saying that each one of the fifty new pieces written for the Moscow competition would be a work of genius, nor do I even propose that the contestants be judged on the merit of their compositions. However, two important goals would be attained: first of all, some instrumentalists might discover an unsuspected talent as composers; secondly, going through the process of composing could only be beneficial to each performer's understanding as an interpreter.

Schnabel would have been in complete agreement. He once wrote, 'Every musician should try to compose, even if he is so disgusted with the results that he destroys every composition immediately after he has written it . . . It is the activity and not the result which is so important.'

Yes, one must try. People think that in order to compose, one has to be a great genius. But you mustn't ask yourself whether you're a man or a god. You are what you are.

Let me give you an example of how a knowledge of composition helps you as an interpreter. Rodin once showed an original Greek sculpture to his friend Paul Gsell, commenting that to all appearances the surface seemed absolutely regular. He then darkened the room, and, laying the statue on its side, ran the light of a little lamp along its edge. And there on the surface could be seen all sorts of indentations which would otherwise have escaped the eye. Now these indentations could be compared to the minute nuances inherent to a musical interpretation, for instance nuances in intonation, and the ability to sense these nuances is dependent upon the interpreter's perception of harmonic structure. Take a fairly simple case: the seventh degree of a scale. As it leads upwards, it has a tendency to be drawn towards the tonic, a tension which should be expressed by a subtle sharpening of pitch. This feeling for the seventh degree helps give character to the key you are in. Once again the English and Americans have found an efficient name for it: 'the leading note' – but the French call it *la note sensible* – the note of sensitivity – and how right it is to describe it in this way! Intonation throughout a piece is intimately related to varying shades of harmonic intensity.

You have laid stress on 'knowledge' of harmony. Don't you think that harmonic perception is at least partly intuitive? I am thinking, for example, of Lotte Lehmann who once confessed to me that she knew nothing of the theory of harmony. Yet she responded with sensitivity to every shade of harmonic inflection in the piano or orchestral part of the work she was singing.

I would agree that harmony is not something purely intellectual. When you have a teacher such as Jean Gallon who, as I've said, helps you not only to understand harmony, but to feel it – then you have an ideal approach.

There is a tendency in the teaching of harmony to focus attention on each chord in isolation. One loses sight of the adventure of harmonic progression. The question is: how does a composer get from place to place, and what unusual events occur during the journey?

To study chords for their own sake, except as elementary exercises, is to see the world in reverse. The effect of every chord depends entirely on its context.

Take Schubert's B♭ major Piano Sonata. In the latter part of the slow movement there is a modulation from C♯minor to an entirely unexpected key. The effect is both startling and radiant; nothing more profoundly beautiful could be imagined – and yet it is no more than a shift to a C major triad.

If we speak of the relativity of keys – of the magical effect Schubert achieves when moving from one key to another – we are dealing with tonality. To me, tonality is a fundamental aspect of music which one cannot sacrifice without suffering an enormous loss. By this I don't mean that music must be strictly tonal. One can resist tonality to a degree, but I don't believe it should be completely ignored. If all twelve notes are treated as equal in colour, it's just as if they were buried away in a cellar without light. The meaningfulness of the different keys resides in their relationships. One could put it in the following way: imagine the key of C major as representing noontime; then, relatively speaking, one could think of C♯ minor as twilight.

It's interesting, by the way, that just as there are twelve notes, there are twelve hours. With major and minor you have twenty-four keys: twenty-four hours. I wonder if Bach thought of that when writing his *Well-Tempered Clavier* in which every Prelude and Fugue has its own mood, its own colour. In China they believe very strongly in the influence of the hours, of the seasons, of the interaction of dark and light. In music it's the same. If you move from major to minor you immediately feel a change of colour and you reflect that in your performance. And if you modulate over many keys, it's as if you go across time. You traverse the daily journey of our planet, and eventually return to your point of repose. You feel the action, you feel the rotation. Otherwise you're just in a neutral world where everything is grey.

During our century – for the first time in musical history – there has been a complete schism with the past. Composers have severed the roots of music which come from antiquity. Schoenberg was the first to want to make the break complete. He feared he could not be sufficiently original without inventing a new system of composition. That is a wrong way of thinking. Every great composer has taken nourishment from the mainstream of his art, and his originality has developed organically. Bach, for instance, learned from Frescobaldi and Vivaldi among others; Mozart from Johann Christian Bach and Haydn.

Verdi was influenced by masters as far back as the Italian Renaissance.

Even Debussy's innovations look back in certain respects to the Renaissance. There is a strong modal influence. In fact, in *Pelléas et Mélisande* the vocal line is almost Gregorian in that the melody seems to come out of the words themselves.

Schoenberg too began in the mainstream. And despite the fact that his early works were a development of Wagner's idiom, some of these, such as Verklärte Nacht, *are not only exceptionally beautiful but bear the special stamp of the composer's personality. I believe that Berg was far more successful in the atonal idiom than his teacher. I've been privileged to hear two first-rate performances of* Wozzeck – *conducted by Kleiber and Abbado – and have found it a tremendously moving experience.*

I agree that *Wozzeck* is a powerful and genuinely felt work. There are indeed many moving moments in it: Marie's lullaby and some of the orchestral interludes. But, for all that, it doesn't bring me the sense of harmoniousness, of enrichment of the soul that I associate with the greatest art, even when – as is sometimes the case with Bach and Beethoven – that art expresses the deepest pain. The music of *Wozzeck* leaves me depressed – and I am not a masochist.

Whatever the merits of atonal music, it is nevertheless expressed through the twelve notes of the scale, and produced by instruments which have moved the heart throughout centuries. But, with some of the electronic sounds propagated today under the guise of music, I fear we are losing touch with our humanity.

What we need today are composers who are musicians and not *noisicians* – composers who aren't impatient to be recognized and who hold their art in such esteem that the music reveals a love of beauty and respect for the ears of their listeners. (Think of the wealth and variety of music given to us by composers living a hundred years ago – from Grieg to Brahms, from Verdi to Bruckner.) What's important is to write something of permanent value whether it's 'modern' or not. To quote Rodin, *'Originalité est un mot vide, un mot de bavard et d'ignorant qui a perdu bien des élèves et des artistes.'* 'Originality is an empty word, a word of the garrulous and the ignorant, which has proved fatal to many students and artists.' When a composer believes that he can produce art that has no roots in the past, it's just as if he were saying that he's the father of God. If the electronic experts indeed believe that they are the founders of all future music, I rather think there is a great future for psychiatrists.

Friends of mine – devotees of electronic music – tell me to keep an open mind. But I don't approach music like a scientific experiment; I respond to it instinctively, and listen to the music I love because it has the miraculous power to connect me immediately with my whole self. When I ask these friends whether the composer of a certain electronic piece would be capable of writing the simplest attractive melody, they say that I'm applying an outmoded criterion to a new art form. But that's one of the criteria which is important to me. Just as my body needs salt, my soul needs melody, and I'm not prepared to let the machines deny it to me.

And the machines cost money. The acoustical research institute IRCAM in France has cost the Government millions. Compare this with what Schubert was able to create on an income that averaged £63 per year.

There's a general modern tendency to think in material terms – as though material installations automatically produce art. Nowadays, whenever I visit a music school, before anyone mentions the curriculum or the nature of the teaching, I am taken to see the various kinds of apparatus. I was recently in Jerusalem and was shown all the gadgets in the Conservatory: an extraordinary collection of electronic equipment which they are extremely proud of, and which was, needless to say, expensive. For me, it's just as if the money had been thrown into the sea. To write music you first need a pencil; then – unless you're Mozart or Schubert – an eraser; and finally, music paper.

You don't even need music *paper, because the old masters lined their own.*

You're right; you just need paper.

XXIII

Education Without Educators

Sometime ago we were looking through Bernard Rudofsky's book Architecture Without Architects *which shows how people in every part of the world have managed to create architecture that is both beautiful and functional without professional help. I believe there is a parallel here with your life, in that despite your lack of formal schooling you are always learning in a real and vital way.*

It's true that my formal education was minimal – I received no more than the poorest worker. But I have an intense curiosity about many things, and, if there's a will to learn, there's a way. I have been helped by my powers of observation. If you are a keen observer and take the time and trouble to try to understand something, you finally develop. My memory, having been trained by music, is good; that helps too.

One sees too often how natural curiosity can atrophy in educational systems which ignore what is of interest and value to the individual. Perhaps even your seemingly boundless curiosity might have been dampened had you been submitted to years of poor institutionalized learning.

I think you're right. There are liabilities in force feeding a young mind too much and too early. I don't want to imply that I am opposed to formal education. I've often regretted not having greater knowledge of a particular subject. But I do think that the education which lasts is the one which is inspired by genuine

231

interest, and genuine interest only occasionally corresponds to what educational authorities think you ought to be taught at a given time. It's not enough to pass an exam or take a degree and then rest on your laurels. The essential thing is to remain eager to learn for the rest of your life.

Your friends have told me stories of the Tortelier-single-mindedness with which you apply yourself to learning something new, whether it be a mathematical principle, the sewing on of a button, or the art of ballet.

> One day while Paul was staying at the flat of his friends, Mr and Mrs Symons, their son, Oliver, assistant ballet master with the Royal Ballet, paid a visit. Paul seized the opportunity to ask Oliver to teach him some basic ballet steps. Lacking tights, he donned pyjamas and slippers, and created a turban for himself out of a scarf. He was put through a variety of strenuous exercises, and groaned as he stretched his 60-year-old muscles to find the equilibrium necessary for each new classical ballet position. But he managed with sufficient skill and determination to merit his teacher's enthusiastic applause.

You often speak of books which have interested you deeply.

I've never read as much as I would have liked; I haven't had the time – either in my youth when I had to earn my own living, or now when I have to study so many scores and give so many concerts. However, when I do read, I read something that's important to me. I absorb it and never forget it.

What sort of reading interests you in particular?

My main interest is in human relations and how to improve them. I've been inspired by the lives of men such as Nansen and Livingstone. Both were famous explorers, but also great humanitarians: Nansen who did so much to help refugees and who organized famine relief for Russia when that country was abandoned by most of the world; and Livingstone, who made a real bridge from the white man to the black man. And I'm drawn to books on history – for instance Michelet's *History of the French Revolution*. How appropriate for today is Michelet's quotation from the Middle Ages: '*Le cœur de l'homme est comme une meule qui tourne sans cesse; s'il n'a rien à moudre il se moud lui-même'* – 'The heart of man is like a mill that turns unceasingly; if there is nothing to grind, it grinds itself.'! That is just what is happening in our time. People have no more religion, no more idealism, no more faith, and so they grind their own hearts. We fight only *against* things; we need something to fight *for*. We have lost a sense of value, and all our forward motion into the science of the future will not bring it back to us. Some time ago I read Baumgardt's *Magellan*. He describes Magellan's efforts, when off the eastern coast of South America, to find a passage through which he could sail to the Pacific Ocean. After much searching he entered what appeared to be such a waterway and proceeded with great hope. But he noticed that the further he went the less salty the water became and the closer together the banks appeared to be; it was in fact the Rio de la Plata. Although his men were close to mutiny, he realized that there was only one way to move forward: to turn back. Modern civilization is in the same predicament. We have taken a wrong turning – only we haven't the good sense to turn back.

Who are your favourite writers of fiction?

I like Zola very much, and Balzac. I especially like the poetry of the Middle Ages – Villon for instance – so full of character and strength. Verlaine is another favourite. And of course I read Shakespeare and see his plays whenever I can.

You have a great love for painting. From where did that come?

I became interested in art when I was very young – that is in admiring great art; I myself have no skill at drawing. I was fortunate in having friends – one of whom was a painter – who shared my enthusiasm. Their knowledge was greater than mine, but the main thing is that their appreciation was genuine. They weren't snobs. If they expressed admiration for Van Gogh and Cézanne it wasn't because it was fashionable to do so. They didn't just *say* that Cézanne has more energy in his brush than Monet; they really *felt* it. When I was 16 or so, I saw these friends every week. We spoke together about art and visited many museums together. It's by seeing many paintings and having friends who understand them that you learn – more than from books.

Which painters are your favourites?

Van Gogh would be among them. I feel his suffering, his
humanity, his originality. But I have a preference for Cézanne
whom I find more harmonious. Sometimes Van Gogh forces his
art almost to a point of exaggeration, something which Cézanne
avoids. If I say that one should respect beauty, I am not advocat-
ing beauty for beauty's sake. Expression is a fundamental
necessity. But when beauty is *included* I am happy. As I have
said, Bach's music can express the deepest sorrow, the deepest
pain, but you cannot say it is not beautiful. That is the achievement of the greatest art.

Among the Italian masters I love Botticelli and Titian; among
the Spaniards, Velasquez and Goya, though I am less attracted
to Goya's dark paintings. I recognize their greatness, but my
personal preference is for art that doesn't insist upon what is
most painful in mankind. That's not to say that I'm blind to
injustice; I see every day that men are far from being angels. But
it is the art of Rembrandt that will always be my favourite,
because, whoever his subject may be, you feel that he's with
him, that he loves him. He's full of compassion; he shares his
suffering. He's not just studying or – as is sometimes the case
with Goya – questioning or even satirizing.

When I look at a work by Rembrandt I feel as if I were living
three hundred years ago and talking with the people he painted.
Once, in Edinburgh, I went into the National Gallery of Scotland
at lunchtime when virtually no one was there. I stood before
Rembrandt's self-portrait and slowly – ever so slowly – moved
my eyes from the shadows in the background across his face
until I met his eyes – those eyes so filled with sorrow. There are
several great moments in life – for instance when you fall in love
with the right person. That was such a moment. I was drawn to
the light of his face as if to a star. I spent half an hour in
conversation with him. It makes me feel better just to look at a
Rembrandt.

When I was on tour in Russia with Pascal and Pau I took them
to see the Rembrandt collection at the Hermitage in Leningrad. I
have already mentioned *The Return of the Prodigal Son* which
hangs there. Another favourite of mine is the *Danaë* – for me,

the most beautiful nude ever painted. You know the story of Danaë locked in the tower. Zeus manages to enter her bed-chamber by transforming himself into a shower of gold. The painting shows her bathed in golden light. Is it the moment when he arrives, or when he leaves her? She is smiling – so I think it must be when he arrives. You feel the warmth of the bed, the temperature of her body, her loving expectancy . . . Rembrandt's first wife Saskia, who died very young, was the model for Danaë. He must have valued this painting highly as he kept it with him all his life. Another of his paintings that I adore is *The Jewish Bride* which is in the Rijksmuseum in Amsterdam. The bride's expression is one of ineffable tender-ness. You already see in her face an intuition that she will one day be a mother – so lightly, so subtly depicted – only a lovely, vague dream in her eyes . . .

I sometimes wonder which composer was, in his own way, most akin to Rembrandt. Bach comes to mind, but Bach is both human and divine, while, for me, Rembrandt is all human. I think that Beethoven is perhaps closest to Rembrandt in spirit; they share a deep, all-pervading humanity.

There is one book which I feel expresses as no other the relationship between art and life, between art and nature. Since I first read it some years ago, it has been a constant inspiration to me. Little wonder – for it is the work of a man who was himself a great creator. If I were appointed by some educational authority to suggest reading material for the school children of the world – not to mention the adults of the world – I would recommend *The Cathedrals of France* by Auguste Rodin. This book is made up of notes written by Rodin in the form of a personal diary – always interesting and often ecstatic. '*Rentrer dans la vérité,*' he tells us; '*retourner à la nature, remonter aux principes; relier le présent au passé.*' What a message for our age of anxiety: 'Enter again into the truth, return to nature, go back to principles, link the present to the past.' This, he says, is 'the process which is necessary if we are to be brought wisdom and happiness.'

Rodin shows us how the art of those who built the cathedrals is rooted in nature. Not only do the cathedrals owe much of their creation to the forests which furnished the wood for the scaffolding, but they are themselves the image of the forest. In

Le Cheval`d'orgueil, Pierre Jakez Hélias writes so wonderfully of trees. To Beethoven every tree said 'Holy, Holy'. I too have learned to revere trees and what they have given us. All his life my father was in contact with wood, which he caressed with tenderness, and I pass my days with my cello, knowing how miraculously wood can be made to vibrate and sing.

'The love of nature,' Rodin says '– this single loving thought – has repaid my whole life . . . Where did I begin to understand sculpture? In the woods when looking at trees, along roads when observing the formation of clouds, in the studio when studying a model; everywhere except in schools . . . The more simple we are, the more complete we shall be, for simplicity signifies unity in truth.' Would that our avant-garde artists – in all fields – might take heed! And Rodin states what could be a credo for us all: '*La beauté éveille le cœur à l'amour, et hors l'amour rien ne vaut*' – 'Beauty awakens the heart to love, and without love nothing is of value.'

I cannot say to what extent I am educated – certainly very little in the quantitative sense. But whatever I have learned has been the product of love, and has therefore been of value to me. There is still so much to learn. How I wish I had more time!

Paul was once having a chat about sociology with his dear old friend Travers Symons. Travers, then aged 97, had been editor of *Purpose* and a contributor to *The New English Weekly*. Paul found it fascinating to explore this subject with him. However, Mary Symons reminded Paul that he had to play that evening. The cello was waiting. Seeing how painful it was for both men to have to cut short their discussion, she offered consolation in the thought expressed by Denis Savrat in *The Three Conventions*, namely, that IDEAS live on throughout generations, a conversation may be continued in a future life. 'Travers,' Paul said in taking reluctant leave of his friend, 'I cannot wait to die so that we can go on with our talk in the next world . . .'

XXIV
Don Quixote III

When I was 15 I enjoyed listening to the jazz of the time and I must confess to my shame that I was very fond of a record called *Chopinata*. This was a jazzed-up version of some Chopin melodies performed by a well-known duo-piano team, Wiener and Doucet. I had no idea that during the same period in America, Arthur Rubinstein was circulating a petition calling for the protection of the great classical masterpieces from ill-treatment for purely commercial purposes. I learned of Rubinstein's petition only some forty years later when, after a magnificent recital he gave in Copenhagen, I asked him to sign a similar petition put forward by the *Mouvement Beethoven* of which I was the founder. He did so at once, covering a whole page with his large signature, but he cautioned me that I would encounter obstacles before succeeding. 'When I began my own initiative,' he said, 'I had the warmest encouragement from my colleagues. However, when my impresario became aware of what I was doing, he warned me not to continue or I wouldn't get any more engagements.' His words were prophetic. The *Mouvement Beethoven* was short-lived and during its brief existence met with much misunderstanding.

Why did you decide to use the name Beethoven?

Because he is the most human of all composers, and therefore the ideal symbol for a crusade against dehumanization. Because his music stands as the supreme example of genuine originality, an originality rooted in the past and breaking through the

traditional musical boundaries of its day as a result of the composer's inner expressive urge. We also thought that Beethoven's
name would be particularly appropriate because we were nearing
the bicentenary of his birth. We envisaged awarding nine prizes
for compositions of symphonies. Our first meeting was held at
the Ecole Normale de Musique in Paris. The Swiss composer
Frank Martin attended it and lent his full support.

Of course the *Mouvement Beethoven* was criticized by the
avant-garde. It was considered a reactionary expression. That
wasn't my idea at all. In fact, nowadays the truly innovative
composer is the one who has the courage to allow himself to be
judged on the basis of his talent as a musician rather than on a
facility in creating effects.

*Isn't it difficult to know just where to draw a dividing line between
music which is genuinely expressive and that which is not?*

Its been said that the earth never lies and that art must not lie
either. If somebody does something artificial it's apparent soon
enough in creation, just as it is in life. It's obvious that there
must always be something of a subjective factor in one's judge-
ment, yet that's no reason to deny ourselves our instinctive
responses. On the contrary, I think it's unnatural and unwhole-
some to listen to the electronic noise produced today and *not*
to react. Some people tend to be so impressed with the avant-
gardists' talk about new art forms that they're afraid to appear
stupid by admitting their sincere feelings.

Another of our aims was to promote world peace through
the universal language which only music can provide. Finally,
as I have said, we wished to protest against the commercial
prostitution of the works of the great composers.

*What criteria would you use for judging whether a transcription is
harmless or an exploitation?*

Bach himself transcribed many of his own pieces for different
instruments – indication enough that there's nothing wrong
with a transcription *per se* if one remains faithful to the spirit of
the original, and if the basic musical elements – harmony,
rhythm and melody – are recognizable. Before the advent of the
gramophone, four-hand piano transcriptions were the chief

way in which symphonies by Brahms and Beethoven became a part of family life. That sort of amateur performance was of the greatest benefit to musical culture. If you love a work and transcribe it for the instrument you play – even if you're an amateur and have to simplify it – as long as you do it with respect, you are not committing a sin. My objections occur when the music is distorted and degraded, when you change its basic character, when you want to give Mozart's G minor Symphony a sexual allure by turning it into a foxtrot.

Unfortunately, when I went to live in Essen in 1969, it proved impossible to maintain the Movement's impetus. My colleagues, who had given their time free of charge, were dispersed, and we couldn't provide the necessary administration. Well, our effort will not have been entirely in vain if it inspires others to do whatever they can to oppose the cheap noise that so often assails our ears.

In modern life commercialization is all-pervasive; you can't escape from it. Not only is the ear assaulted, but the eye as well. Take a walk in any of the world's great cities from New York to Tokyo and you are surrounded by publicity meant to catch your attention.

Didn't you once protest publicly against advertisements for Coca-Cola?

Ah yes; I was giving a master class in Weikersheim on the 'Romantic Road', and noticed to my disgust that this lovely old town was fairly plastered with Coca-Cola posters. So one evening my students and I formed a *Ligue Anti-Coca-Colique* and set about restoring Weikersheim's eighteenth-century beauty by removing some of the most offending posters. Alas, Coca-Cola is imposed upon people everywhere. Even in remote parts of Brazil people drink it, when they could well do with something more nourishing. We should add to the *Book of Genesis* 'And God created the Coke'.

Of course we're subject to so many forms of thought control – not least when watching television.

Apropos of that, I once visited an elderly couple who lived in a small village in the English Lake District. The man apologized for having missed my last master class on television, although he had seen all the previous ones. He explained that since his retirement he had devoted as much time as possible to his hobby of making clocks from slates upon which he drew beautiful designs. 'One Sunday we were looking at the telly,' he said, 'and the programmes were all so interesting that we spent the whole afternoon watching them. So the next morning I sold the damned set. That's why I couldn't see your programme.' There you have the real peril of television: it's dangerous when it's bad, and it's worse when it's good – because however interesting it may be, nothing can compare with creation. A man is not supposed only to sit and watch; a man is supposed to act. It's not enough for him to say 'I love you'; he's supposed to prove it. If one remains transfixed before the screen throughout a lifetime, on his tombstone will be inscribed, 'Here lies Mr Viewer; he was well-informed . . .'

If we aren't careful, life will become a series of surfaces like the television screen, surfaces which are sterile and artificial. In our society the individual is minimized; he is nearly reduced to a cipher. Science is all-pervasive. Chemists serve us pills as if they were giving us bread; biologists prepare their version of the man of the future. Matisse put it well when he said that in the old days the tool was the continuation of the arm, but nowadays the arm is the continuation of the tool.

Hope may lie in the fact that every social phenomenon tends to produce a compensatory reaction. Today there are many young people who object to the computerized society. The question is whether they can find some positive means to create a more meaningful society for their own children.

This brings us to the larger issue of social justice on an economic level – a concern that has always been with me. It's in my blood, just as it was in my father's and grandfather's, and I've never hesitated to speak my mind on the subject. In my twenties my dear Feuillard cautioned me that if I continued in this way I might harm my prospects of a career. I was sincerely sorry to have upset him, as he had done so much for me. However, my need to take a stand on questions of social justice was too strong to be suppressed. My subsequent travels have made me all the more aware of the shockingly unfair distribution of wealth on our planet. A shameful disparity between rich and poor exists not only in the Third World. Even in Paris, in London, one finds people sleeping on the streets. What is the solution? In China, for instance, despite all their difficulties, they have to a large extent alleviated such misery. True, they don't have our high standard of living; you don't see the same beautiful cars and supermarkets. But at the lower end of the scale you don't find so many people suffering from want. It's no small thing to have warm clothing and enough to eat.

What would you consider to be an ideal kind of government?

There are three possibilities: a democracy like Switzerland, a kibbutz, or an ideally run Communist state.

Which Communist state?

The one that doesn't exist. The one in which there is both political freedom and equal distribution of wealth. But let us not forget that repression of individual liberty exists not only in Communist countries, but in the many dictatorships supported by the so-called 'free world'.

Rather than trying to prove which political regime is right or wrong, rather than forever talking about 'systems' – none of which work very well – wouldn't it be better to concentrate our attention on the world's economy as a whole? Shouldn't we take the bull by the horns and denounce the monstrous diversion of wealth into military expenditure – all for the sake of an illusory national security? And to what do we owe this tragic waste of resources? To nothing but fear: the fear the Russians have of the Americans, and the Americans of the Russians. Such fear poisons life. We sense it even here in Europe. People feel threatened by some vague danger from the outside without knowing what it is. Little wonder, with Armageddon literally hanging over our heads! There are already over 50,000 nuclear warheads; however, we're repeatedly told that we'll only be safe if we produce yet more weapons. It's an endless cycle which can only lead to catastrophe.

Jung compared the stockpiling of nuclear weapons to giving a boy of six a bag of dynamite as a birthday present. This, he said, 'forces a psychological question on mankind: Is the mental and moral condition of the men who decide on the use of these weapons equal to the enormity of the possible consequences?'

It's clear that with all their 'rational calculations' our statesmen have led us into a diabolical predicament. We need a renewal of faith. We need to trust to our intuition about the values of human life. This explains the grass-roots movements springing up spontaneously in so many places where people from all walks of life march together to express their right to exist without being subject to the threat of nuclear holocaust.

I feel as they do, and as a musician it's only natural that I should try, no matter how limited my means, to use music to express my concern.

I have written four anthems dedicated to world peace. The inspiration for the first came about in the following way. I had been immersed in the biography of Nansen – a story that, as I have said, never ceases to move me. I happened to be reading this very book while in an aeroplane which ran into deep fog and circled the airport several times while attempting to land. I began to think that we might not be destined to land at all. The image of Nansen was before me, and I promised myself that if we were to land safely I should dedicate more of my efforts to the humanitarian principles which he so nobly exemplified. In fulfilment of this pledge I conceived an anthem in tribute to the United Nations and called it *Le Grand Drapeau* – 'The Great Flag' – the flag which knows no national boundaries. It was played in London for the twentieth anniversary of the first General Assembly of the United Nations, and has been performed several times for English and French television.

My second anthem, *The Blue Berets* is a vivacious march, honouring the UN peace-keeping forces. The third is a hymn called *Vers la Paix*. This time my text is set not to a melody of my own, but to Beethoven's *Ode to Joy*. I chose Beethoven's incomparable tune because it's in everybody's ears, and it immediately awakens a feeling of universal brotherhood. And I have now composed a fourth anthem: *May Music Save*

Peace for which once again I have written both words and music.*

On occasion I've also spoken to my audiences of my concern. As I said recently in Milan: 'The art of Johann Sebastian Bach represents the highest achievement of mankind: it is sovereign – sovereign as is the idea which pursues me, which will not leave me, the idea of universal peace. We must work together against the peril of nuclear war if we want our grandchildren to be able to listen to Bach's music.'

How has the public reacted to these speeches?

Normally very positively. Only once – in Denver – did someone shout, 'Stop talking about politics and get on with the music' – but he was drowned by the applause. In any case I am not speaking of politics; I'm speaking of survival. You can be Labour, Tory, Democrat, Republican, communist or capitalist – we're all threatened equally. Security has become indivisible among the peoples of the world. That's what the politicians are so slow to understand.

I don't have an inflated idea of my abilities; I can't imagine that my anthems, my speeches, my letters are suddenly going to alter the course of history. If they find a vibration in the minds and hearts of some people, I shall have already accomplished something. It's a bit like composing: you hope for the best result, but the activity is important in itself. I cannot just sit back and do nothing. If I am concerned, I act.

I have found in my own personal experience that individual action is both more possible and effective than one would think.

The Chinese have a saying: 'It is worthwhile to have lived if one has grown a tree.' If we all try, for better or worse, to grow our own trees, at least we can live more meaningfully, and if we're numerous enough perhaps we can, after all, affect man's destiny in a positive way.

Centenary of the *Concerts Lamoureux*
PAUL TORTELIER SINGS his 'HYMN for PEACE'.
Three hundred people were turned away at the door of the Salle Pleyel for

*See Appendix III.

the concert given by Paul Tortelier . . . He arrived on stage, his lean face lit up by a broad smile with which he greeted his audience. He then shared with them the entire richness of his instrument . . . Three movements from Bach's Sixth Suite: generous sonority, phrases leaping with life, indomitable energy, peasant-like rusticity, vital warmth – the cellist's eyes fiery and dreamy staring into the infinite . . . And then a performance of Haydn's C major Concerto: sparkling, borne on air . . . varied and playful in all its freshness and poetry. Silencing the acclamation with a motion of his hand, Tortelier addressed the public in a ringing voice: 'Music does not stop at music. I wanted to perform for you today my Hymn for Peace, based on the *Ode to Joy*, in a version for voice and eight cellos. That not being possible for practical reasons, I will nevertheless sing it to you, because we must put music to the service of peace . . .' And without accompaniment he sang the three verses of his moving hymn: 'All men on earth are alike when they feel the grip of fear . . . All men on earth are alike when they feel the threat of death . . . May all men soon be brothers to achieve a lasting peace.' Further applause. It only remained for Beethoven himself to speak, and Tortelier proceeded to conduct the *Eroica* with his customary ardour and intensity . . .

Le Monde,
8 December 1981

Aware as I am of the dangers that face the world, my own life has been, and continues to be, one of profound happiness. Every moment is full; I am never bored. Living in this way has had at least one beneficial effect: people tell me that I've forgotten to grow old.

If you were able to live your life over again is there anything you would wish to change?

Details, yes – many of them. But I would not want to change the main direction my life has taken – nor *could* I have done so. It seems that I was born under two stars: my mother's which destined me to play the cello, and my father's which impelled me to dedicate myself to ideals. Even if all my efforts in this latter respect prove fruitless, I cannot resist the spirit which moves me.

One day I brought my petition for the *Mouvement Beethoven* to Rudolf Kempe. That wonderful musician was sympathetic to my aims, as I knew he would be. Yet he felt it was useless to make a protest of this sort. 'After all,' he said, 'the forces of commercialism are far too ingrained for such idealistic efforts to have any effect.' 'If the risk is so great that we shall indeed become ciphers,' I asked, 'is it not all the more important that we protest? How else can we live meaningfully?'

He looked at me quizzically for a moment and said,' I hope you don't mind if I say that you are really something of a Don Quixote.'

And I replied, 'I don't mind at all.'

My Creed

Divin Amour t'inspirera
Lois naturelles tu suivras
Lait maternel tu boiras
Confort point ne t'affaiblira
Patience point ne te manquera
La Vérité tu rechercheras
La Bonté tu vénéreras
La Beauté t'illuminera
Sa bonne étoile te guidera
Le Temps ton plus grand bien sera
De la Mort ne te soucieras
De la Joie tu t'empareras

———

Love, which is divine, shall inspire thee
The Laws of nature shall be thy laws
Mother's milk shall nourish thee
Comfort shall not sap thy strength
Thou shalt have patience
Thou shalt seek truth
Thou shalt venerate goodness
Beauty shall illuminate thee
Its good star shall guide thee
Time shall be thy greatest treasure
Thou shalt not fear death
Thou shalt seize upon joy

Appendix I

Compositions by Paul Tortelier

Composition	Publisher
Song with piano: *Un Grand Sommeil Noir* (Verlaine), 1935	Office d'Editions Musicales
Three Pieces for Oboe and Two Cellos, 1936	Office d'Editions Musicales
Elégie for Cello and Piano, 1937	Delrieu, Nice
Spirales for Cello and Piano, 1943	Durand, Paris
Concerto for Cello and Orchestra No. 1, 1943	
Trois P'tits Tours for Cello and Piano, 1943	Consortium (formerly Gallet), Paris
Suite for Solo Cello in D minor, 1946	Salabert, Paris
Sonata for Cello and Piano in D minor, 1947	Durand, Paris
Saxe for Cello and Piano, 1947	Delrieu, Nice
Concerto for Two Cellos or Cello and Violin or Two Violins, 1950	Chester Music, London
Prelude for Solo Cello in D minor, 1950	

Composition	*Publisher*
Two *Ballades à Chameau* for Two Cellos, 1950	
Concerto for Cello and Orchestra No. 2, 1954	
Symphonie Israelienne, 1956	
Toccata for Cello and Piano, 1958	Delrieu, Nice
The Great Flag, words and music, Hymn for the United Nations, 1959	
Six Cadenzas (for concertos by Boccherini, C. P. E. Bach, Haydn [D major], Schumann, 1959	Delrieu, Nice
Two Caprices for Two Cellos and Piano, 1961	
Violin Concerto, 1965	
Two Songs with Piano: *Sensation* (Rimbaud), *Fleur de Neige* (folk text), 1967	
Offrande for String Orchestra, 1970	Editions Transatlantiques, Paris
The Blue Berets, March for peace, words and music, *circa* 1970	
Pishnetto for Cello and Piano, 1970	Chester Music, London
Recital Etudes for Cello and Piano, 1972	
Alla Maud: Waltz for Two Cellos and Orchestra (or Piano), 1973	
Nine Miniatures for Two Cellos in *How I Play*, *How I Teach*, 1975	Chester Music, London

Composition	*Publisher*
Cello Books No. 1 and No. 2 (first position pieces), 1975	Chester Music, London
Two Cadenzas (Haydn C major Concerto), *circa* 1975	
Danse sur le mode Gréco-Chinois for Piano trio; or Flute, Violin, two Cellos and Piano, 1976	
Concerto for Piano and Orchestra, 1976	
Variations and Dance for Flute and Piano, 1978	
Danaë: Waltz for Two Cellos and Piano, 1980	
Sancho's Tears for Viola and Cello, 1980	
Towards Peace on the theme of the *Ode to Joy* for mixed choir, words and music, 1982	
May Music Save Peace, anthem for mixed choir, words and music, 1982	
Variations on *May Music Save Peace* for Cello and Piano, 1982	
Sonata Brève for Cello and Piano, 'Bucéphale', 1983	Delrieu, Nice

Editions:

Bach: Six Suites for Solo Cello	Augener (Stainer & Bell, London; Galaxy, New York) first edition 1966, second edition 1983

Composition	*Publisher*
Sammartini: Sonata for Cello and keyboard in G major	Delrieu, Nice, 1959
Valentini: Sonata for Cello and keyboard in E major	Chester Music, London, 1977
Solmisation Contemporaine	Heugel, Paris, 1965
How I Play, How I Teach	Chester Music, London, 1975

Appendix II
Paul Tortelier Discography

This discography in no way claims to be a *complete* listing of the recordings made by Paul Tortelier as cellist, conductor and, on occasions, commentator, though it does embrace his most significant contributions to the record catalogue during the past three decades or more.

The order of works recorded is alphabetical by composer. To clarify the rôles that this versatile artist variously assumes, Paul Tortelier's name is not credited on the line of participating artists when he appears as cello soloist. His name is credited only when he conducts, in which case his name appears after that of the orchestra, or if he recorded in the dual capacity as orchestral/ensemble director as well as soloist, in which instance the symbol † appears beside his name.

Record numbers only have been quoted. UK records available at the time of going to press are indicated with an asterisk (*e.g.* UNS 207*). Available cassette equivalents of discs are indicated by (TC) (*e.g.* ASD 4075*(TC)). The numbers of long-deleted 78 rpm recordings appear in italics (*e.g. DB 11191*). Foreign record numbers are listed solely as an approximate guide to equivalent non-UK releases.

The c/w (coupled with) line provides a comparatively quick method of locating other music on the record. Titles of works indicate that they are by the same composer as that of the listed work. If the coupling is of music by another composer his name is given in capital letters. The ubiquitous *etc.* denotes the existence of more works on the record than is possible to itemise in

253

a single line. Two prominent recital discs, *Soirée musicale* and *Encores*, are indicated solely by their collective titles. When there is no *c/w* line either the work occupies the entire record or Paul Tortelier does not participate in the rest of the record's contents.

Where the same work has been recorded more than once the performances are listed one under the other in approximate chronological order of recording.

Numerous extracts from the above LP recordings have been available in various forms at different times of which the only significant disc currently available is SEOM 19*. This "Paul Tortelier sampler" comprises extracts from Bach (SLS 798), Beethoven (SLS 836), Chopin & Rachmaninov (ASD 2587), Fauré & Tortelier (HQS 1289), Grieg (ASD 2954), Elgar (ASD 2906), Walton (ASD 2924/ESD 1077631), R. Strauss (SLS 880) and Paganini (ASD 3015).

Abbreviations

arr	arranged
CBSO	City of Birmingham Symphony Orchestra
CO	Chamber Orchestra
ed	edited
LPO	London Philharmonic Orchestra
LSO	London Symphony Orchestra
O	Orchestra
PhO	Philharmonia Orchestra
PO	Philharmonic Orchestra
rev	revised
RPO	Royal Philharmonic Orchestra
SO	Symphony Orchestra
trans	transcribed

Record Company Prefixes

Angel (USA)	S
CBS (UK)	61000 & 79000 series
Classics for Pleasure (UK)	CFP
Columbia (France)	33 FCX
Columbia (UK)	33 CX
Columbia (USA)	ML
Concert Hall Society (USA)	CHS
Discocorp (USA)	RR
Erato (Europe)	LDE, STE, STU
HMV (UK)	ALP, ASD, BLP, CSD, ESD, HQS, SEOM, SLS, SXLP, XLP
	C, DA, DB

Musical Masterworks Society (USA)   MMS
Pathé (France)   *PDT*
Pathé Marconi (France)   063, 069
Philips (UK)   ABL, ABR, GBL
Piccadilly (UK)   FTF
Supraphon (Europe)   LPV, SUA
Unicorn (UK)   UNS
World Records (UK)   CM, ST, T

All prefixes indicate long play 33⅓ rpm records except those in italics which are 78 rpm discs.

	UK record numbers	Other record numbers
C. P. E. BACH		
Cello Concerto No. 3 in A, W.172		
London CO/Paul Tortelier† (c/w HAYDN)	UNS 207*	
J. S. BACH		
Adagio (from Toccata, Adagio & Fugue, BWV.564) (arr. Siloti, rev. Casals)		
Maria de la Pau (Soirée musicale)	ASD 3283	
Orchestral Suite No. 3 in D, BWV.1068		
Scottish CO/Paul Tortelier (c/w COUPERIN, RAMEAU)	ASD 3321	
Prelude No. 8 in E flat minor (Well-Tempered Clavier) arr. Hartmann		
Tasso Janopoulo (c/w RAVEL)	DB 11191	
Sonatas for cello & harpsichord Nos. 1–3, BWV 1027–29		
Robert Veyron-Lacroix		LDE 3266 STE 50166
Suites for unaccompanied cello Nos. 1–6, BWV 1007–12		
(i)	SLS 798*	069 10828/30
(ii)	SLS 1077723*(TC)	
BEETHOVEN		
Cello Sonatas Nos. 1–5		
Eric Heidsieck	SLS 836*	
No. 3 in A, Op.69		
Maria de la Pau (c/w SCHUBERT)	ASD 4075*(TC)	
(12) Variations on Ein Mädchen oder Weibchen, Op.66		
Karl Engel		DA 5051/2
(12) Variations on See, the conquering hero comes, G.157		
Karl Engel		DA 5042/3

	UK record numbers	Other record numbers

BOCCHERINI
Cello Concerto in B flat (*ed. Grützmacher*)
  English CO/Maud Martin-Tortelier (*c/w*
    HANDEL, PAGANINI etc)   ASD 3015

BOELLMANN
Symphonic Variations, Op.23
  RPO/Yan Pascal Tortelier (*c/w*
    SCHUMANN etc)   ASD 3728*   069 07047

BRAHMS
Concerto for violin, cello & orchestra in A
  minor, Op.102
  Christian Ferras/PhO/Paul Kletzki   ALP 1999 & ASD 549
                                    T 699 & ST 699
                                    CFP 40081

Cello Sonatas Nos.1 & 2, Opp.38 & 99
  (*i*) Karl Engel   ALP 1233
  (*ii*) Maria de la Pau   ASD 3612

Piano Quartet No. 3 in C minor, Op.60
  Myra Hess/Joseph Szigeti/Milton Katims ABR 4063   ML 4712

String Quintet No. 2 in G, Op.111
  Isaac Stern/Alexander Schneider/Milton
    Katims/Milton Thomas   ABL 3184   ML 4711

BRUCH
Kol Nidrei, Op.47
  RPO/Yan Pascal Tortelier (*c/w*
    SCHUMANN etc)   ASD 3728*

CHOPIN
Cello Sonata in G minor, Op.65
  Aldo Ciccolini (*c/w RACHMANINOV*)   ASD 2587*

Prelude in E minor, Op.28/4 (*arr. Bazelaire*)
  (*i*) Tasso Janopoulo (*c/w SARASATE*) DB 11116
  (*ii*) Shuku Iwasaki (*Encores*)   HQS 1289*

F. COUPERIN
(Les) Goûts-réunis au nouveaux concerts
  No. 8 Concert en sol majeur (*arr.*
    Oubradous)
  Scottish CO/Paul Tortelier (*c/w Pièces etc*) ASD 3321

  No.13 Suite for two celli (*arr. Bazelaire*)
  Maud Martin-Tortelier   LPV 474
                                      SUA 10351

Pièces en Concert (*arr. Bazelaire*)
  Principals of Scottish CO/Paul Tortelier†
    (*c/w BACH etc*)   ASD 3321

	UK record numbers	Other record numbers
DEBUSSY		
Cello Sonata in D minor (1915)		
(*i*) Gerald Moore	*DB 9509/10*	
(*ii*) Jean Hubeau		ERA 9214
		LDE 3201
Minstrels (Preludes, Book 1) (*arr. Bergman*)		
Maria de la Pau (*Soirée musicale*)	ASD 3283	
DELIUS		
Concerto for violin, cello & orchestra (1915)		
Yehudi Menuhin/RPO/Meredith Davies	ASD 3343*	S 37262
DVORAK		
Cello Concerto in B minor, Op.104		
(*i*) Zurich Tonhalle/Otto Ackermann		MMS 2006
		MMS 124
(*ii*) PhO/Sir Malcolm Sargent	ALP 1306	
	XLP 30018 & SXLP 30018	
(*iii*) LSO/André Previn (*c/w Rondo*)	ASD 3652*(TC)	
Rondo in G minor, Op.94		
(*i*) Shuku Iwasaki (*Encores*)	HQS 1289*	
(*ii*) LSO/André Previn (*c/w Concerto*)	ASD 3652*(TC)	
ELGAR		
Cello Concerto in E minor, Op.85		
(*i*) BBC SO/Sir Malcolm Sargent	BLP 1043	
(*ii*) LPO/Sir Adrian Boult	ASD 2906*(TC)	
FAURE		
Après un rêve (*arr. Casals*)		
Shuku Iwasaki (*Encores*)	HQS 1289*	
Cello Sonatas Nos. 1 & 2, Opp.109 & 117		
(*i*) Jean Hubeau (*c/w Elégie*)	T 638	LDE 3193
		STE 50101
(*ii*) Jean Hubeau		STU 70554
(*iii*) Eric Heidsieck (*c/w Elégie etc*)	ASD 3153	069 12894
Elégie in C minor, Op.20		
(*i*) PhO/Herbert Menges (*c/w SAINT–SAENS etc*)	ALP 1336	
(*ii*) Jean Hubeau (*c/w Sonatas*)	T 638	LDE 3193
		STE 50101
(*iii*) Erik Heidsieck (*c/w Sonatas etc*)	ASD 3153	069 12894
(*iv*) Toulouse Capitol O/Michel Plasson		167 73071
Papillon in A. Op.77		
(*i*) Shuku Iwasaki (*Encores*)	HQS 1289*	
(*ii*) Eric Heidsieck (*c/w Sonatas etc*)	ASD 3153	069 12894
Serenade in B minor, Op.98		
Eric Heidsieck (*c/w Sonatas etc*)	ASD 3153	069 12894
Sicilienne, Op.78		
Maria de la Pau (*Soirée musicale*)	ASD 3283	

	UK record numbers	Other record numbers
GIARDINI		
Tamborino & Gigue		
(c/w *COUPERIN & HINDEMITH*)	LPV 474	
	SUA 10351	
GRANADOS		
Intermezzo (Goyescas) (*arr. Cassado*)		
Shuku Iwasaki (*Encores*)	HQS 1289*	
GRIEG		
Holberg Suite, Op.40		
(2) Elegiac Melodies, Op.34		
Northern Sinfonia O/Paul Tortelier (c/w		
TCHAIKOVSKY)	ASD 2954	
Cello Sonata in A minor, Op.36		
Robert Weisz (c/w *SCHUBERT*)	CM 26	
	HQS 1398	
HANDEL		
Sonata in G minor for two cellos & orchestra		
(*arr. Feuillard & Paul Tortelier*)		
Maud Martin-Tortelier/ECO/Paul		
Tortelier† (c/w *BOCCHERINI, VIVALDI*		
etc)	ASD 3015	
HAYDN		
Cello Concerto in C, Hob.VIIb/1		
Württemberg CO/Jorg Faerber (c/w		
Concerto in D)	ASD 4157*(TC)	069 07594
Cello Concerto in D, Hob.VIIb/2		
(*i*) Colonne O/Jean Fournet	*DB 11167/70*	
(*ii*) London CO/Paul Tortelier† (c/w		
CPE BACH)	UNS 207*	
(*iii*) Württemberg CO/Jörg Faerber (c/w		
Concerto in C)	ASD 4157*(TC)	069 07594
HEKKING		
Chanson mélancholique		
(?) (c/w *LAVAGNE*)	*PDT 68*	
Villageoise		
Marie de la Pau (*Soirée musicale*)	ASD 3283	
HINDEMITH		
Cello Concerto No. 2 (1940)		
Czech PO/Karl Ančerl (c/w		
COUPERIN etc)	LPV 474	
	SUA 10351	
HONEGGER		
Cello Concerto		
French National Radio O/Georges		
Tzipine		33FCX 665
KARJINSKY		
Esquisse		
Marie de la Pau (*Soirée musicale*)	ASD 3283	

	UK record numbers	Other record numbers
KODALY		
Sonata for solo cello, Op.8		
(c/w TORTELIER)	ASD 3458*	
LALO		
Cello Concerto in D minor (1876)		
CBSO/Louis Frémaux	ASD 3209*	
LAVAGNE		
Concerto romantique (1942)		
Lamoureux O/Eugène Bigot (c/w		
HEKKING)		PDT 66/8
MARTIN		
Petite symphonie concertante (1945)		
London CO/Paul Tortelier (c/w		
ROUSSEL etc)	UNS 233	
MASSENET		
Elégie, Op.10		
Shuku Iwasaki (Encores)	HQS 1289*	
MENDELSSOHN		
Cello Sonatas 1 & 2, Opp.45 & 58		
Maria de la Pau		069 16282
Chant populaire (Song without words, Op.53/5) (arr. Hartmann)		
Maria de la Pau (Soirée musicale)	ASD 3283	
Piano Trio No.1 in D minor, Op.49		
Kyung-Wha Chung/André Previn (c/w SCHUMANN)	ASD 3894*(TC)	
MOZART		
Oboe Quartet in F, K.370		
(i) Marcel Tabuteau/Isaac Stern/William Primrose	33CX 1090	33FCX 227
(ii) Marcel Tabuteau/A. Pernel/K. Tuttle (c/w Piano Quartet)		RR 547
Piano Quartet in E flat, K.493		
William Kapell/Arthur Grumiaux/Milton Thomas (c/w Oboe Quartet)		RR 547
NIN		
Granadina (Chants d'Espagne) (arr. Kochanski)		
Maria de la Pau (Soirée musicale)	ASD 3283	
PAGANINI		
Moto perpetuo, Op.11		
Shuku Iwasaki (Encores)	HQS 1289*	

	UK record numbers	Other record numbers
PAGANINI (*contd*)		
Variations on a theme by Rossini		
(*i*) for two cellos & orchestra (*arr. Paul Tortelier*)		
Maud Martin-Tortelier/ECO/Paul Tortelier (*c/w BOCCHERINI, HANDEL etc*)	ASD 3015	
(*ii*) for cello and piano (*arr. Paul Tortelier*		
Shuku Iwasaki (*Encores*)	HQS 1289*	

POPPER
Dance of the Elves, Op.39 (*ed. Fournier*)
  Maria de la Pau (*Soirée musicale*)   ASD 3283

RACHMANINOV
Cello Sonata in G minor, Op.19
  Aldo Ciccolini (*c/w CHOPIN*)   ASD 2587*

Vocalise, Op.34/14
  Maria de la Pau (*Soirée musicale*)   ASD 3283

RAMEAU
Les Indes galantes   ASD 3321

RAVEL
Pièce en forme de Habañera (*arr. Bazelaire*)
  (*i*) Tasso Janopoulo (*c/w J. S. BACH*)   DB 11191
  (*ii*) Shuku Iwasaki (*Encores*)   HQS 1289*

Piano Trio in A minor (1915)
  Yan Pascal Tortelier/Maria de la Pau
    (*c/w SAINT–SAENS*)   ASD 3729*

RIMSKY–KORSAKOV
The flight of the bumblebee (Tsar Saltan)
  (*arr. Rose*)
  Maria de la Pau (*Soirée musicale*)   ASD 3283

ROUSSEL
Sinfonietta, Op.52
  London CO/Paul Tortelier (*c/w MARTIN etc*)   UNS 233

SAINT–SAENS
Allegro appassionato for cello & orchestra, Op.43

	UK record numbers	Other record numbers
(*i*) CBSO/Louis Frémaux (*c/w Concerto No.1 etc*)	ASD 3058*	
(*ii*) Maria de la Pau (*c/w Sonata No. 1 etc*)		069 73016

Cello Concerto No.1 in A minor, Op.33

	UK record numbers	Other record numbers
(*i*) Zurich Tonhalle/Walter Goehr		CHS 1180
(*ii*) PhO/Herbert Menges (*c/w FAURE etc*)	ALP 1336	
(*iii*) CBSO/Louis Frémaux (*c/w Allegro etc*)	ASD 3058*	
(*c/w TCHAIKOVSKY etc*)	ESD 1077621*(TC)	

	UK record numbers	Other record numbers
Cello Sonata No.1 in C minor, Op.32		
Maria de la Pau (*c/w Arrangements etc*)		069 73016
(The) Swan (Carnival of the animals)		
(*i*) Shuku Iwasaki (*Encores*)	HQS 1289*	
(*ii*) Robert Johnston (*c/w Concerto No. 1 etc*)	ASD 3058*	
(*iii*) Maria de la Pau (*c/w Sonata etc*)		069 73016
Arrangements for cello & piano		
(Les) Cloches du soir, Op.85		
Etienne Marcel – Act 3 Prelude		
Samson and Delilah – Mon coeur s'ouvre		
& Dance of the Dagon Priestesses		
Suite, Op.16 – Serénade		
Violin Concerto No. 3 – Andantino		
Maria de la Pau (*c/w Cello Sonata No.1 etc*)		069 73016
Trio in F, Op.18		
Yan Pascal Tortelier/Maria de la Pau (*c/w RAVEL*)	ASD 3729*	

SARASATE

Zapateado, Op.23/2

(*i*) Tasso Janopoulo (*c/w CHOPIN*)	*DB 11116*	
(*ii*) Shuku Iwasaki (*Encores*)	HQS 1289*	

FRANCOIS SCHUBERT

The Bee, Op.13/9

Maria de la Pau (*Soirée musicale*)	ASD 3283	

FRANZ SCHUBERT

Sonata in A minor, D.821 (Arpeggione)
  (*rev. & trans P. Fournier*)

(*i*) Robert Weisz (*c/w GRIEG*)	CM 26	
	HQS 1398	
(*ii*) Maria de la Pau (*c/w BEETHOVEN*)	ASD 4075*(TC)	

String Quintet in C, D.956
  Isaac Stern/Alexander Schneider/Milton

Katims/Pablo Casals	ABL 3100	
	GBL 5624	
	61043*	
	79602*	

SCHUMANN

Cello Concerto in A minor, Op.129
  RPO/Yan Pascal Tortelier (*c/w*

BOELLMANN etc*)	ASD 3728*	069 07047

Piano Quintet in E flat, Op.44
  Myra Hess/Isaac Stern/Alexander
    Schneider

Milton Thomas (*c/w BRAHMS*)	ABL 3184	ML 4711

Piano Trio No.1 in D minor, Op.63

(*i*) Jean Hubeau/Henri Merckel (*c/w Trio No.3*)		LDE 3153
(*ii*) Kyung-Wha Chung/André Previn (*c/w MENDELSSOHN*)	ASD 3894*(TC)	

	UK record numbers	Other record numbers
SCHUMANN (*contd*)		
Piano Trio No. 3 in G minor, Op.110		
Jean Hubeau/Henri Merckel (*c/w Trio No. 1*)		LDE 3153

SHOSTAKOVICH
Cello Concerto No.1 in E flat, Op.107

Bournemouth SO/Paavo Berglund (*c/w WALTON*)	ASD 2924*	
(*Not a Tortelier coupling*)	ASD 4046*(TC)	

R. STRAUSS
Don Quixote, Op.35

(*i*) Leonard Rubens/RPO/Sir Thomas Beecham	DB 6796/6800	
	DB 9357/61	
(*ii*) Giusto Cappone/Berlin PO/Rudolf Kempe	ALP 1759 & ASD 326	
	T 609 & ST 609	
	CFP 40372*(TC)	
(*iii*) Max Rostal/Staatskapelle Dresden/ Rudolf Kempe	SLS 880	
	ASD 3074	
	SXLP 30428	S 60363

TCHAIKOVSKY
Pezzo capriccioso, Op.62

Northern Sinfonia O/Yan Pascal Tortelier		
(*c/w Rococo Variations etc*)	ASD 2954	
(*c/w SAINT–SAENS etc*)	ESD 10077621*(TC)	

Variations on a Rococo theme, Op.33

(*i*) RPO/Norman Del Marr	C 3776/7	
(*ii*) PhO/Herbert Menges (*c/w FAURE etc*)	ALP 1336	
(*iii*) Northern Sinfonia O/Yan Pascal Tortelier (*c/w GRIEG etc*)	ASD 2954	
(*c/w SAINT–SAENS etc*)	ESD 1077621*(TC)	

TCHEREPNIN
Duo for violin & cello, Op.49
Yan Pascal Tortelier

Piano Trio, Op.34
Yan Pascal Tortelier/Alexandre
Tcherepnin

Suite for solo cello, Op.76	CSD 3725	063 10912

TORTELIER

(The) Great Flag[1]	FTF 38506	

(3) Miniatures for two cellos

Maud Martin-Tortelier (*Soirée musicale*)	ASD 3283	

[1] This record, "The essential Paul Tortelier", includes spoken extracts including an introduction to *The Great Flag*. It has not been possible to trace a copy to determine performers.

	UK record numbers	Other record numbers
Offrande[2]		
London CO/Paul Tortelier (*c/w MARTIN etc*)	UNS 233	
Pishnetto		
Shuku Iwasaki (*Encores*)	HQS 1289*	
(Le) Pitre		
Gerald Moore (*c/w DEBUSSY*)	*DB 9509*	
Suite in D minor for solo cello (1944/45) (*c/w KODALY*)	ASD 3458*	
Valse No. 1 'Alla Maud'		
Maud Martin-Tortelier/Maria de la Pau (*Soirée musicale*)	ASD 3283	

VALENTINI
Cello Sonata No.10 in E		
Shuku Iwasaki (*Encores*)	HQS 1289*	

VIVALDI
Cello Concerti (*ed. Malipiero*)		
in C, RV.400; in B minor, RV.424; in C minor, RV.401		
London Mozart Players/Philip Ledger (*c/w Double concerto etc*)	ASD 3914*(TC)	
Cello Concerto in D, Op.3/9 (*arr. Dandelot*)		
English CO/Paul Tortelier† (*c/w BOCCHERINI etc*)	ASD 3015	
Concerto in C for violin, two celli & strings, RV.561†		
Concerto in G minor for two celli & strings, RV.531		
Maud Martin-Tortelier/†Jacques Francis Manzone/London Mozart Players/ Philip Ledger (*c/w Cello concerti*)	ASD 3914*(TC)	
(6) Sonatas for cello & harpsichord, Op.14		
Robert Veyron-Lacroix		LDE 3340 STE 50240 STU 70240

WALTON
Cello Concerto (1957)		
Bournemouth SO/Paavo Berglund (*c/w SHOSTAKOVICH*)	ASD 2924*	
(*Not a Tortelier coupling*)	ESD 1077631*(TC)	

WEBER
Adagio and Rondo (*arr. Piatigorsky*)		
Maria de la Pau (*Soirée musicale*)	ASD 3283	
Violin Sonata No. 5 in A, J.103 (*arr. Piatigorsky*)		
Tasso Janopoulo		*SK 103*

[2] This record also includes Paul Tortelier's spoken introduction to *Offrande* as well as some of his thoughts on Beethoven.

Appendix III

'May Music Save Peace'

Paul Tortelier, 1983

* Alternative wording to the first four words and to bar 21: 'God, thou on high'.

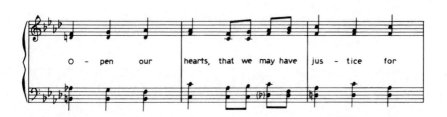

O - pen our hearts, that we may have jus - tice for

all, _____ and hail _____ the rise of the day

bring-ing the reign of love. _____ God if Thou art,

save our Great Ship and May Mu - sic save Peace.

Index